OREGON'S CUISINE OF THE RAIN

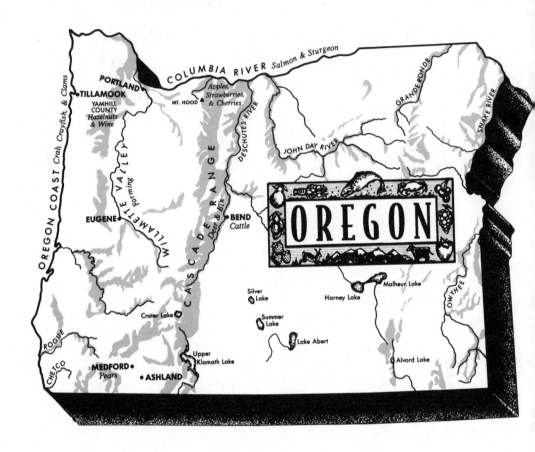

OREGON

COLUMBIA RIVER *Salmon & Sturgeon*

OREGON COAST *Crab, Crayfish, & Clams*

PORTLAND
•TILLAMOOK
YAMHILL
COUNTY
*Hazelnuts
& Wine*

MT. HOOD ▲ *Apples,
Strawberries,
& Cherries*

DESCHUTES RIVER

GRANDE RONDE

SNAKE RIVER

JOHN DAY RIVER

WILLAMETTE VALLEY *Farming*

CASCADE RANGE

Deer & Elk

EUGENE•

•BEND
Cattle

Malheur Lake

Silver
◊ Lake

Harney Lake

OWYHEE

Crater Lake ◐

Summer
Lake

Lake Abert

ROGUE

Upper
Klamath Lake

Alvord Lake

CHETCO

MEDFORD •
Pears

• ASHLAND

OREGON'S CUISINE OF THE RAIN

From Lush Farm Foods to Regional Recipes

Karen Brooks

ADDISON-WESLEY PUBLISHING COMPANY
Reading, Massachusetts   Menlo Park, California   New York
Don Mills, Ontario   Wokingham, England   Amsterdam   Bonn
Sydney   Singapore   Tokyo   Madrid   San Juan
Paris   Seoul   Milan   Mexico City   Taipei

Library of Congress Cataloging-in-Publication Data

Brooks, Karen.
    Oregon's cuisine of the rain : from lush farm foods to regional
  recipes / Karen Brooks.
        p.   cm.
    Includes index.
    ISBN 0-201-63282-9
    1. Cookery, American—Pacific Northwest style.   2. Cookery—
Oregon.   I. Title.
TX715.2.P32B76   1993
641.59795—dc20   92-34431
                                                                    CIP

Jacket design by Christine Raquepaw
Cover and text illustrations by Dennis Cunningham
Text design and map by Karen Savary

1 2 3 4 5 6 7 8 9 -MA-96959493
First printing, February 1993

To my mom, Ethel Fleishman,
for being my best friend and partner

Contents

ONE

Hazelnut Hotcakes, Apple Cider Syrup, and Other Morning Glories *1*

TWO

Seductive Tarts, Intriguing Pâtés, and Other Small Plates *17*

THREE

Oyster Bisque, Mussel Chowder, and Other Seasonal Soups *35*

Acknowledgments

For more than a thousand days and nights I sat at my computer writing *Cuisine of the Rain*. While watching the daily legion of joggers running in sweaty ecstasy by my house, which is located at the entrance to one of America's largest woodland parks, I agonized over every detail in these recipes: Which ones were original enough for the book? How many minute directions to include in the cooking instructions? And did I forget any of the state's culinary calling cards?

I laughed a lot, too, usually at my own particular brand of obsession. Along the way, dozens of people brainstormed and debated with me over some fabulous food. Most of all, I will never forget their magnanimous support.

I could have never completed this book without the massive encouragement from my parents, Ethel and Alan Fleishman, and my brother, Craig. My mom acted as full-time consultant, taster, proofreader, ego booster, and devil's advocate; my dad listened patiently at least twice a week while I talked recipes, recipes, recipes to my mom in St. Louis, Missouri, graciously paying what I imagine were frightening phone bills. And my brother, an attorney in Denver, Colorado, was always available to give me sound advice. His children, Jason, Brett, and Jodi Fleishman, provided me with my best distraction—the reality check for love and humor.

I unlocked Oregon's culinary secrets with the help of Portland writer and native expert Tim Sills. Emily Moore, one of the Northwest's leading-edge chefs, and Harriet Reed Greenwood, a legend on the Portland restaurant scene, also contributed writing and research assistance.

Addison-Wesley's Elizabeth Carduff contributed everything a writer could hope for in an editor: a sharp eye for details, a supportive spirit, and an innate perception of the book's vision. Production coordinator Tiffany Cobb was a dream-team player for the deadline-weary. I am also eternally indebted to my friend and agent Richard Pine, who made it possible for me to hang up my black belt in worrying.

My friends were always on hand for impromptu energy. During a year-long illness they did it all: hauled me to markets in search of Oregon's fine edibles, proofread the manuscript, and delivered supreme advice with marathon phone sessions. My loving thanks to Gideon Bosker, Lisa Shara Hall, Shirley Kishiyama, Josie Mosely, Trink Morimitsu, Joan Strouse, Victoria Frey, Peter Leitner, Joel Weinstein, Nancy Row, Renardo Barden, Susan Orlean, Amy Godine, Matt Kramer, Marty Hughley, Miriam Seger, Roger Porter, Jeff Bachrach, Sue Witter, Barry Johnson, the Alexis Bakouras family, Chi-Wei Chang, Patricia Allison, Sara Perry, Kip Richardson, and Gloria and Jerry Epstein.

My friend Jeff Brown generously shared his knowledge of the Oregon wine scene. I'll always remember Scott MacRae's tireless spirit-boosting and Benjamin Brink's patience with my hairdo neurosis during a shoot for promotional photographs. Also thanks to Jon Zimmer for making house calls on my ailing computer, and to my hairdresser Maxene Jackson for weekly infusions of support.

My restaurant critic colleague David Sarasohn provided editorial consultation that was invaluable to the success of this book.

Finally, I am eternally grateful to the other friends and culinary wizards who generously contributed their original recipes to this book: Lena Lencek, Larry Kirkland, Chris

Maranze, Stu Levy, Nancy Briggs, Juanita Crampton, Pattie Hill, Ron Paul, George Tate, Greg Higgins, Amelia Hard, Dennis Baker, Millie Howe, James Beals, Pat and Mike Vidor, Karl Schaefer, Linda Faes, Nick Pierano, Jane Burkholder, Bob Sitton, Pat Failing, Naomi Kaufman Price, Kathleen Towers, and Veronique Vitt.

The New Oregon Eating Experience

After you use this book, hide it. It's not that you'll want people to think you personally invented Hot Three-Berry Cobbler with Sour Cream Ice Cream, although that wouldn't be bad. And it's not that you have to worry about getting pages messy. Recipes that started with just-picked berries can handle a little dirt. It's that a vital ingredient in Oregon cuisine, as in Oregon life, is keeping quiet about it. Otherwise, a state that features Chinook salmon in its rivers, huckleberries in its mountains, chanterelle mushrooms in its forests, and the world's best pears in its orchards could get crowded.

For a long time, Oregon has been a secret worth keeping. Everyone knows about the rain—the endless months of misty mornings and muddy landscapes. Yes, it's a badge of honor not to carry an umbrella here; that's strictly for the tourists. And yes, storm watching is a major activity on the Oregon coast. But the rain gives us our soul, our sense of place. It also gives us endless raw materials for fashioning a whole new way of cooking.

Oregon's Cuisine of the Rain brings to your table recipes at the forefront of Oregon's thriving food scene. Many creations are my own response to the region's riches. Others were hard won on the dinner-party front, originating from bases that warmly celebrate the local bounty and leave no doubt that Oregon cooks are inspired. The remaining innovations come from the visionary chefs who helped to pioneer Oregon cuisine. In the pages that follow, you'll sample the signature dishes that won critical acclaim in the restaurant reviews I've written over the past twelve years. Their enthusiasm has filtered into the home kitchen, where cooks routinely transform everyday ingredients into an honest creation with a distinct Oregon flavor. Each season is a springboard for a new dish: a dozen varieties of wild mint scent summer's salads; delicate oysters sweeten winter's bisques; wine-red cranberries emblazon fall's tart chutneys; and Chinook salmon, its sweet, pink flesh grilled over hot coals, announces the arrival of spring.

Oregon may or may not be, as one national magazine proclaimed, the garden capital of the world. But few would argue that the rich, rain-soaked soil furnishes farms and forests with a variety of edibles most cooks only dream about. This is a place where blackberry brambles ramble so freely that locals consider them weeds, where crab pots and clam shovels are as indispensable to summer as bathing suits, and where 90 percent of America's hazelnuts grow alongside rickety farmhouses and carpets of elegant Pinot Noir grapes. Oregon is so verdant with produce—from superior apples to prize-winning zucchini—that part of every crop is sold for a pittance to anyone with a U-pick bucket. The same relentless rainfall feeds uncountable miles of Oregon rivers and streams, which are home to the state's most accessible offering, fresh fish—from steelhead trout to white sturgeon.

Word of this bounty has, of course, leaked out before. "When I recall the taste sensations of my childhood," remembered James Beard about Oregon, "they lead me to the great razor clams, the succulent Dungeness crab, the salmon, crawfish, mussels and trout of the Oregon coast."

Beard, who knew the local rules, never wrote extensively about Oregon's food. He did, however, come back to Oregon every summer of his life, presumably to get something to eat.

It is mandatory for anybody flying into Oregon to announce that they've never seen any place so green. It's not surprising that when they can get a closer look, they find they've never seen anything like Gathered Greens and Field Flowers in Walnut Vinaigrette. And it's hard to claim that Oregon has hidden its fruit under a basket when Harry and David of Medford have been selling their individually wrapped produce for decades, at prices that turn apples and pears into luxury gift items. The food has always been here. What's new are the recipes, and people who are attacking the Oregon larder with influences ranging from Burgundy to Thailand to Tex-Mex.

You can see it in the high temple of Oregon food, The Heathman Hotel in downtown Portland, where the menu runs from power breakfasts of Hazelnut Corn Cakes with Wild Blackberry Compote to dinners of Grilled Venison with Cranberry-Pepper Sauce. The menu changes regularly, depending on what's fresh and what new inspiration has shown up in the kitchen. You also see it in what might be the ultimate of custom cooking: lunch served once a day, for two people only, at Briggs and Crampton's Catering and Table for Two in Portland. The reservation list runs into the next fiscal year, and once you have tasted the owners' Chanterelle Tart with Sugar-Roasted Walnuts, you understand why people fly in from Tucson for an extraordinary afternoon meal, imaginatively designed and artfully flavored, a virtual calling card of Oregon cuisine.

In addition to the wave of restaurants inventing Oregon cuisine, the state is speckled with microbreweries—small, independent companies that handcraft beers and ales from Oregon-grown hops and clean Cascade Mountains water, potions regularly compared to the satin experience of London's finest. Cooks looking for a headier glass turn to Portland's Clear Creek Distillery, which puts out an eau-de-vie ranked with the renowned fruit brandies of France, Switzerland, and Germany. Fashioned from Bartlett pears grown on the flanks of Mount Hood, the postcard mountain looming over Portland's eastern horizon, this sensuous liqueur is the darling of the new Oregon kitchen. It sharpens sauces, glazes ducks, and fortifies fruit tarts. Just as essential is Clear Creek's apple brandy, a potent perfume for an apple crisp or a pâté of figs and chicken livers.

What's also new, over the past two decades, are some of the finest vineyards on the West Coast, winning national and international recognition with a crop of premium, award-winning Pinot Noirs and Chardonnays. Local restaurants, in fact, are often gauged on the quality of their regional wine selection. Beyond its sipping value, the fruit of the Northwest vine is a key element in the elevating of Oregon sauces and marinades to something beyond the ordinary.

David Lett, of Eyrie Vineyards, helped pop the cork on an Oregon wine boom with a stunning late-'70s showing in a blind tasting of his Pinot Noir against Burgundies. Since then, Lett has set off a second explosion by bringing to Oregon—and to the United States—the Italian Pinot Grigio grape, producing a soft, dry Pinot Gris that is the best thing in the world to drink with salmon.

It is not surprising that an Oregon wine maker sets out to enhance the taste of salmon. The fish is the great challenge in Oregon food, the test of anyone who cooks or even eats, and every restaurant has its own response to the challenge. The answers range from Sweet-and-Sour Salmon with Fennel Greens to King Salmon Hash, exploding with the smoky scent of Pacific alder wood. Stumbling out of a Portland supermarket, a stunned New Yorker once exclaimed, "They sell salmon in there like it was hamburger!" The difference is, when Oregonians cook salmon, it can taste like an autumn sunset.

The heart of Oregon cuisine is out on the hillsides where the state's cooks do their shopping. Pink orange salmonberries, a species of wild raspberries rarely found in markets, hide in the low foothills of both the Coast Range and the Cascades, beckoning sweetly to jam and pie connoisseurs. Between the rugged lines of those two geographic landmarks lies the Willamette Valley, where elderberries and blackberries thrive so shamelessly that cultivated crops are considered commercially unfeasible.

To find the elusive and majestic blue huckleberry, known to locals as wild blueberries, one must journey far above the civilized chaos of the valley to the rarefied air of the high Cascades. As big as a baby's thumb, juicier than a pomegranate, and holding a flavor that could inspire music, this September jewel flourishes along the sunlit southwestern meadows that frame Oregon's Mount Hood and Washington's Mount Adams. As they have for centuries, Northwest Indian families carry buckets of wild blues home each fall, drying them for a later date with winter desserts.

The same sort of informal harvesting occurs throughout Oregon. Mount Emily, for example, in the northeast corner of the state, is famed for its exquisite-tasting morel mushrooms. Selling in supermarkets for no less than sixteen dollars a pound, morels have become a signature of the new Oregon table. Three hundred miles west, Oregon's winding coastline invites crowds of shellfish harvesters. To indulge their habit, devotées of crab, mussels, clams, and even urchin roe compete with the annual deluge of foragers combing the state's beaches.

Nothing captures Oregon's stunning richness better than the novel *Sometimes a Great Notion*, the 1960s masterpiece by author Ken Kesey, who lives on a rural Oregon dairy farm: "All the hillside, all the drying Himalaya vine that lined the big river, and the sugar-maple trees farther up, burned a dark brick and over-lit red. The river split for the jump of a red-gilled silver salmon, then circled to mark the spot where it fell. Canvasback and brant flew south in small, fiery, far-away flocks. And in the shabby ruin of broken cornfields rooster ringnecks clashed together in battle so bright, so gleaming polished-copper bright, that the fields seemed to ring with their fighting."

Oregon's Cuisine of the Rain can help you feel and taste that brightness. It is a chronicle of Oregon's march to the top of America's culinary heap and a roundup of the original recipes that are carving out new territory. In the pages that follow, you'll find the definitive guide to the best that Oregon has to offer. This book also makes Oregon's bounty a movable feast. Increasingly, the ingredients that stock the local kitchen are readily available around the country. For the few that can't be found elsewhere, turn to The Taste of Oregon (page xxv) for substitutions and mail-order sources.

One of the most remote states in the union is finally on the gastronomic map. The rest of the country is discovering what we've always known but never talked about: Oregon is food heaven, blessed with fresh ideas about cooking.

Just remember to keep the secret.

The Taste of Oregon

 The following foods and spirits are the backbone of the Oregon eating experience. Many of the region's riches are exported around the country. Find them. They're often no farther away than the nearest quality market. Substitutions are possible, of course, and I give you plenty of alternatives here. But if a hankering for the genuine article sets in, consider the mail-order sources below.

Much of Oregon's superior bounty comes from the Hood River Valley, one of the country's great fruit-orchard belts. Here, 17 miles of spectacular pears and apples are bordered by 11,245-foot Mount Hood and the Columbia River, where Chinook salmon and mammoth sturgeon run through a narrow, winding gorge.

Another superior growing region is the Willamette Valley, over 100 miles of verdant farmland, misty hills, and wineries southwest of Portland. Sloped between the Coast Ranges to the west and the Cascades to the east, the valley has warmer, drier, and sunnier conditions than the rest of the state. Ideal weather conditions and a longer growing season combined with rich soil and cooling breezes have created one of North America's most fertile farm regions.

Apple Cider

Oregon has a reputation for pressing superb cider from unblemished apples bursting with tangy juice. The best ciders come from Willamette Valley growers using old-fashioned family methods. The exceptional E and E Cider, for example, relies on the same old winepress and hand-bottling techniques it used in 1939; the company's rousing cider comes from original Jonathon and Rome Beauty farm trees. Other families use their own blends, pressing delicious ciders from Gravensteins, Spartans, or whatever good cider apples they have in their orchards.

Oregon cider is widely available in local markets. Cooks use it to add a zesty fruitiness to their kitchen creations. The thick, tangy beverage can be reduced to make a delicious breakfast syrup (see Apple Cider Syrup on page 8) and it is used as a poaching or braising liquid for seafood and meats. Beyond this, it makes a wonderful glaze for roasting game.

Because it keeps refrigerated for two weeks, Oregon cider is not shipped to other states. But any good, unpasteurized cider—usually found at natural-food stores—may be substituted.

Apples

Oregon sits in one of the world's best apple-growing regions. The Willamette and Hood River valleys supply a magnificent range of varieties, most of them of exceptional quality. While some of the best varieties (listed by season below) may be difficult to find, good substitutes are always available. During late summer and fall, check your local newspaper for markets, roadside stands, and U-pick farms carrying interesting varieties.

SUMMER APPLES

Gravenstein A medium to large apple that varies in color from green to green yellow with pale red stripes to red, the Gravenstein is juicy, crisp, and highly flavorful. As an all-purpose or cider apple, it is one of the best. Substitute McIntosh, Winesap, or Granny Smith.

EARLY FALL APPLES

Jonagold This Golden Delicious and Jonathon hybrid is gaining popularity on the national scene. Sweeter, softer, and more golden than Jonathon, it is a good eating apple. It's also better than the standard Delicious types for baking, cooking, and juicing. Substitute Gravenstein or Jonathon.

Jonathon Small to medium-sized and round, this variety ripens from green to deep red. Peak flavors emerge when the skin shows a green background color. With its distinctive tang and crisp texture, the Jonathon is an excellent apple for eating, baking, and juicing, but a weak choice for applesauce. Substitute Newton Pippin, Winesap, Granny Smith, or Jonagold.

McIntosh As it matures, this medium-sized, cherry red apple changes from tart and crisp to mild, sweet, and juicy. Through all its phases, it's a good choice for eating, baking, juicing, and making applesauce. Substitute Newton Pippin or Granny Smith.

Newton Pippin Originally developed in New England during the late 19th century, this small, solid green apple comes with an occasional red blush. Very crisp, tart, and somewhat dry, it is excellent for cooking and baking, but less successful for cider and applesauce. Substitute Granny Smith or underripe McIntosh or Gravenstein.

Royal Gala One of the Hood River Valley's most popular varieties, the Royal Gala has a crisp texture and mild flavor with a good tang. This fine all-purpose apple is medium to large in size, with a color scheme that runs from green to yellow green and red. Substitute Jonathon, Jonagold, or Granny Smith.

LATE FALL APPLES

Granny Smith Medium to large and a bright, hearty green, the Granny is Oregon's most popular commercial variety. Firm with a tart-sweet flesh, it is perfect for eating and all baking needs, although it is not as good for cider and applesauce. It can be substituted for most other varieties used for baking.

Mutsu Medium-sized and green yellow to golden in color, this hybrid, a cross between the Golden Delicious and the Japanese Indo, develops flavor in cloudy or rainy weather, making it a natural for Oregon's Willamette Valley. It is a firm apple with juicy, dense flesh—very good for baking, desserts, and cider. Substitute Gravenstein or McIntosh.

Rome Beauty Small to medium-sized, round, and cherry red when ripe, this is not an eating apple. It is excellent for baking, however, as it holds its shape beautifully, and is a good all-purpose cooking apple. Substitute Newton Pippin (except for applesauce) or McIntosh.

Spitzenburg This "old-fashioned" Oregon variety has it all: spicy, aromatic, tangy, and very sweet with crisp flesh. Small to medium-sized with green or yellow stripes alternating with red, it is an outstanding all-purpose apple. Substitute Granny Smith, McIntosh, or Gravenstein.

Winesap Medium-sized with deep red color, this apple is tart, crisp, and very juicy, making it an excellent choice for cooking, baking, and cider. Substitute Granny Smith, Jonathon, or Newton Pippin.

The following are mail-order sources that will ship Oregon apples throughout the country:

Pinnacle Orchards
P.O. Box 1068
Medford, OR 97501
(503) 772-6271
1-800-547-0227
AE/Visa/MC
Homegrown apples, pears, and a variety of Oregon regional food specialties.

Norm Thompson Outfitters, Inc.
"Cravings"
P.O. Box 3999
Portland, OR 97208
1-800-547-1160
AE/Visa/MC/DC/CB
Large catalog of Oregon fruits, food products, and specialty items. Call for catalog.

Asparagus

Oregon's sandy soil and soft, cool spring weather offer ideal conditions for growing a vivid wild variety of asparagus that thrives in fields throughout middle and eastern Oregon. Crisp, tender, uniformly compact, and completely free of bitter overtones, Oregon asparagus spears are superior to their sometimes flavorless and stringy California cousins. Widely distributed in the West during late spring and early summer, Oregon asparagus can be found as far east as Colorado.

Bay Shrimp

This very sweet, tiny Oregon native is caught in bays and offshore pockets up and down the coast between April and October. Cleaned and cooked immediately, bay shrimp are sold fresh or frozen to fish markets throughout the West. The terms *shrimp meat* and *salad shrimp* refer to these succulent, bright pink morsels. Although they freeze fairly well, the flavor and texture are much better fresh. Gulf or Atlantic shrimp meat may be substituted.

Jake's Famous Products
4252 S.E. International Way
Milwaukee, OR 97222
(503) 220-1895
1-800-777-7179
FAX (503) 659-3170
Visa/MC/AE/DC
Five-pound minimum for shipping. Fresh bay shrimp available April 1 to mid-November; frozen bay shrimp available year-round.

Berries

Oregon is home to some of the best berries on the planet. Even in the heat of summer, they thrive and become incredibly sweet; moist, mild winters help keep berry plants vital during dormancy. Wild berries grow in nearly all parts of the state. Backyard blackberry picking is an August ritual, followed by mountain camping trips to stalk Oregon's incomparable huckleberry. U-pick farms are the place to find raspberries considered among the world's best. But the real berry royalty is the Willamette Valley strawberry: small, extremely sweet, and so melting and juicy that it doesn't last long even when fresh.

Most local berries freeze well and are shipped throughout the country. Oregon cooks typically stash away extra berries in freezer bags for winter baking.

BLACKBERRY

Oregon's prolific wild blackberry (called dewberry in the East) is a roundish, medium-sized berry of biting sweetness with a citrus tang. Purple red to soft black in color, it grows on large, brambly bushes with lots of hidden stickers. But most cooks are familiar with Oregon's cultivated Thornless Evergreen blackberry, a long, purple black variety with compact seeds and a sweet citrus flavor. Most frozen blackberries on the market are Thornless Evergreens. Loganberries, marionberries, and boysenberries—all cultivated relatives—may be substituted.

BLUEBERRY

Oregon's crunchy, sweet cultivated blueberry is no stranger to the food world: The state is fourth in the nation in blueberry production. Local blues, which freeze beautifully, inspire cooks to experiment. They pair them with duck, tuck them into cornbread, or cook them down into glorious chutneys, relishes, and syrups.

BOYSENBERRY

Large and tangy with a reddish color that turns deep purple black when ripe, these big-seeded fruits are the largest member of the blackberry family. They are excellent for baking, preserving, and freezing, but are too tart for out-of-hand eating.

CRANBERRY

A wet climate and rich acid soil are essential for cranberry cultivation; Oregon's coastal wetlands have plenty of both. Bogs just south of the mouth of the Columbia River, near Coos Bay on the south central coast, produce excellent cranberries, firm and magnificently tart. A passion for experimental cranberry recipes originated in this part of the state and eventually the fever spread to urban kitchens. This versatile berry can be successfully frozen for over a year.

GOOSEBERRY

The unsung, extra-tart, green to purple gooseberry was an Oregon favorite earlier in the century when a backyard bush or two would provide plenty of round, puckery fruit for pies and conserves. But stemming each berry became too time-consuming for modern cooks, and the gooseberry practically vanished from the local repertoire. Oregon cooks, however, are rediscovering the merits of a berry that is as tart as a lime but also as sweet as a plum. Gooseberries are widely available canned and occasionally available frozen.

HUCKLEBERRY

The Oregon huckleberry is actually a wild mountain blueberry. Twelve varieties grow in the state, mostly along the coast or in the mountain back country. Local cooks make plentiful use of the coast huckleberry, a tight, dark blue, intensely flavored berry. This variety is also known as the Evergreen or box blueberry.

The great peaks of Oregon's Cascade Mountains—Mount Hood, Mount Adams, Mount Jefferson, and Mount Saint Helens (especially before the 1980 eruption)—are the place to find the juicy, succulent, maroon-colored mountain blueberry, or broadleaf huckleberry. This variety is fabulous for pies, cobblers, jams, and syrups. If huckleberries are unavailable, substitute blueberries.

LOGANBERRY AND LOGANBERRY LIQUEUR

A good, deep flavor and a high acid content make these dark red, medium-to-large berries exceptional for jams, jellies, and wines. The berries are also used to produce a delicious, portlike spirit called Whidbey's Liqueur. It comes from Whidbey Island, off the coast of Washington just north of Seattle. A popular cooking ingredient with Northwest cooks, Whidbey's Loganberry Liqueur can be used in place of other fruit liqueurs for baking. The liqueur is widely available in Oregon, Washington, and Idaho. It can also be special ordered from liquor stores in your area.

MARIONBERRY

Large and bright black, probably the longest and best bearing of the blackberries, this sweet-tart original is one of Oregon's signature fruits. It was developed during the 1950s at Oregon State University. Juicy and excellent in flavor, it is particularly valued for eating, desserts, and preserving because of its very small seeds.

RASPBERRY

There's no denying the thrilling flavor and dynamic versatility of perfectly ripe raspberries, especially from Oregon. The state's delicate, exquisite red raspberries are grown almost exclusively in berry heaven: the Willamette Valley. These berries are good for eating and terrific for sauces or preserves. They ripen in early summer and sometimes last well into July, with second fall crops in September.

Purple raspberries—best used for preserving, baking, and purées—arrive slightly later. They are larger and softer, first ripening in late June. Golden raspberries, a rarer but exceptional late-summer variety, are more subtle in flavor with a summery, melonlike taste that echoes their golden hue. The Willamette Valley also produces black raspberries, or black caps, tart, deep purple, tight, small domelike berries with an intense, plummy taste. A prized jam berry, black caps can be found at various U-pick farms around the state.

STRAWBERRY

Oregon's favorite berry arrives before summer officially begins and disappears before the end of June. Cultivated primarily in the rich valley of the Willamette River, local strawberries are highly perishable and must be quickly eaten, frozen, or preserved so their fleeting season can be enjoyed to the utmost. To discover the true delights of Oregon strawberries, visit the state in early June.

Brandies and Liqueurs

It is no coincidence that pear brandy, apply brandy, and other fruit liqueurs have captured the imagination of local cooks. The intoxicating essence of Oregon fruits has been captured in an eau-de-vie from Steve McCarthy's Clear Creek Distillery in Portland. The company's exquisite pear brandy, or *eau-de-vie de poire,* is made only from perfectly ripened Bartlett pears harvested in McCarthy's family orchards in the Hood River Valley. Its rounded flavors are suspended in a bracing, glass-clear, 80 proof liquid that is like golden-toned fire.

The autumn straw color of Clear Creek's apple brandy, distilled exclusively from McCarthy's crop of Golden Delicious and aged at least two years in old French Limosin oak Cognac barrels, heralds a clean scent of blossoms and an apple-rich taste, at once mellow and crisp. A rarer framboise eau-de-vie has the fresh summery scent of extra-ripe raspberries and a robust, citrusy tang.

Also inspiring is Clear Creek's grappa (called *marc* in France). It is made from the leavings, or pomace, of Muscat grape pressings gleaned in the fall from local wineries. An intricacy of tropical and lavender essences precede the bite of anise in the clean, woodsy flavor of this offering, hailed by connoisseurs as one of the world's best grappas.

McCarthy's secret is choosing only the very best fruit at the peak of its ripeness, something about which his European counterparts are not so meticulous. His brandies are true eaux-de-vie: made solely from fruit, and without the addition of caramelized sugar for color. They are cold-filtered and bottled at the small, urban distillery, then corked, sealed, and labeled by hand.

Federal regulations prohibit the shipping of high-proof liquors directly to retail customers. The best way to obtain these "waters of life" is to ask a local liquor store to contact a distributor who is currently carrying them. Or call or write the distillery directly to obtain a list of distributors.

Clear Creek Distillery
1430 N.W. 23rd Avenue
Portland, OR 97210
(503) 248-9470
Visa/MC
Specialties are pear brandy,
Calvados apple brandy, and
grappa. Tours and tastings
offered at distillery.

Cheeses

In most American households, the name *Tillamook* is synonymous with Cheddar cheese. For the past 82 years, the Tillamook Creamery, located in Tillamook County on the Oregon coast, has been turning out a smooth, distinctive cheese. Thirty million pounds of Tillamook Cheddar make their way around the world annually.

A lesser-known fact is that western Oregon (and western Washington State) harbors other world-class cheese makers, and a burgeoning artisan industry, producing exquisite cow and goat cheeses, is taking hold in eastern Oregon and other parts of the Northwest. For example, the Rogue River Valley Creamery, known for its sharp Cheddar and superb butter since the 1930s, produces an Oregon blue cheese of exceptionally rich flavor and buttery smoothness. Manufactured from the milk of Holstein cows, Oregon blue has been recognized repeatedly in European competitions as America's best blue cheese.

Other cheeses from the region are also gaining in stature. A process called hand-cheddaring makes the Cheddars and jacks from Bandon's Food of Bandon, Oregon, among the country's creamiest and best crafted. A wonderfully sharp and clean-tasting feta made from the impeccably fresh milk of well-tended goats comes from Tall Talk Dairy in Canby, Oregon. Proprietors Esther and Harlan Peterson have also developed a superb goat's milk cream cheese. Their cheeses are available at specialty-food markets in Oregon and are distributed nationally by Neiman-Marcus. The Blue Heron French Cheese Company in Tillamook sells enticingly flavored Brie cheeses and French-style Camemberts. The company runs a mail-order operation that handles products from the nearby area, including wonderful smoked sausages, pepperonis, and jerkys.

Additional innovators on the scene include Rolling Stone Chevre in Parma, Idaho, 150 miles from Oregon's eastern border. The company is known for creamy, handcrafted fresh goat's milk logs and exquisite cheese tortes. Creative cow and goat cheeses flavored with juniper, lavender, or fennel are the specialty of Quillisascut Cheese Company in eastern Washington. And Sally Jackson of Washington's Okanagan Highlands produces delicious raw handmade cheeses using milk from her tiny herd of goats and cows.

A mild, fragrant Gouda popular with Oregon chefs hails from the major fruit and dairy region around Yakima in eastern Washington. Another regional favorite is produced by the agriculture department of Washington State University at Pullman. The school trains its students in cheese making by producing one of the country's best-loved Cheddars, Cougar Gold. The cheese is renowned for its marvelous pungent creaminess.

All the dairies and creameries listed below happily ship their cheeses and dairy products, and will send brochures and price lists on request.

Bandon's Food
P.O. Box 1668
Bandon, OR 97411
1-800-548-8961
FAX (503) 347-2012
Hand-cheddared Cheddars
and jacks; flavored cheeses
such as Cajun, onion,
jalapeño, and smoked.

Blue Heron French Cheese Company
P.O. Box 598
2001 Blue Heron Drive
Tillamook, OR 97141
(503) 842-8281
1-800-275-0639
Visa/MC
Brie, flavored Bries, Camembert, and soft-ripened French-style cheeses. Large catalog of Oregon food products also available.

Quillisascut Cheese Company
Loralea and Richard Misterly
2409 Pleasant Valley Road
Rice, WA 99167
(509) 738-2011
Specialty goat and cow's milk cheeses, fresh and aged, plain or flavored with herbs and spices.

Rogue River Valley Creamery
P.O. Box 3606
311 N. Front
Central Point, OR 97502
(503) 664-2233
Oregon Blue Cheese (aged 90 days), Cheddars, jacks, flavored jacks, low-fat cheeses. Cheeses shipped November to March only; butter not available by mail-order.

Rolling Stone Chevre
Charles and Karen Evans
27349 Shelton Road
Parma, Idaho 83660
(208) 722-6460
Handmade fresh goat cheeses (*chevre*) in various sizes and flavors; some aged goat cheeses available.

Tillamook Creamery Association
P.O. Box 313
Tillamook, OR 97141
(503) 842-4481
1-800-542-7290
FAX (503) 842-3102
Visa/MC
Tillamook Cheddars, jacks, and low-salt cheeses.

Washington State University Creamery
Washington State University
101 Food Quality Building
Pullman, WA 99164-6392
(509) 335-4014
Cougar Gold Cheddars, mild through extra-sharp; also jack and some specialty cheeses available.

Cherries

Cherries arrive in early July from the great orchard valleys of the Willamette and Hood rivers. Delicate, orange red pie (or sour) cherries are too tart for eating but perfect for cobblers, pies, and preserves. Their brief season is soon followed by big, sweet eating cherries: deep red Bings, purple black Lamberts, and the pink-blushed, golden Rainiers and Royal Annes, so juicy it's hard to believe they can still be crisp. The eating varieties are just as delectable and versatile. Local cooks turn them into gorgeous compotes and jams or toss them with hearty meat and game dishes.

Oregon cherries are available seasonally in the Northwest, British Columbia, and northern California. Occasionally, they are shipped farther east. Both pie and sweet cherries freeze well at home (pit them first) and can be used for winter cooking; but they will be too mushy to be eaten out of hand.

Sun-dried cherries, with their intense balance of berry sweetness and earthy chew, are a hit with Oregon chefs, paired with game and smoked meats or used to enliven chocolate dishes, custards and fresh fruit desserts. Sun-dried cherries can be ordered from the following sources:

Orchard Crest Farms
Wayne and Myrna Simmons
3287 Orchard Heights Road N.W.
P.O. Box 5515
Salem, OR 97304
(503) 362-4381
Sweet pickled cherries; gourmet Oregon prunes.

Oregon Harvest and Gifts
Sandy and Juanita Temple
P.O. Box 1269
McMinnville, OR 97128
(503) 472-8686 or 835-3843
Dark and golden sun-dried cherries, chocolate sun-dried cherries, gift packages.

Clams

The aroma of fresh clams steamed in white wine with garlic, shallots, and fresh herbs says "Oregon seafood" to many natives. But the state's prolific clam beds have been largely fished out. As a result, most of the steamers available for commercial sale today come from the beaches of Washington State and British Columbia.

The manila is the Northwest's most popular clam. Tasty, tender, and easy to cook, this small variety has a lightly scored shell and characteristic radial stripes from base to edge. Larger butter clams and the littleneck variety of quahogs (pronounced kó-hogs) are still found at low tide on many Oregon beaches; although not as quick to steam open as the manila, the quahog is popular among weekend clammers. East Coast quahogs, which range in size from the smallest topnecks and littlenecks to the larger cherrystone and chowder clams, may be substituted for their Pacific cousins. Use the smaller types for steaming and the meatier ones for bisques, stews, and chowders.

The fragile-shelled razor clam, a long, flat variety known for its delicate flavor and melting texture, is a traditional Oregon favorite. For years it thrived on the Oregon coast. But during the 1980s, with pollution on the rise and over-clamming out of control, the mollusk became a rare find for commercial and weekend clammers. With clamming regulations now in place, however, razors are emerging again on Oregon's beaches and menus.

Pacific coast clams will be shipped by overnight air from the following sources:

Jake's Famous Products
(see bay shrimp)

Josephson's Smokehouse
(see smoked seafood)
Also one-pound vacuum-packed razor clams; two-pound packages undiluted clam chowder.

University Seafood and Poultry
(see fillet fish)
Manila clams from Hood Canel off Washington's Puget Sound and Oregon razor clams when available.

Dungeness Crab

For Oregonians, an outing to the coast between late fall and early winter is a great adventure. This time of year, storm watching is nothing less than a sport. The daring also like to head for the beach and picnic on fresh Dungeness crab.

The Dungeness is one of the world's premier shellfish. Local cooks don't like to fancy it up too much; they serve it just cooked and cracked, with nothing more than a little drawn butter and natural sea juices as a sauce.

Dungeness crabs are about 8 to 10 inches in length with their claws folded. A native Pacific rock crab found up and down the coast from San Francisco to Alaska, they weigh up to three pounds. Caught in southern waters during the colder winter months and off the Alaskan coast in spring and summer, the crab's population rises and falls dramatically in cycles that run in 7- and 10-year increments. Prices and availability fluctuate as the crabs go through their natural resurgences. When unavailable, substitute blue crab or fresh snow crab.

The outlets listed below will ship freshly cooked Dungeness by overnight air. Or find a local seafood purveyor who imports impeccably fresh crab; the delicate Dungeness loses plenty in flavor and texture when frozen.

Jake's Famous Products
(see bay shrimp)
Season runs year-round
between Oregon, Alaska, and
Canada. Will ship fresh or
frozen.

Pure Food Fish Market
Lee Brillhart
1511 Pike Place Market
Seattle, WA 98101
(206) 622-5765
1-800-392-FISH
FAX (206) 622-2050
Visa/MC
Will ship fresh from October to
February or frozen year-round.
Call for catalog.

Fennel

In grocery stores across the country, it is often called anise. But to Oregonians, the licorice-scented fall vegetable that looks like wild celery is fennel. Fennel was introduced to western Oregon early in the century by northern Italian vegetable farmers. Its perfumed crunch has won favor with local cooks as a salad ingredient or a baked side dish. Chopped fennel can also add a deep, robust savor to long-simmered meat and game.

Fresh fennel was once only found in Asian or Italian produce markets. But specialty-food markets and supermarket chains are beginning to stock it, too. If not readily available in your area, ask the produce manager of your favorite grocery store to order it. Or substitute celery with a little ground aniseed (fennel seed is too strong and not licorice-flavored) for a fresh fennel accent.

Figs

Many Italian families settled in Oregon's fertile farmlands early in this century. They introduced their native foods and gardening techniques to the region. One of their gifts to the Northwest was the fig. At least three types of fig tree were planted in Oregon's rural plots and backyards. The trees survived the region's damp winters and left a thriving legacy of neighborhood figs that still grow honied and luscious in hot years.

White, or Calimyrna, figs, favored by backyard enthusiasts, are round and green with a pinkish blush and sugary sweet flavor when ripe. They are most familiar in their dried form, available as a golden brown imported fig "bracelet" packaged in Greece or Turkey. Dark, plummy Black Mission and suave, red Turkish figs are also found fresh on yard trees throughout Oregon. There's even a commercial fig orchard or two, although the local climate is generally too cold in the winter to support an industry.

Fresh figs are available around the country at specialty-produce shops and some supermarkets from mid-August to October. If you must substitute dried figs in a recipe calling for fresh, reconstitute them by pouring boiling water (or warm wine or other liquor) over them just to cover and let steep in a warm place, covered, for several hours or overnight. Keep in mind that dried figs are sweeter than fresh ones. Moreover, their texture is more chewy than soft. It is best not to substitute Calimyrna for Black Mission (or vice versa) in a recipe calling for dried figs; substitute dates for Calimyrnas and raisins or prunes for Black Missions.

Fillet Fish

Oregon cooks are spoiled by their proximity to superior fishing waters. For decades they've been able to craft imaginative seafood dishes with a wealth of impeccably fresh fish. Although salmon (see separate entry) is the star of the region, many other fish varieties are prized for their flavor and versatility.

ALBACORE TUNA

Albacore is the Northwest's native tuna. It migrates between North America and Japan and is usually caught off the

Oregon coast in August. Yellowfin and bluefin tuna are excellent substitutes.

LINGCOD

Despite its name, lingcod is not really a cod. Officially it's a member of the greenling family. Prized for its firm flesh and meaty flavor, it can be traded for most Atlantic cods or haddocks.

PACIFIC HALIBUT

Nothing can surpass the succulent firmness of perfectly cooked, porcelain white Pacific halibut from cold Northwest waters. It can be pricey and hard to get during its brief commercial seasons—usually early or mid-spring; mid- and late summer; and mid-fall or early winter. But it's worth some time and trouble to find this royal fish fresh. Freezing produces a watery, dry-fleshed distant relation, good only for fish and chips. Atlantic and California halibut, although lacking the mellow sweetness of the Pacific variety, can be substituted if more easily obtainable.

PACIFIC RED SNAPPER

This is not a true snapper, but rather a deep-water Pacific rockfish with a gorgeous coppery red skin and a flavor similar to that of Pacific rock cod. More than four dozen rockfish varieties have taken up residence in the Pacific Northwest's salt waters. This one, often called red snapper, is favored for its mild, rich flesh and meaty fillets. Any of the various Atlantic ocean perches may be substituted.

PETRALE SOLE

The delicate yet meaty petrale sole is probably the tastiest of the soles and flounders fished off the Oregon coast. Some of the firmer flounders or fresh Atlantic turbot may be substituted.

The following fish purveyors ship excellent Northwest seafood around the country:

Jake's Famous Products
(see bay shrimp)
Lingcod, black cod, and varieties of rockfish

Josephson's Smokehouse
(see smoked seafood)
Fresh halibut, lingcod, Pacific snapper, albacore tuna, and petrale sole, in season.

Pure Food Fish Market
(see dungeness crab)
Pacific rock cod, lingcod, and yellow-eyed rockcod

University Seafood and Poultry
1317 N.E. 47th
Seattle, WA 98105
(206) 632-3700 or 632-3900
Visa/MC
Lingcod, petrale sole, Pacific snapper, halibut, and a good variety of other seasonal selections.

Fruit Preserves, Syrups, and Confections

Indecently Delicious Cranberry Marmalade. Wild Mountain Cross Blackberry Jelly. Amaretto Peach Syrup. Fresh Apple-Hazelnut Butter. Marion Marnier Syrup. And on and on. The list of local preserves, syrups, fruit honeys, nut butters, vinegars, and confections created by small artisan producers reads like a celebration of Oregon's brimming cornucopia.

A marvelous variety of concoctions, from old family recipes to new inspirations, is erupting from the kitchens of regional farmers and home cooks all over the state. Luckily, many of these jarred gems are available through mail-order sources. Some of the best are listed below:

Golden Orchards
Route 1 Box 332
Hillsboro, OR
(503) 647-5769
Checks accepted.
Peach marmalade, butter, and conserve; Oregon raspberry and marionberry preserves.

Made in Oregon
5 N.W. Front
Portland, OR 97209
(503) 273-8498
1-800-428-9673
FAX (503) 273-8318
Visa/MC
Large selection of specialty jams including marionberry, elderberry, and boysenberry. Fruit butters run from pumpkin to apple. Call or write for catalog.

Game

Prod a native Oregonian and you're likely to get a recounting of yearly hunting trips with an uncle or granddad, along with a few family recipes featuring quail, pheasant, or venison.

Oregon pioneers began a well-established hunting tradition at the turn of the century. Many of their descendants, along with thousands of newcomers, still pursue that tradition each fall. Local chefs find that many regional ingredients—from hazelnuts and fresh apple cider to wines from Oregon vineyards—are beautiful complements to the robust variety of game flavors. So it's no surprise that all kinds of game show up on the menus of Oregon's finest restaurants.

Depending upon the age of the animal or bird, wild game may require different cooking methods than farm-raised meat or poultry. Young wild game usually takes less cooking time, responding well to quick searing, sautéing, broiling, or grilling. Meat from older animals needs longer, slower cooking: braising or slow roasting with aromatic accompaniments after an initial searing is best.

The game recipes in this book are based on cooking methods for younger or farm-raised animals. But cooking times can be lengthened, heats lowered, and some liquid added to adjust the recipes for older meats.

If you don't know a hunter, ask your local butcher how to get farm-raised birds, rabbit, and venison.

The following distributors ship overnight throughout the country:

Native Game Company
P.O. Box 1046
1105 W. Oliver
Spearfish, SD 97783
(605) 642-2601
1-800-952-6321
Visa/MC
Venison, elk, and game birds such as pheasant, quail, and squab. Minimum order of $75.

University Seafood and Poultry
(see fillet fish)
Pheasant, quail, and squab—fresh when available, or frozen.

Greens, Fresh-Cut Herbs, and Edible Flowers

Nowhere is it more appropriate to eat the fruit of the land than in Oregon, where the harvest of wonderful edibles seems endless. Therefore, it is fitting to find that the wild greens of mountains, meadows, marshes, and fields have become integral to regional salads. Many growers are now cultivating greens that flourish in the wild: sorrel, dandelion greens, peppery cresses, and mustards, for example. Markets also carry blends of indigenous and imported greens. Chrysanthemum leaves, mizuna, anise hyssop, and radicchio or the other chicories are often found in the mix. These greens provide an exciting interplay of bitter and tart, crunchy and leafy, in salads that inspire creative impulses.

The irreplaceable accents of fresh herb flavor—the clean bite of lemon thyme, for example, or the sweet pungency of pineapple sage—have helped define the character of Oregon's culinary style. Many local markets and gourmet produce outlets now feature locally grown culinary herbs of delightful variety. Whimsy and beauty meet during spring and summer when local chefs introduce tiny edible flowers: fragile violas and forget-me-nots, hearty bachelor's buttons, or the fragrant, vivid calendulas and fuschias.

Fresh-cut herbs and herb plants, baby lettuces, wild and cultivated specialty greens, and edible flowers are available by mail from the following source:

The Posey Patch
Mike Posey
Phone orders only:
(503) 254-5280 (Portland, OR)
or (206) 286-2150 (Vancouver,
WA) Fresh herbs and herb
plants, salad mixes, baby
lettuces, edible flowers.

Hazelnuts

To Oregonians, a hazelnut is a filbert is a hazelnut. For years locals favored the name *filberts*. It comes from the French for Saint Philibert, whose name day on August 20 is close to the harvest date for the nut. The English term *hazelnut*—officially adopted by Oregon growers in the '80s—arrived in America with the early settlers.

Whatever you call it, this small, round, armor-shelled kernel is truly Oregon's native nut. It has thrived here since the early 19th century and was proclaimed the official state nut in 1989. With local farmers producing about 98 percent of the nation's crop, it's no wonder the sweet, seductive nut has become a staple on local menus. Hazelnuts add a deep-toned crunch to everything from Oregon lamb to pear and blue cheese salads, and they are integral to the region's signature desserts.

Hazelnuts can be bought in various grades and sizes. They come shelled (shells off) or unshelled, and shelled nuts are sold blanched (skins off but still raw), raw and unblanched (skins on), or roasted (skins removed). Sizes are small, medium, large, and extra-large.

Hazelnuts and hazelnut products can be ordered from these excellent sources:

Dundee Orchards
P.O. Box 227
Dundee, OR 97115
(503) 538-1063
Giant-sized whole nuts, plus less expensive broken ones for baking; creamy or crunchy hazelnut butter.

Westnut, Inc.
P.O. Box 125
Dundee, OR 97115
(503) 538-2161
Five-pound packs of shelled whole nuts; also sliced and diced hazelnuts. Chocolate-hazelnut torte also available. Ask for the "Oregon Hazelnut Primer," a 32-page information and recipe book.

Honey

Oregon's agricultural paradise has a particularly delicious side benefit, a bountiful array of indigenous honeys. Yields are small compared to Hawaii or the Midwest, but the state's great variety of flowering plants, bushes, and crops are the source for distinctive varieties.

Early in the spring, beekeepers concentrate on wild-flower honey from the dandelions, pussywillows, and cherry blossoms in southern Oregon. Hives are then moved to the Willamette Valley and coastal foothills, where exceptional honeys are gleaned from raspberry flowers and holly blooms.

As summer progresses, some hives are placed on the slopes of the Cascades for fireweed, thistle, and snowberry blossoms. Others go to central and eastern farms for alfalfa, buckwheat, mint, pumpkin, and carrot blossoms (Oregon is one of the nation's top producers of carrot seeds). One company even produces honey from poison oak flowers. The bee-keepers claim it will detoxify the sting of the plant.

Unusual honeys are available, pure and unpasteurized, from the following apiaries:

Bee's Knees Honey Factory
Charles Lilley, president
520 S.W. Yamhill Street
Suite No. 8
Portland, OR 97204
(503) 640-5757
Visa
Ships any quantity of 16 different honeys, from 4-ounce jars to 55-gallon drums. Mr. Lilley recommends the light holly honey. Gift packs available.

Oregon Apiaries
1118 N. College
Newberg, OR 97132
(503) 538-8546
Exceptional honey cremes whipped with Oregon berries. Also a variety of wild honeys.

Ruhl Bee Supply
Cheryl Johnson, manager
12713 N.E. Whittaker Way
Portland, OR 97230
(503) 256-4231
Visa/MC
Large variety of Oregon honeys and honey products, including honeycomb and honey candy. Factory tours, tasting room, and demonstration hive.

Lamb

Oregon lamb is succulent and mild, rich in savor and aroma, tender, and very lean. No wonder it has won acclaim over most domestically raised and imported varieties. In fact, the goal of Northwest lamb producers (particularly the highly regarded Superior Farms Hermiston, Oregon) has been to raise the world's leanest yet most flavorful meat. The proposition was reasonable given the Willamette Valley's lush ryegrass pastures.

Local lambs are raised on a meadow diet, making them stronger and less susceptible to illness than feedlot lambs raised on grain and hay. The bucolic conditions also allow them to gain weight without putting on excess fat. The lambs are usually "finished" on corn and roughage in sunny eastern Oregon to add a richer tone to their flesh. Then they're carefully selected and butchered. Fat is trimmed to $\frac{1}{4}$ inch instead of the $\frac{1}{2}$-inch layer left on most domestic lamb.

Local cooks are fond of the regional lamb, and it's rare to find a good restaurant here that doesn't showcase it. A favorite summer backyard barbecue feast is a butterflied leg of lamb marinated in fresh herbs, Walla Walla Sweet onions, and Oregon Pinot Noir and then grilled blush pink throughout.

Oregon lamb is often processed with other similarly raised animals from Washington, Idaho, and Utah and is sold all over the West as "Northwest lamb." Although not always available east of the Rockies, it is a good bet your local butcher or meat department has heard of Carlton Packing Company. The company's lamb can be obtained through a local wholesale distributor.

Another processor of quality Oregon (and Northwest) lamb is Talarico's Meat and Seafood Market of Portland, Oregon. They carry fresh Oregon lamb; thick loin chops are their specialty. And if you're interested, they also have fresh natural veal. Addresses and phone numbers for both firms are given below.

Carlton Packing Company
P.O. Box 580
10600 N.W. Westside Road
Carlton, OR 97111
(503) 852-7166

Talarico's Meat and Seafood Market
8502 SW Terwilliger
Portland, OR 97219
(503) 246-7619
Visa/MC
$25 minimum order with credit card

Mushrooms

Winter's final gusts in early March mean one thing: the imminent appearance of the morel. This is Oregon's elusive and best-loved wild mushroom, known for its profoundly earthy overtones. And when summer begins its cool slide toward fall, the golden, rich, prolific chanterelles emerge to enrich the autumn table, sometimes popping up in wooded foothills as late as December. Oregonians traditionally seek these two delectable fungi over all others, often trekking to the mountains to hunt them. But the state hosts more than a dozen other choice varieties. Oregon, in fact, is one of the world's richest and most productive mushroom regions.

Robust porcini, staples of Italian and French cuisines, are shipped both fresh and dried to Italy and France (where they are known as cèpes). (In this country, porcini are commonly called boletes or boletus mushrooms.) And America's Asian communities look to Oregon as a source for the deep-flavored matsutake, or pine mushroom. This highly prized Japanese fungus is considered a rare find, but it thrives in Oregon's pine and fir forests.

Abundant Oregon truffles, available in both white and black varieties, are not nearly as pungent as the venerable Italian and French types. But hundreds of undiscovered species are in the area. Conventional wisdom says that resourceful digging will produce local varieties equal in quality to their European relations.

The quirky names of some other delicious natives— lobster mushroom, chicken of the woods, cauliflower, hedge-hog, black trumpet, yellow foot, bear's tooth—are enticing descriptions for cooks. They add interest and depth to local cookery and come with the knowledge that mushrooms picked in Oregon are generally handled more carefully than European imports. These gems of the woods are of highest quality.

You can order wild (and some cultivated) forest mushrooms from these very good and knowledgeable purveyors:

Full Moon Mushroom Company
Barbara and Mike Maki
P.O. Box 6138
Olympia, WA 98502
(206) 866-9362
Cultivated oyster and shiitake mushrooms; mushroom kits to grow your own.

Peak Forest Fruit
Lars Norgren, mushroom broker
2614 S.E. 22nd Avenue
Portland, OR 97202
(503) 232-7044

All types shipped in season; something wonderful always available. Morels are usually available April to July; chanterelles from September to December; cèpes are available throughout the year. Dried mushrooms are year-round.

Sosio's
1527 Pike Place Market
Seattle, WA 98101
(206) 622-1370
Matsutake, chanterelle, morel, and other mushrooms shipped fresh in season.

Mussels

Roger Sardina of Umpqua Aquaculture is known affectionately in these parts as Roger the Mussel Man. Almost single-handedly, he has carved a niche for wild and cultivated mussels in Oregon's seafood cookery. About ten years ago, Sardina was a marine biology student who scraped wild mollusks off the rocks near his seafront home, selling them to restaurants and resorts. As Sardina's reputation grew, so did his cultivation plans. Today he grows large quantities of a plump, succulent, golden-orange descendant of the original. Sardina's cultivated mussel is a hard-shelled variety that populates West Coast waters from Baja to British Columbia. It has benefited from his care. The cultivated mussels are fatter and sweeter than the wild ones and they have a less spiny beard.

Once the Oregon palate was hooked on mussels, another delicious variety, the Penn Cove, appeared on the market. It is farmed on Whidbey Island in the northern part of Washington State's Puget Sound in an area called Penn Cove. This smaller, thinner-shelled "blue" mussel was brought here from the Baltic Sea on the hulls of sailing ships. Its fragile shell could not withstand the pounding seas off the Oregon coast, but finds a perfect home in the calm bays around the cove. It is more delicate in taste than Sardina's Umpqua mussel.

Look for these ebony-shelled mollusks at your fish market. If not available, contact the following sources:

Jake's Famous Products
(see bay shrimp)
Will ship Penn Cove or
Umpqua mussels as available.

Umpqua Aquaculture
Roger Sardina
P.O. Box 287
Winchester Bay, OR 97467
(503) 271-5684
FAX (503) 271-5743
No mail orders.

University Seafood and Poultry
(see fillet fish)
Will ship Penn Cove mussels
as available.

Nut Oils

Europeans discovered long ago that the rich, unctuous nutti-
ness of fresh, cold-pressed hazelnut and walnut oils adds
a sumptuous earthiness to sauces, vinaigrettes, and condiments. North Americans have developed a more recent enthusiasm, buying imported European oils to enrich the new
American cuisine. Now an Oregonian firm, Paradigm Foodworks, is marketing some of the country's first domestic nut
oils. Oregon's hazelnuts and walnuts are cold-pressed without additives into fragrant, first-quality oils full of pungent
nut flavor and bearing a light, glossy sheen.

Sold as Oregon Crude hazelnut and walnut oils, the oils
are available from Northwest retail outlets or by mail-order.

Paradigm Foodworks, Inc.
5775 S.W. Jean Road—Suite No. 106A
Lake Oswego, OR 97035
(503) 636-4880
1-800-234-0250
FAX (503) 636-4886
Visa/MC
Nut oils, dessert sauces,
and a variety of cooking and
baking chocolates.

Oysters

The briny-sweet flavor of fresh oysters has graced Oregon's tables for at least a century. Many restaurants and
seafood shops now feature a dozen or more varieties
grown exclusively in the Northwest. Many come from
farms up and down the Oregon coast, or from Washington's

Willapa Bay, one of the largest oyster-producing bays on the West Coast.

Most cultivated Northwest oysters are the so-called Pacific type. A delicately fluted oyster with a well-defined cup, it is actually a Japanese transplant. Pacific oysters have 15 percent more meat (not water) per ounce than East Coast and Gulf varieties, making them popular with shellfish purveyors across the nation and reasonably easy to find in most areas.

Oysters pick up distinctive flavors from the composition of environmental waters. Because they grow in different bays and inlets, Pacific oysters are distinguished by a range of tastes, from coppery bright and briny to soft, mellow, and silvery. Since oysters' individual characteristics are defined by their home waters, they're given corresponding names: Umpqua oysters, Netarts Bay oysters, Yaquina Bays, Tillamook Bays, Quilcenes, and so on. An exquisitely delicate and altogether different oyster, grown from the seed of the French belon, or flat type, is cultivated by Roger Sardina of Umpqua Aquaculture (see Mussels).

The Northwest's only indigenous oyster is the Olympia. Very sweet and more delicate than the Pacific, the Olympia was once prolific on the West Coast. It was nearly wiped out by overpicking early in the century. Because of its fragile nature, it is now only farmed in very small coastal pockets, particularly near Olympia, Washington, on the southern elbow of Puget Sound.

If you've never had the pleasure of trying the crisp, oceany tastes and pliant, buttery textures of Pacific Northwest (and particularly Oregon) oysters, it's worth the effort of asking for them in local restaurants and seafood markets; West Coast oysters are widely distributed and you may be surprised at how easy they are to find. If you can't locate them in your area, write or call the following mail-order sources. But remember, as with all oysters, Pacific Northwest types are best eaten in the cooler months (November through April or May), since they become soft, "spawny," and sometimes thoroughly unpalatable when picked from their homes during warmer seasons.

Jake's Famous Products
(see bay shrimp)

Pure Food Fish Market
(see dungeness crab)
Quilcene, Willapa Bay
Shoalwater Bay,
Kumamotos and Belon oysters

Umpqua Aquaculture
(see mussels)
Excellent Pacific oysters and
Umpqua flat oysters available,
but not by mail order.

University Seafood and Poultry
(see fillet fish)
Wide variety of Pacific oysters
including Hama Hama and
Quilcene. Also Kumamoto
and Olympia oysters when
available.

Pears

Oregon's exquisite pears figure prominently in the local food scene. This "queen of fruits" mates beautifully with local cheeses, hazelnuts, wild greens, game, and other regional ingredients. Although considered a "hard" fall fruit, pears are more fragile than apples and require more careful handling. They are best ripened off the tree, individually wrapped and stored for a few days in a moderately cool, dark place. When ripe, they should be firm but beginning to yield under finger pressure; check the tops first to avoid bruising the fruit. Pears tend to lose their full flavor and creamy texture soon after ripening, so use them quickly and ripen only what you plan to use.

Oregon ranks third in national pear production. Some of the world's best pears are grown here, especially the sweet, fragrant Comice. Only a few places on the planet have the right conditions for growing great Comice pears. Oregon's Rogue River Valley, located in the southwestern part of the state, is one of them. There, the combination of cold winters, clay soils, and mild spring weather is perfect for the Comice.

Boscs, Seckels, and Bartletts also thrive in the Rogue River Valley. Across the state, the northern Hood River Valley produces wonderful examples of more obscure varieties. It also supplies much of the world with winter pears (Anjous,

Boscs, and Bartletts) of exceptional quality. Most of the following varieties are widely distributed in markets around the country.

ANJOU OR D'ANJOU

Mild and sweet, this short, round, green pear is the most popular winter variety. It is mainly an eating pear, excellent for salads or a dessert plate, but not recommended for cooking or baking. Anjous keep better than other pears. They can be kept at home in a cold spot through March or April.

BARTLETT AND RED BARTLETT

Known in Europe as the Williams pear, the Bartlett is the most pear shaped of pears, having a distinctly rounded bottom and full, tapered top. The first pear to ripen in the fall, it has a mellow tartness that is perfect for all purposes: canning, desserts, cooking, and eating. The Red Bartlett can be used in the same ways as its green gold cousin, and its beautiful red skin is a welcome color accent to fall and winter menus.

BOSC OR BEURRE BOSC

Extremely sweet with a melonlike fragrance, this tall, elegant, russet-toned pear is almost crisp when ripe. It's a delightful dessert pear, eaten just ripe and served alongside a glass of port and a robust cheese (a buttery Oregon Blue would be perfect). Boscs also hold their flavor and shape when cooked, making them particularly well suited to poaching and sautéing.

COMICE

Called the planet's best pear by aficionados (its full name, *doyenne du comice* means "best of show" in French), this round, slightly tapered variety possesses a very fragrant, rosy perfume and the creamiest of textures. The thin, light green skin is easily bruised, making delicate handling a must. This is not an ideal cooking pear. It is best eaten out of hand or used in salads and chutneys.

For a taste of the genuine Oregon pear, consider the mail-order sources below:

Harry and David
Bear Creek Corporation
Medford, OR 97501
1-800-345-5655
Visa/MC
Oregon's oldest and most reliable shipper of specialty pears. Other fruits, baked goods, and candies also available.

Pinnacle Orchards
441 South Fir Street
Medford, OR 97501
1-800-547-0227
Visa/MC/AE
Three or four varieties of pears plus apples and other Oregon foods such as nuts, cheeses, sausages, and preserves.

Norm Thompson Outfitters, Inc.
(see apples)

Prunes

Oregon has earned a reputation for its prunes and three varieties are worth knowing: the marvelously tart Italian prune and the sweet-tasting Brooks and Parsons prunes. Italian prunes (known as prune plums when fresh) have been raised here since the 1880s. Although they make up less than 1 percent of the nation's total prune crop, they are highly prized by cooks for their plummy tartness. Oregon, in fact, is the only place in the country where they are still grown.

The large-pitted Brooks and the sugary Parsons prunes were developed in the 1920s by two Oregonian horticulturalists when winter's impediments made it nearly impossible to get fresh fruit. At that time Oregonians, especially those of French and German descent, used prunes to add summery warmth to winter dishes. Now that fresh fruit is always available, the honied tang of prunes has become a signature flavor of Oregon cuisine. Taking their cues from the Europeans, local cooks use prunes in desserts based on custard, hazelnuts, or chocolate. Or they soak them overnight in fruit brandies and serve them with chicken, duck, or quail.

Oregon prunes (especially the Italian variety) are available under various brand names across the country. If the package doesn't say "from California," the prunes are probably from Oregon. The unusual, tart-sweet Italians are the best find, but any good-quality prunes may be substituted.

Rhubarb

This crisp, tart, ruby red plant is so suited to Oregon's western valleys that its growing season there is one of the nation's longest. That's why local rhubarb is found in produce aisles March through September. Rhubarb contributes to the regional cooking style in ways unimagined by old-time makers of pies, cobblers, and jams. It provides the edge in a fruit soup, the sparkle in a fish sauce, and the homey undertone in a contemporary dessert.

For optimum flavor and color after cooking, choose stalks that are approximately $\frac{3}{4}$ inch to 1 inch thick in the center. Also look for a deep rose color that whitens near the base and intensifies in redness toward the tapered top. Larger stalks, while providing good volume, may be woody and not especially flavorful; thin, young branches, despite good tartness and color, often cook down to almost nothing.

Cut off and discard the leaves, which are mildly toxic. Cook the cut-up stalks in a small amount of liquid over low heat. You'll need some sweetening to tame the tartness; try an Oregon honey for a change of flavor.

Salmon

The role of salmon in the development of the Pacific Northwest cannot be overestimated. Salmon fishing is one of the world's largest and most sophisticated industries and it runs from the Oregon coast to North Alaska.

The region's various salmon species have a peculiar life cycle. Every spring and fall they are compelled to "run" in a particular river at a time unique to their ancestral families.

They swim against all odds and hardships to spawn in the very same headwaters where they were born and where they will die. Oregon's Native American tribes knew these runs well; much of their survival depended upon annual salmon catches. The runs are now closely tracked by industries and local chefs in search of the best catches. Families of each species are targeted for "harvest" as they begin their runs. Some rivers hold the spawning grounds for two or three different kinds of salmon. For example, Oregon's greatest river, the Columbia, is known for spring and fall runs of Chinook, or king, salmon. The Columbia River also has a fall run of Coho, or silver, salmon.

The quality of salmon is determined by its species name and the river in which it runs. For example, the term *Columbia River spring Chinook* refers to the firm, hearty red meat of the rich-fleshed king salmon, the largest of the salmon types. An early spring run also connotes a higher oil content, the result of the cold waters. A fall Coho from the Columbia, on the other hand, will be a smaller, somewhat leaner fish caught in warmer waters. Its rosy pink flesh is made flavorful by a long summer season of feasting on smaller marine life.

Other popular species include the medium-sized Sockeye, with very succulent, deep red flesh. Used mostly for canning, it is an excellent, sweet-flavored eating fish, prized on the East Coast as the best salmon for making lox. But the sockeye has been on the endangered species list. The ocean-caught Chum salmon, found in Oregon off Tillamook Bay on the central coast, is sometimes considered a lesser variety because of its paler color. Chums, however, are highly regarded for smoking.

Pink salmon are smaller and not as rich as Chinooks or Cohos. But they have a delicate taste and are perfect for grilling whole in late summers. Chinook and Coho are closely related and may be used interchangeably in most salmon preparations.

Many outlets in both Oregon and Washington provide mail-order services for shipping fresh, whole salmon by overnight mail. Among them are:

Jake's Famous Products
(see bay shrimp)
5-pound Chinook salmons

Josephson's Smokehouse
(see smoked seafood)
8-pound Coho salmon or
10-pound Chinook salmon

Pure Food Fish Market
(see Dungeness crab)

Sausage

Before there was a good source of locally made sausage, Oregon chefs let creativity be their guide. They combined left-over meat, poultry, and game with Oregon wines, fruits, nuts, and herbs to make distinctive charcuterie and sausages. Into this tradition stepped Portlander Fred Carlo, owner of a small retail shop called Salumeria di Carlo. A New York transplant who honed his culinary art in Italy's Friuli region, Carlo established himself as the region's sausage king during the 1980s. Carlo's signature creations have become mainstays in local recipes: spicy chicken sausage; pork sausage with brandied raisins; zingy chorizo with red wine; and melting, home-cured prosciutto.

Other artisan meat processors and smokehouses around the state are concentrating on quality jerkys, salamis, pepperonis, and sausages. The following companies will ship around the country:

Debby D's Sausage Factory
2210 N. Main Street
Tillamook, OR 97141
(503) 842-2622
Visa/MC
Sausages, salamis, and home-style pepperonis; smoked salmon is a specialty.

Salumeria di Carlo
Fred Carlo
3739 S.E. Hawthorne
Boulevard
Portland, OR 97214
(503) 239-4860 or 221-3012
Handmade specialty sausages without fillers or preservatives.

Tillamook Country Smoker
P.O. Box 128
Bay City, OR 97107
(503) 377-2222
1-800-325-2220
FAX (503) 377-2746
Sausage, smoked meats, pepperonis, and jerkys.

Smoked Seafood

Before gold seekers invaded the West, salmon was the Northwest's most precious commodity. Smoked over alder-wood fires, the pink fish was flamboyantly displayed as a sign of wealth at Native American potlatches, which could be called the original power lunches. Alder wood is still preferred by local salmon smokers. The mellow, honied smoke of this prolific Northwest tree is a great match for the rich flavor of cured salmon. It is far superior to the cloying fruit woods or the harsher hickory.

Three styles of smoking prevail—cold smoking (for lox), hot smoking (for kippered salmon), and jerky (also known as squaw candy). Each style has variations particular to the smoker. In cold smoking, salmon fillets are cured with a dry salt rub placed in a salt brine for three days. The salmon is then rinsed and hung up or laid flat for twelve hours in a chamber filled with smoke from coals smoldering in a nearby firebox. The temperature never exceeds 80 degrees F—a higher temperature would begin cooking the meat. Buttery cold-smoked salmon is sometimes called Nova lox or simply lox on the West Coast. East Coast lox and Scandinavian gravlax are simply salt-cured without smoke for two or three days. Refrigeration is essential at all times after smoking or curing; cold smoking is not a cooking process designed for long preservation of the fish. Cold-smoked salmon freezes well, however.

Hot-smoked, or kippered, salmon is cured briefly in a wet salt brine, sometimes with sugar and spices added, then laid or hung for about five or six hours in a smoky chamber that climbs to 180 degrees F. Drier and flakier than cold-smoked salmon, hot-smoked salmon partially preserves the flesh. In this manner, the texture is more like the traditional Indian smoked fish. Still, the fillets should be refrigerated if kept more than a day or two. They can also be frozen for several months if well wrapped.

Salmon jerky, or squaw candy, is often made at home by cooks fortunate enough to have an abundance of fresh fish. Jerky need not be smoked, although commercial smokers usually follow the same procedures as for hot smoking. They leave the fish in the smoking chamber for up to four days. The fish is then filleted and cut into strips to be cold-smoked for another 24 hours. Jerky is still flaky when done, but hard and somewhat leathery. It keeps beautifully for weeks on the shelf.

The local passion for smoked fish doesn't end with salmon. Just about every type of Oregon seafood has had at least one experimental journey through the smoker. Some have become staples of the regional style. Sturgeon and the oily black cod, or sablefish, for example, are among Oregon's finest smoked seafood options. Shellfish is popular, too. Oysters, mussels, scallops, and clams are usually smoked in their natural salt and placed in a cold smoker for up to 4 hours.

A variety of smoked, pickled, and otherwise preserved fish are available from the following sources:

Jake's Famous Products
(see bay shrimp)
Hot-smoked salmon; smoked rainbow trout; smoked salmon or trout pâtés; smoked white sturgeon.

Josephson's Smokehouse
P.O. Box 412
Astoria, OR 97103
(503) 325-2190
1-800-772-3474
FAX (503) 325-4075
Visa/MC
One of the oldest, most reliable, and best-loved smokehouses in the Pacific Northwest. Cold-smoked lox, salmon jerky, traditional smoked Chinook, Sockeye, and Coho salmon, sturgeon, oysters, albacore tuna, and trout. Send for mail-order catalogue.

Norm Thompson Outfitters, Inc.
(see apples)

Sturgeon and Sturgeon Caviar

Its Loch Ness monster appearance has not helped the situation one bit. Let's face it: To most Americans, sturgeon is somewhere between a shark, a catfish, and a huge, armored eel. Yet this prehistoric Columbia River resident is a real delicacy known for its rich flavor and meatlike versatility. It is sweet and juicy, with a flavor that brings to mind scallops or lobster, and its flesh is dense and firm. It is delicious roasted, grilled, poached, or cooked in stews and chowders.

For thousands of years, the Pacific sturgeon has grown to enormous size and age in the larger rivers that empty into the Pacific along the Oregon coast. Because sturgeon spawn only when over six feet long and eight to ten years old, they are not a commercial fish. Actually, they are caught accidentally in nets meant for salmon.

Caviar from the roe of the Columbia River sturgeon has gained critical attention on the international scene. Produced by only by a few smoked-fish processors, the salty, jet black roe has been favorably compared with the much more expensive Russian Beluga and Sevruga caviars, as well as some of the new Chinese caviars. It is made only when enough eggs can be taken from roe-laden females brought in with spring- and fall-run salmon.

Oregon cooks became fond of the roe in the early '80s, when salmon and sturgeon were plentiful in the Columbia River. But now, as salmon runs shrink and regulations increase, local cooks must share a smaller supply with the rest of the world. Josephson's of Astoria has smokehouses right on the banks of the Columbia River. The company makes sturgeon caviar regularly and holds back enough to ship to mail-order customers all over the United States and Canada.

Josephson's Smokehouse
(see smoked seafood)
Sturgeon caviar available in 1-
to 8-ounce jars.

Walla Walla Sweet Onions

If cooks know only one offering from the Pacific Northwest, it is probably the justifiably famous Walla Walla Sweet onion. Sweet enough to eat like an apple, the large, delicate Walla Wallas lack the tear-making sulfur that creates the bite in most onions.

Its season is short, arriving briefly from spring to mid-summer. Cooks waste no time making use of it, often caramelizing it in its own sugar or baking it in tarts and breads. Walla Wallas can be the main focus of a summer ragout or simply served raw in sandwiches and salads.

Walla Walla Sweets are grown just over Oregon's northern border in the central dry farmlands of eastern Washington near Walla Walla. Their legacy in the region reportedly began around the turn of the century. As the story goes, a French soldier turned Washington farmer used seeds of a truly sweet onion from the island of Corsica. The Walla Walla area was subsequently settled by many Italian farmers who developed early, mid and late strains of their favorite onion, extending the growing season to about three and a half months.

Although onions with similarly honied tones—Hawaii's Maui onions or Georgia's Vidalias, for example—vie with Walla Wallas for the crown as the country's absolutely sweetest onion, locals believe that the Walla Walla's pungent flavor combined with its unsurpassed sweetness make it the world's best onion. Substitute others if you will, but the Walla Walla Sweet is widely available in many areas of the country during late July and August. If you don't find them near you, contact the following source and have some sent:

Walla Walla Gardener's Association
210 N. Eleventh Street
Walla Walla, WA 99362
(509) 525-7070 or 525-7071
1-800-553-5014
Visa/ MC
Will ship 10-pound and
20-pound boxes July through
the first week in August.

Walnuts

Prior to 1953, Oregon produced 10 percent of the nation's English walnuts. In the mid-1950s, a succession of heavy winter freezes wiped out nearly all the state's commercial walnut orchards. But small groves survived on some farms and many backyards still have an old spreading walnut tree or two. Oregon no longer ships walnuts in any great quantity, but local cooks still enjoy delicious fresh nuts for baking and general cooking purposes from neighborhood trees.

A small resurgence of walnut production is taking place in central Oregon. Orchardists are beginning to grow and export some excellent black walnuts.

Wine

In his *Wines of North America,* Robert Parker calls Oregon vineyards "America's new wine stars." Since the explosion of Pacific Northwest viniculture during the past twenty years, attention has focused on the startling Chardonnay and Pinot Noir grapes produced in the region. The Northwest climate allows the grapes to mature more slowly and thus retain more natural acidity. The vintners are fiercely independent and generally produce wine with a clear European character.

Chardonnay and Pinot Noir are not the only fine varietals grown in Oregon. The Riesling is light and flowery, with a crisp palate-clearing character. The previously little-known Pinot Gris makes a vibrant semidry summer cooler and is exploding in popularity.

The most consistent producers of Pinot Noir include Eyrie, Adelsheim, and Veritas, but others do as well as a good vintage. Shafer produces a wonderful Pinot Blanc blush. Excellent Chardonnays are produced by Shafer, Eyrie, Tualatin, Adelsheim, and Sokol Blosser, but again, they are not restricted to these. Delightful Rieslings are made by Sokol Blosser, Shafer, and Ponzi. Eyrie and Ponzi produce fine Pinot Gris wines.

Years to seek include 1983 Pinot Noir; 1985 and 1987 Pinot Noir, Chardonnay and Riesling; and 1988 Pinot Gris.

A visit to Yamhill County, otherwise known as Oregon's wine country, is a fall ritual for locals and tourists. Located about forty minutes from Portland, this county's wineries can be reached via Highway 99W, the state's official wine road. Many are set on the picturesque southern slopes of hills that offer splendid vistas of the fertile Willamette Valley, the Coast Range, and the Cascades. For maps, recommended tour routes and other information, contact the Oregon Winegrowers Association at 1200 N.W. Front Avenue, Suite 400, Portland, OR 97209, (503) 228-8403. Or call the Oregon Wine Advisory Board in Portland at (503) 228-8336.

CHAPTER ONE

HAZELNUT HOTCAKES, APPLE CIDER SYRUP, AND OTHER MORNING GLORIES

Autumn Pear Waffles with Frangelico Maple Syrup

Since Oregon produces most of the nation's hazelnuts as well as some of the world's best-tasting pears, this dish is a logical marriage of major industry and majestic notions. It's the creation of chef Harriet Reed Greenwood, whose innovative Oregon roadhouse cooking is legendary on Portland's breakfast circuit. Reed's creative touch extends to garnishing: She often serves these waffles with a dollop of whipped cream flavored with hazelnut liqueur.

Makes about 8 waffles; serves 4

For the pear topping:
Juice of $\frac{1}{2}$ lemon
2 ripe but firm pears

For the maple syrup:
1 cup pure maple syrup
$\frac{1}{4}$ cup hazelnut liqueur

For the waffles:
2$\frac{1}{4}$ cups unbleached all-purpose flour

1 tablespoon baking powder
$\frac{1}{2}$ teaspoon salt
1 tablespoon sugar
3 large eggs, at room temperature, separated
$\frac{1}{4}$ cup vegetable oil or unsalted butter, melted
1$\frac{1}{2}$ cups milk
2 tablespoons Frangelico (hazelnut) liqueur

1. To make the topping, fill a large bowl with water and add the lemon juice. Peel the pears, cut them in half lengthwise, and remove the cores. Cut each pear half into 6 lengthwise slices. Place the slices in the water as they are cut to prevent them from darkening.

2. To make the syrup, combine the maple syrup and hazelnut liqueur and set aside until ready to serve. Or combine and warm in a saucepan just before serving.

3. Preheat an oven to 200 degrees F. Heat a waffle iron until the indicator light shows it is ready to use.

4. To make the waffle batter, in a large mixing bowl combine the flour, baking powder, salt, and sugar. Slightly beat the egg yolks in a mixing bowl. Stir in the oil or melted butter, milk, and liqueur. Set aside. In a separate bowl, beat the egg whites until soft peaks form. Make a well in the center of the dry ingredients. Pour the egg yolk mixture into it all at once. Stir quickly and lightly (do not beat), using only a few strokes. The batter will still have a few lumps. Fold in a small amount of the egg whites to lighten the batter, then gently fold in the remaining whites until barely blended.

5. Cover about two-thirds of the waffle grid with batter. Close the lid and let the waffle cook until steam no longer rises from the iron, about 4 minutes. Remove the waffle and keep it warm by laying it directly on the rack of the preheated oven. Repeat with the remaining batter.

6. When all the waffles have been made, drain the pear slices. Transfer the waffles to warm serving plates. Top each waffle with pear slices. Serve the syrup on the side.

From Harriet's Eat Now Cafe

 # Gingerbread Pancakes with Apple Compote

Make no mistake: These deeply cinnamoned cakes, snappy with molasses, will entice anybody out of a warm bed on a Sunday morning. The fresh apple compote is an inspired touch and a welcome change from maple syrup. Look around your market for an apple with plenty of character. Possible choices include Red Gravenstein, Spitzenberg, or McIntosh.

Makes about sixteen 3-inch pancakes; serves 4

For the compote:

6 tart apples, peeled, cored, and sliced

1 cup water

$\frac{1}{4}$ cup firmly packed light brown sugar

1 tablespoon ground cinnamon

1 teaspoon ground ginger

$\frac{1}{2}$ teaspoon ground nutmeg

$\frac{1}{8}$ teaspoon ground cloves

$\frac{1}{8}$ teaspoon salt

For the pancakes:

$\frac{1}{2}$ cup each unbleached all-purpose flour and whole-wheat flour

$\frac{1}{2}$ teaspoon each salt and baking soda

$\frac{3}{4}$ teaspoon baking powder

2 teaspoons ground ginger

1 teaspoon each ground cinnamon and nutmeg

1 cup buttermilk

2 tablespoons molasses

1 large egg, lightly beaten

1 tablespoon vegetable oil or unsalted butter, melted

Sour cream or crème fraîche (page 236) for garnish

1. To make the compote, combine all the compote ingredients in a saucepan and bring to a boil. Reduce the heat to low, cover with a tight-fitting lid, and simmer for 30 minutes. Remove the lid and simmer until all the water is absorbed and mixture is thick and chunky, about 30 minutes longer. Remove the pan from the heat and set aside to cool.

2. To make the pancake batter, sift together the flours, salt, baking soda, and baking powder into a large bowl. Add the ginger, cinnamon, and nutmeg. In a separate bowl, stir together the buttermilk, molasses, egg, and oil. Make a well in the center of the dry ingredients. Pour the buttermilk mixture into it all at once. Stir quickly and lightly (do not beat), using only a few strokes. The batter will still have a few lumps.

3. Heat a lightly greased griddle or a large skillet over medium-high heat (350 to 375 degrees F). Ladle the batter by heaping tablespoonfuls (about $\frac{1}{8}$ cup) onto the hot

OREGON'S CUISINE OF THE RAIN

surface. When bubbles appear on the surface, after about 1 minute, turn the cakes and brown on the other side.

4. Serve the pancakes piping hot, topped with 1–2 teaspoons of the compote and a dollop of sour cream.

From Harriet's Eat Now Cafe

 # Thin Cream Cheese Pancakes with Marionberry Syrup

Marionberries are a cross between the loganberry and the wild mountain blackberry. They have the same color and basic flavor as the wild blackberry, but fewer and larger seeds and a natural sweetness usually reserved for the ripest of wild blackberries. Berry syrups, such as the following, have become a signature of the Oregon breakfast table. Here the purple red topping makes a nice cover for delicate cream cheese pancakes. If you can't find marionberries, substitute blackberries, strawberries, or any other seasonal berry.

Makes about sixteen 3-inch pancakes; serves 4

For the syrup:
**3 cups marionberries or
   other seasonal berries
$\frac{1}{4}$ cup sugar, or to taste
1 tablespoon fresh lemon
   juice**

For the pancakes:
**1 cup unbleached all-
   purpose flour, sifted
1 tablespoon sugar
$\frac{1}{2}$ teaspoon salt
$\frac{3}{4}$ teaspoon baking powder
$\frac{1}{2}$ teaspoon baking soda
$\frac{1}{2}$ cup (4 ounces) cream
   cheese, at room temperature**

**$\frac{1}{2}$ cup buttermilk, at room
   temperature
2 tablespoons unsalted
   butter, melted, or
   vegetable oil
1 teaspoon pure vanilla
   extract
2 large eggs, lightly beaten**

For the garnish:
**1 cup marionberries or
   other seasonal berries
1 cup plain yogurt or sour
   cream sweetened with
1 tablespoon honey**

1. To make the syrup, place the berries, sugar, and lemon juice in a food processor fitted with the steel blade and process for 10 seconds. Taste for sweetening and add more sugar if desired. To remove the seeds, strain the mixture into a bowl through a fine-mesh sieve, pushing with the back of a spoon. Set aside.

2. To make the pancake batter, sift together the sifted flour, sugar, salt, baking powder, and baking soda into a large bowl. Combine the cream cheese, buttermillk, melted butter, vanilla extract, and eggs in the food processor fitted with the steel blade. Process briefly, just enough to blend the ingredients thoroughly. Make a well in the center of the dry ingredients. Pour the buttermilk mixture into it all at once. Stir quickly and lightly (do not beat), using only a few strokes. The batter will still have a few lumps.

3. Heat a lightly greased griddle or a large frying pan over medium-high heat (350 to 375 degrees). Ladle the batter by heaping tablespoonfuls (about $\frac{1}{8}$ cup) onto the hot surface. When bubbles appear on the surface, turn the cakes and brown the other side.

4. Serve the pancakes piping hot with a garnish of the berries and a dollop of the sweetened yogurt or sour cream. Serve the syrup at room temperature on the side.

From Harriet's Eat Now Cafe

 # Hazelnut Corn Cakes with Wild Blackberry Compote

Old-fashioned breakfast basics mingled with new Oregon twists are a morning specialty at The Heathman Hotel. With its silver service in a setting of turquoise elegance, the dining

OREGON'S CUISINE OF THE RAIN

room is the grandest setting in all of Portland for the consumption of flapjacks. The cakes derive their rich texture from toasted hazelnuts ground as fine as flour. The hot blackberry topping, with its ginger accent, is a modern touch. When blackberries are out of season, serve with maple syrup. Or try the Apple Cider Syrup on page 8.

Makes about twelve 6-inch corn cakes; serves 4 to 6

1 cup water
1 cup milk
1 teaspoon unsalted butter, melted
$\frac{1}{4}$ cup yellow or stone-ground cornmeal
1 cup unbleached all-purpose flour
$\frac{1}{2}$ cup finely ground roasted hazelnuts (page 236)

$\frac{1}{2}$ teaspoon salt
1 teaspoon sugar
1 teaspoon baking powder
1 egg, lightly beaten
Wild Blackberry Compote (page 233), or maple syrup and unsalted butter

1. Combine the water and milk in a heavy saucepan and bring to a boil. Stir in the butter and cornmeal. Remove from the heat, cover, and let stand for 10 minutes.

2. Place the flour, hazelnuts, salt, sugar, and baking powder in a mixing bowl and stir to combine. Beat the egg into the cornmeal mixture. Using a wire whisk, gradually whisk the cornmeal mixture into the dry ingredients. Mix until smooth, adding more water if necessary to achieve the thickness of heavy cream.

3. Heat a lightly greased griddle or a large frying pan over medium-high heat (350 to 375 degrees). Ladle the batter by $\frac{1}{4}$ cupfuls onto the hot surface. When bubbles appear on the surface, turn the corn cakes and brown the other side.

4. Serve the corn cakes piping hot with the Wild Blackberry Compote.

From The Heathman Hotel

Apple Cider Syrup

In the early '80s, Portland offered few prizes as coveted as a seat at Indigine's brunch table. Chef Millie Howe, who now concentrates solely on dinner, offered highly original alternatives to stardard fare, including this terrific option to maple syrup. Try it over pancakes or waffles or drizzle it over vanilla ice cream piled high with hot, sautéed apple slices. For the best flavor, use fresh, unpasteurized cider. The syrup will keep for more than one week when poured into sterilized and sealed jars. Store them in a cool, dark place.

Makes about 1 quart

2 gallons fresh apple cider
2 cinnamon sticks
12 cloves

1 lemon, thinly sliced
$\frac{1}{2}$ cup honey

1. Combine all the ingredients in a large heavy-bottomed pot and bring to a boil. Boil until the mixture is reduced to approximately 2 quarts. Then lower the heat and simmer until thickened and reduced to approximately 1 quart syrup. This process will take several hours.

2. Pour the syrup through a fine-mesh sieve into a sterilized mason jar and keep tightly covered until ready to use. Serve at room temperature or heat in a saucepan just before serving. To keep more than 1 week, seal in sterilized jars.

From Indigine

 # Aged Gouda and Sherried Apple Omelets

Gouda is a popular Oregon cheese. The region's best buy comes from Yakima, Washington. It's a rich, aged, golden cheese that brings to mind the taste of caramel and toasted walnuts. Any

good-quality Gouda, however, will match well with the smoky scent of sherry and the sweet flavor of apples and tarragon. Gravensteins, Newton Pippins, or any other crisp, tart apples will work well here.

Serves 2

For the filling:
2 tablespoons unsalted butter
2 large apples, peeled, cored, and sliced lengthwise
2 tablespoons dry sherry

For the omelets:
6 large eggs
2 tablespoons water
1 tablespoon minced fresh tarragon, or 1 teaspoon dried tarragon
2 tablespoons unsalted butter, preferably clarified (page 239)
1 cup grated Gouda

1. Preheat an oven to 400 degrees F.

2. For the filling, melt the butter in a large heavy-bottomed skillet over medium-high heat until slightly golden. Add the apples and sauté for 1 to 2 minutes. Add the sherry and sauté over high heat for 1 minute. Reduce the heat to low, cover with a tight-fitting lid, and cook for 5 minutes. Using a slotted spoon, transfer the sautéed apples to a plate and reserve. Return the skillet to the burner and raise the heat to high. Slightly reduce any liquid remaining in the pan, then pour the thickened liquid over the reserved apples.

3. It is best to make the omelets individually. In a bowl, whisk the eggs with the water and tarragon. Over medium heat, melt half of the butter in an 8-inch oven-proof omelet pan or heavy skillet. When the skillet is hot, pour in half of the eggs. Cook, tilting the pan and occasionally pushing the set eggs aside with a spatula or fork so the omelet cooks quickly. When the bottom is set but the center is still moist and runny, spoon half of the

(continued)

reserved apples evenly over the top and then half of the Gouda. Place the pan in the oven until the filling is set, 10 to 15 seconds.

4. Remove the skillet from the oven, fold the omelet in half, and serve immediately. Repeat the process to make the second omelet.

From Harriet's Eat Now Cafe

 # Goat Cheese and Poached Pear Omelets

Northwest cheese makers are turning out an exciting variety of goat cheeses—some traditional, some innovative, some good enough to rival their European counterparts. The movement inspired this original omelet, perfect for a romantic breakfast for two. Fresh lavender, which flourishes in Northwestern gardens in early summer, gives the omelet a wonderful perfume. Dried lavender is available in most herb shops.

Serves 2

For the filling:
2 ripe unblemished pears, preferably Bosc, Bartlett, or Anjou
½ cup Zinfandel or pear wine
½ cup water
1 tablespoon sugar
2 teaspoons pesticide-free fresh or dried lavender sprigs, optional

For the omelet:
6 large eggs
2 teaspoons water
2 tablespoons unsalted butter, preferably clarified (page 239)
2 to 4 ounces Montrachet or other mild fresh goat cheese
½ cup sour cream or crème fraîche (page 236) for garnish

1. To make the filling, peel, core, and cut the pears into 8 to 12 sections, depending upon their size. Set aside. In a saucepan, combine the wine, water, sugar, and lavender. Bring to a boil, reduce the heat to low, and simmer for 10 minutes.

2. Add the pears to the saucepan. Raise the heat and bring the liquid to a simmer, then remove from the heat. Let the pears steep in the pan until they are tender but still firm, about 15 minutes. Using a slotted spoon, remove the pears to a dish and set aside. Discard the poaching liquid.

3. It is best to make the omelets individually. In a bowl whisk the eggs with the water. Heat an 8-inch omelet pan or heavy cast-iron skillet over high heat for 1 minute. Melt half of the butter in the pan and heat until golden. Pour half of the eggs into the pan. Cook, tilting the pan and occasionally pushing the set eggs aside with a spatula or fork so the omelet cooks quickly. When the eggs are just about set, distribute half of the Montrachet and one fourth of the pears over the omelet. Fold the omelet in half and transfer to a serving plate.

4. Top the omelet with a dollop of sour cream and an equal amount of the poached pears. Repeat the process to make the second omelet.

From Harriet's Eat Now Cafe

 # King Salmon Hash

Here, tender flakes of smoked salmon replace the traditional roast beef leftovers. Oregon salmon is typically alder smoked, which gives it a seductive scent. But any good smoked salmon will work beautifully here.

Serves 4 to 6

For the hash:
6 tablespoons unsalted butter
1 medium red onion, finely chopped
1 teaspoon finely chopped garlic
3 cups cooked, peeled, and shredded russet potatoes
1¼ pounds smoked salmon, skinned, boned, and flaked
½ cup sour cream
1 teaspoon fresh lemon juice
1 tablespoon prepared horseradish
1 tablespoon finely chopped fresh parsley
Salt and freshly ground pepper

For the garnish:
¼ cup sour cream
2 scallions, finely chopped

1. To make the hash, melt 3 tablespoons of the butter in a heavy skillet over medium heat. When the butter melts, add the onion and sauté until still slightly crunchy, about 3 to 5 minutes. Add the garlic and sauté lightly for 1 minute. Remove the onion and garlic from the pan and set aside. In the same skillet, place the remaining 3 tablespoons butter and the potatoes. Cook until the edges begin to crisp, about 5 minutes. Remove from the heat.

2. Place the salmon in a bowl. Add the sautéed onions and garlic, cooked potatoes, sour cream, lemon juice, horseradish, and parsley. Season to taste with salt and pepper. Mix well but do not pack the mixture.

3. Return the mixture to the skillet and cook, tossing gently to prevent the contents from sticking to the pan, until heated through, about 5 minutes. Remove to a warm plate.

4. Garnish the hash with the sour cream, sprinkle with the scallions, and serve.

From The Heathman Hotel

Chinook Salmon Lox

Fresh bagels, velvety cream cheese, and lox that is thick, soft, and smoky with a faint hint of salt are the soul of any respectable Sunday brunch. Good-quality lox can be found in most areas, but few compete with the flavor of home-cured lox fashioned from Oregon's superb Chinook salmon. The following recipe comes by way of visionary restaurateur Michael Vidor, the brains behind two of Portland's signature restaurants: L'Auberge and Genoa. The preparation is easy but requires a home smoker or a kettle grill. Serve the lox with pumpernickel or rye bread, cream cheese, and thinly sliced onions.

Serves 10 to 12

$\frac{1}{4}$ **cup sugar**
$\frac{1}{4}$ **cup salt**
1 Chinook salmon, about
  7 pounds, filleted with
  the skin on

Vegetable oil

1. Stir together the sugar and salt in a small bowl. Sprinkle the mixture lightly over both sides of the salmon fillets. Select a dish long enough to hold the salmon fillets flat. Line it with a piece of plastic wrap. Put the 2 fillets in the dish, skin side out and with no pieces overlapping, and cover with plastic wrap. Place a heavy weight on top and refrigerate for 2 days. Periodically drain off any liquid that accumulates in the dish.

2. Remove the salmon from the refrigerator and wipe with paper towels until all of the moisture is removed. Lightly coat both sides of the salmon with vegetable oil.

3. Cook the salmon in a smoker (if you are using a kettle grill, see step 4) heated to not more than 130 degrees F just until the flesh is slightly firmed, about 45 minutes.

(continued)

Remove the fish from the smoker, let cool, and chill until ready to use.

4. To smoke in a kettle grill, follow steps 1 and 2. Heat enough charcoal briquettes to fit under a 6-inch cast-iron skillet. Wet enough alder, apple, hickory, or other clean wood chips to fill the skillet and place them in it. Place a nonflammable hot plate over the coals and set the skillet on top. When the chips begin to smoke, place the salmon atop a clean grill rack or on a cake rack positioned about 5 to 6 inches above the chips. Cook until the salmon is just firm enough to slice, 30 to 45 minutes. Be careful not to overcook the fish or to have so much smoke that it penetrates the flesh. There should be just enough smoke to cook the salmon. Remove the fish from the grill, let cool, and chill until ready to use.

5. To serve, carefully remove the skin and cut the fish into paper-thin slices, working from head to tail. Arrange the slices on a plate. Wrap any unused lox in plastic wrap and store in the refrigerator for up to 2 weeks.

From the kitchen of Michael Vidor

 # Potatoes, Smoky Ham, and Sweet Onions

This urban variation on a rustic Oregon theme brings together smoky ham, red potatoes, and sweet onions in a lusty break-fast special.

Serves 6

2 pounds red potatoes
1 pound smoked country
   ham steak
About $\frac{1}{2}$ cup vegetable oil or
   safflower oil
2 Walla Walla Sweet onions
   or yellow onions, thinly
   sliced

Salt and freshly ground
   pepper to taste
$\frac{1}{2}$ cup water

1. Place the unpeeled potatoes in a saucepan with water to cover. Bring to a boil and boil until almost tender, about 15 minutes. Drain, remove the skins, and cut the potatoes into slices $\frac{1}{8}$ inch thick.

2. Remove any excess fat from the outer edge of the ham steak. Cut the steak into 1-inch pieces.

3. Preheat an oven to 350 degrees F.

4. Place 3 tablespoons of the oil in a large skillet over medium-low heat. Add half of the onions and sauté until golden, about 15–20 minutes. Add half of the potatoes and season to taste with salt and pepper. Add half of the ham steak pieces and sauté until the potatoes are golden on both sides, about 8 to 10 minutes, adding a little oil if necessary to prevent sticking.

5. Transfer the mixture to an ovenproof casserole. Repeat the process with the remaining ingredients and add to the casserole as well. Pour the water evenly over the top. Bake, uncovered, for 20 minutes or until the water is absorbed. Serve hot.

CHAPTER TWO

SEDUCTIVE TARTS, INTRIGUING PÂTÉS, AND OTHER SMALL PLATES

Crab Cakes with Aged Cheddar and Pear Chutney

This Oregon twist on a Maryland classic crowns patties of Dungeness crab with grated Cheddar from Oregon's Tillamook creamery. A zip of pear chutney, dabbed on top, provides the concluding spark.

Makes 8 crab cakes; serves 4

1 pound cooked Dungeness crabmeat or other sweet crab meat, any cartilage removed, flaked
1 tablespoon Dijon mustard
Large pinch of cayenne pepper
$\frac{3}{4}$ cup sliced scallions
1 large egg, beaten
$\frac{1}{2}$ cup good-quality mayonnaise

2 tablespoons peanut, vegetable, or corn oil
2 cups fresh bread crumbs
1 cup grated aged Cheddar cheese
$\frac{1}{2}$ cup Pear-Currant Chutney (page 222) or other fruit chutney

1. Preheat a broiler.

2. Combine the crab meat, mustard, cayenne pepper, scallions, egg, and mayonnaise in a mixing bowl. Stir to mix well. Divide the mixture into 8 equal portions. Shape each portion into a ball and then flatten it into a $\frac{1}{2}$-inch-thick patty. Set aside.

3. Warm the oil in a large heavy skillet over medium-high heat. Place the bread crumbs in a shallow bowl. Dip each crab cake into the crumbs and shake off any excess. Slip the cakes into the hot skillet, a few at a time, and cook, turning once, until golden brown and cooked throughout, 2 to 3 minutes.

4. Transfer the cooked cakes to a flameproof platter or aluminum foil–covered baking sheet. Top each cake with 1 tablespoon of the Cheddar cheese. Place under the broiler and heat, just until the cheese melts, about 1 minute.

5. Serve the crab cakes piping hot, dabbed with chutney.

From The Heathman Hotel

 # Steamed Clams with Garden Herbs

On summer mornings in the Northwest, clam diggers dot the shoreline like sea gulls. Shovel and pail in hand, they're spurred on by memories of irresistible sand dwellers. The prize: heaping pots of freshly steamed clams, mesmerizing beachside bonfires, and the hum of conversation. Whole clams steamed in broth invigorated by local wine and garden herbs are a classic regional preparation. Serve with hot sourdough bread on the side to sop up the juices.

Serves 4

4 pounds steamer clams in the shell, well washed and drained
2 tablespoons unsalted butter
$\frac{1}{4}$ cup chopped mixed fresh herbs such as thyme, oregano, tarragon, and basil

2 tablespoons minced garlic
2 cups Pinot Gris or other dry white wine
Juice of 1 lemon
Salt and freshly ground pepper
Lemon wedges and fresh herb sprigs for garnish

1. Scrub the clams with a stiff brush. Let them stand for about one hour in several changes of cold water to remove their sand. Drain into a colander until ready to use.

(continued)

2. Place the butter, chopped herbs, and garlic in a large saucepan. Simmer over medium heat for 2 to 3 minutes.

3. Add the wine, lemon juice, and clams and bring to a boil. Cover and cook until the clams open, 3 to 5 minutes. Discard any clams that do not open. Season to taste with salt and pepper.

4. Divide the clams and the broth among individual serving bowls. Garnish with lemon wedges and herb sprigs.

From The Heathman Hotel

 # Oysters in Basil Nests with Quail Eggs

Tiny Olympias, the Northwest's only native oysters, are regional gems. To do more than just eat 'em raw would be, as one writer put it, courting the "thin wedge on the edge of heresy." The following dish is a handsome starter that's easy to assemble. Look for the quail eggs in Asian grocery stores.

Serves 4

1 bunch fresh basil
12 oysters in the shell
Rock salt as needed
$\frac{1}{4}$ cup hazelnut oil

12 quail eggs
$\frac{1}{4}$ cup freshly grated
  Parmesan cheese
Lemon wedges for garnish

1. Preheat a broiler.

2. Remove the stems from the basil and discard. You should have about 2 cups leaves. Cut the leaves into fine shreds.

3. Shuck the oysters, placing the oyster meats in a bowl and reserving the shells. Lay 12 oyster shells on a bed of rock salt in a shallow baking pan. Make a small nest of the shredded basil in each shell. Add the hazelnut oil to the shucked oysters and lightly toss. Place 1 oyster in each shell. Carefully break 1 quail egg into each shell. Sprinkle a little Parmesan cheese over the top of each egg.

4. Place the pan under the broiler until the eggs set and the oysters are warm. Serve immediately with lemon wedges.

How to shuck an oyster: Hold each oyster rounded side down, slip an oyster knife or other small sturdy knife into hinged side and twist the knife to pry open the shell. Run the knife along the upper and lower shells to detach the muscles.

From The Heathman Hotel

 # Seviche of Salmon, Crab, and Oysters

Seviche means raw fish that is "cooked" through marination in citrus juice. This South American specialty has been embraced by Northwest cooks, who experiment boldly with the local catch. Light but substantial, it is perfect as a first course or luncheon entrée. It is simple to assemble, but requires up to 24 hours to marinate. Vary the fish as desired to find the best seasonal options, but make sure to use absolutely fresh seafood. The best versions are made by cooks who taste and adjust the marinade repeatedly until a ravishing blend of hot and tart flavors emerges.

Serves 8

1 large red onion, sliced into
  thin rings
1 tablespoon salt
2 pounds salmon fillets
$\frac{1}{2}$ pound sea scallops
$\frac{1}{2}$ pound shucked oysters
2 cups water, boiling
$\frac{1}{4}$ pound Dungeness crab
  meat or other sweet crab
  meat, any cartilage
  removed, shredded
Juice of 6 large lemons
Juice of 8 limes
2 large cloves garlic,
  crushed

2 tablespoons chopped fresh
  cilantro
Salt and freshly ground
  pepper, optional
2 small fresh hot red chili
  peppers
6 to 8 jalapeño or serrano
  peppers, preferably fresh,
  but rinsed canned chilies
  will do
2 heads leafy greens,
  separated into leaves and
  chilled
Paper-thin red onion rings
  for garnish, optional

1. Carefully separate the thin onion rings and place them in a large mixing bowl. Sprinkle with the salt and add water to cover. Let stand for 30 minutes. Rinse and drain, then set aside in the bowl.

2. Cut the salmon into uniform strips about $\frac{3}{8}$ inch wide and $1\frac{1}{2}$ inches long. Place the salmon, scallops, and oysters in a colander. Pour the boiling water over the top. Shake the colander to drain off excess water. Add the drained seafood and the crab meat to the reserved onion rings and toss to mix. Scatter the mixture over the bottom of a wide, shallow baking dish.

3. In a small bowl, stir together the lemon and lime juices, garlic, cilantro, and, if desired, salt and pepper to taste. Taste and adjust the seasonings. Pour the marinade over the seafood, making sure each piece is partially immersed in the liquid.

4. Remove the stems from the red chilies and jalapeños. Cut the peppers in half and discard the seeds. Slice the chilies into long, thin strips and add them to the fish mixture.

5. Cover the pan with plastic wrap and refrigerate for 6 hours or overnight. When the fish is ready, it will have turned white. Taste the marinade occasionally, adding more seasonings or citrus juice as necessary.

6. Line individual plates with the leafy greens. Spoon the seviche over the lettuce and garnish with paper-thin onion rings, if desired.

 ## Bay Shrimp Pâté

Tiny crustaceans known as bay shrimp or "Oregon shrimp meat" are a prized catch on Northwest coastlines, valued for their delicate texture and mild, sweet flavor. These are the qualities that shine brightly in this dainty, subtle, and buttery pâté with a brisk undertone of dill. Serve with thinly sliced sourdough bread and a bottle of white Zinfandel.

Serves 12

3 cups bay shrimp or any
   small shelled shrimp
   (about $1\frac{1}{3}$ pounds)
$\frac{3}{4}$ cup good-quality
   mayonnaise
$\frac{1}{2}$ cup coarsely chopped
   onion

2 tablespoons chopped
   fresh dill, or 2 teaspoons
   dried dill
1 pound (2 cups) clarified
   unsalted butter (page 239)
Kosher salt
Lemon wedges for garnish

1. Drain the shrimp and squeeze to eliminate any excess moisture.

2. In a food processor fitted with the steel blade, combine the shrimp, mayonnaise, onions, and dill. Process until

(continued)

barely puréed. Fold in the clarified butter and add salt to taste.

3. Line a 4-cup loaf pan with plastic wrap. Pour the shrimp mixture into it. Cover and chill overnight.

4. Remove the pâté from the pan by inverting the mold on a flat plate. Discard the plastic wrap. Slice and serve with lemon wedges.

From Indigine

 # Chicken Liver Mousse with Figs and Apple Brandy

Some things are so grand you never quite get used to them. Fresh figs growing a few feet from your door are one of them. Such is the glory of the Northwest, where fig trees often come with the neighborhood. Voluptuous when eaten fresh and temptingly sweet when dried, figs find their way into all kinds of Northwest innovations. Here a creamy chicken liver spread takes its character from dried figs macerated in regional apple brandy. The results are nothing less than smashing, especially served with toast points or crackers and a robust wine.

Serves 4 to 6

6 dried figs, stemmed and sliced

$\frac{1}{4}$ cup apple brandy or Calvados

6 ounces ($\frac{3}{4}$ cup) unsalted butter, at room temperature

1 small onion, chopped

$\frac{1}{2}$ pound chicken livers, trimmed of discolored areas and fat

$\frac{1}{4}$ teaspoon dried thyme

$\frac{1}{4}$ teaspoon ground mace

$\frac{1}{4}$ teaspoon freshly ground white pepper

$\frac{1}{4}$ to $\frac{1}{2}$ teaspoon salt

1. In a small bowl, combine the figs and brandy and let stand for 2 hours. Drain off the brandy and reserve it along with the figs.

2. Melt 2 tablespoons of the butter in a medium-heavy skillet over medium heat. Add the onion and sauté until tender, about 10 minutes. Add the livers and sauté until just pink in the center, 3 to 5 minutes. Remove from the heat. Transfer the onion and livers to a food processor fitted with the steel blade; set the skillet aside. Add the thyme, mace, pepper, salt, and reserved figs. Process until smooth. Taste and adjust the seasonings. Leave the mixture in the processor.

3. Place the skillet over medium-high heat and pour in the reserved brandy. Deglaze the pan by stirring and scraping the solidified juices from its bottom and sides. Add the deglazed juices into the liver mixture and process to mix.

4. Cut the remaining butter into pats, and add to the processor. Process until very smooth. Taste and adjust the seasonings.

5. Place the mousse in a bowl or crock, cover with plastic wrap, and chill until ready to serve.

From Cafe des Amis

 # Game Pâté with Cranberry-Ginger Chutney

Eastern Oregon is the land of juniper, jackrabbit, venison, and sagebrush. Game hunting is still a popular sport in these parts, with local shops pulling in good weekend business from city

dwellers. Rumor has it that more time is spent preparing for and talking about the adventure than on the hunt itself. The following recipe is a must should the wily sportsman get lucky. The pâté is best made at least 24 hours in advance. Serve with crusty bread, feisty chutney, and assorted condiments—Dijon mustard, capers, sliced red onions, and small sour pickles.

Serves 12

$\frac{3}{4}$ **pound ground lean rabbit or chicken**

$\frac{3}{4}$ **pound ground lean venison or pork loin**

$\frac{3}{4}$ **pound whole chicken livers or rabbit livers, trimmed of discolored areas and fat**

$\frac{3}{4}$ **pound bacon, ground**

3 cloves garlic, finely minced

3 shallots, finely minced

A few gratings of whole nutmeg, or $\frac{1}{2}$ teaspoon ground nutmeg

1 teaspoon chopped fresh thyme, or $\frac{1}{2}$ teaspoon dried thyme

1 tablespoon juniper berries

$\frac{1}{2}$ **teaspoon hot-pepper flakes**

2 large eggs, lightly beaten

$\frac{1}{4}$ **cup heavy cream**

2 tablespoons Cognac

1 cup fresh bread crumbs

Salt and freshly ground pepper

Small amount of vegetable oil

1 pound prosciutto, thinly sliced

Cranberry-Ginger Chutney (page 223) or other fruit chutney

1. Combine all the ingredients, except the vegetable oil, prosciutto, and chutney, in a mixing bowl. Mix thoroughly. Warm a small amount of vegetable oil in a sauté pan over medium-high heat. When the pan is hot, cook a small amount of the pâté. Taste the cooked mixture; it should give you an idea of how the finished pâté will taste. Adjust the seasonings. Cook another small amount of the mixture, if necessary, to test the adjusted seasonings.

2. Preheat an oven to 375 degrees F.

3. Line the bottom and sides of a $2\frac{1}{2}$-quart ceramic pâté mold with the prosciutto slices. Overlap the slices to cover the entire inside surface of the mold and allow 2 inches of prosciutto to hang over the edges. Fill the lined mold with the pâté mixture, pressing it down to eliminate any air pockets. Shape the mixture so that it extends $\frac{1}{2}$ inch above the rim of the mold. Fold the overhanging prosciutto slices over the top to enclose the pâté completely. Cover the top with aluminum foil.

4. Place the mold in a roasting pan and pour in water to reach 1 inch up the sides of the mold. Bake until the internal temperature registers 140 degrees F on an instant-read thermometer and the top of the pâté is firm to the touch, about $1\frac{1}{2}$ hours.

5. Remove the mold from the roasting pan. Place a heavy pan or a baking sheet weighted with a stack of plates on top of the pâté. Let cool for 1 hour or until the pâté is room temperature. Run a knife blade around the edge of the pâté and carefully invert it onto a flat plate. Wrap it tightly with plastic wrap and refrigerate overnight.

6. To serve, cut the pâté into slices. Offer the chutney on the side.

From The Heathman Hotel

 # Goat Cheese with Green Olives, Black Peppercorns, and Red Chilies

The splendid array of Oregon-produced goat cheeses has inspired some simple, delicious offerings, such as the following. Serve with crackers or crusty bread and fresh fruit as a first course or light lunch.

Serves 6

6 small wedges goat cheese	$1\frac{1}{2}$ tablespoons chopped
12 unpitted green olives	fresh oregano or
1 cup olive oil	2 teaspoons dried oregano
2 cloves garlic, minced	2 teaspoons crushed
1 dried red chili pepper, broken into small pieces	peppercorns

1. Place the wedges of goat cheese in a glass pie plate or serving dish. Surround with the olives.

2. In a small bowl, stir together all the remaining ingredients to make a marinade. Pour the marinade over the cheese and olives. Cover and marinate for several hours in the refrigerator.

3. Remove from the refrigerator 1 hour before serving. Using a slotted spoon, carefully remove the cheese and olives from the marinade and serve.

From Indigine

Pears Stuffed with Blue Cheese and Hazelnuts

Hazelnuts and Oregon's fabulous blue cheese figure prominently on the menu at Bread and Ink Cafe, one of Portland's premier neighborhood restaurants. In a '40s-style interior with vintage poker-table chairs and frost green walls, chef Pattie Hill mingles local nuts and cheeses in a procession of original dishes that includes the following. The pears may be stuffed in advance, but be sure to bring them to room temperature before serving.

Serves 8

1 bunch watercress
$\frac{1}{4}$ cup unsalted butter, at
   room temperature
$\frac{1}{4}$ pound cream cheese, at
   room temperature
$\frac{1}{2}$ pound blue cheese, at
   room temperature
$\frac{1}{2}$ cup heavy cream
1 cup chopped roasted
   hazelnuts (page 236)

$\frac{1}{2}$ teaspoon freshly ground
   white pepper
2 tablespoons pear brandy
2 quarts water
Juice of 1 large lemon
8 ripe but firm and
   unblemished Comice or
   Bartlett pears

1. Discard the stems from the watercress sprigs and pat the leaves dry. Measure $\frac{1}{4}$ cup leaves; chop them finely and set aside. Chill the remaining whole leaves until serving time.

2. Place the butter, cream cheese, and blue cheese in a mixing bowl. Using an electric mixer set on low speed, beat until creamy. Slowly beat in enough of the cream to lighten the mixture. Add the hazelnuts, pepper, pear brandy, and chopped watercress. Mix until just blended. Set aside. (If preparing ahead of time, refrigerate until ready to use, then bring to room temperature.)

3. Fill a large bowl with water and add a few tablespoons of lemon juice. Cut the pears in half lengthwise. Cut off a quarter-size slice from the rounded side of each pear half so the pear halves will sit firmly on a plate when served. With a melon ball scooper, scoop out the core and enough of the center to make a small well. Combine the water and lemon juice in a large bowl. As each pear is cut, drop it into the water and let it stand until ready to fill.

4. To serve, make a bed of the chilled watercress leaves on a serving platter or small individual plates. Spoon an equal amount of the mousse into each pear well. Arrange the pears atop the watercress and serve immediately.

From Bread and Ink Cafe

Autumn Pear and Goat Cheese Tart

*A marriage of fresh goat cheese and poached pears is hard to
contest. Consider this chic little tart in the fall, when pears are
peaking. It's a savory dish, perfect as a first course or as an
alternative to a fruit and cheese plate. If you're looking for
an unusual dessert, use a sweeter pastry such as Pâte Sucrée
(page 189) and garnish each portion with a dollop of sweetened crème fraîche (page 236). The recipe comes from my
friend Jane Burkholder, owner of I Dolci Bakery and one of
Portland's most formidable pastry chefs.*

Serves 4 as a main course or 6 as a first course

**9-inch Pâte Brisée tart shell,
partially baked (page 187)**

For the poached pears:
**1 vanilla bean
2 cups water
1 cup dry white wine
1½ cups sugar
Juice of 1 lemon
1 cinnamon stick
4 ripe Anjou or Bartlett
pears, peeled, halved
lengthwise, and cored**

For the custard:
**1 vanilla bean
¼ pound mild goat cheese, at
room temperature
1 tablespoon unbleached all-
purpose flour
2 large eggs
¼ cup half-and-half**

1. Prepare the tart shell and partially bake as directed.
Let cool.

2. To poach the pears, cut the vanilla bean in half lengthwise
and scrape out the seeds into a large, heavy saucepan;
save the pod for another use. Add the water, wine, sugar,
lemon juice, and cinnamon stick. Bring the mixture to a
boil. Reduce the heat to low and add the pears, cut sides
up. Simmer until the pears are tender but still firm, about
10 minutes. Remove from the heat. Using a slotted spoon,

remove the pears from the liquid and set aside on a plate to cool. Discard the poaching liquid.

3. Preheat an oven to 350 degrees F. Position a rack in the middle of the oven.

4. To make the custard, cut the vanilla bean in half and scrape out the seeds into a small bowl; save the pod for another use. Place the goat cheese in a mixing bowl. Using an electric mixer set on low speed, beat until smooth. Add the flour and then the eggs, one at a time, beating well after each addition. Scrape down the bowl sides and add the half-and-half and vanilla bean seeds. Beat until thoroughly combined.

5. Arrange the cooled pears in the pie shell, hollow sides down. Spoon the custard evenly over the pears.

6. Bake the tart until the custard sets, about 20 minutes. Remove to a wire rack to cool. Serve at room temperature.

From the kitchen of Jane Burkholder

 # Chanterelle Tart with Sugar-Roasted Walnuts

Fall in the Northwest is met with great expectations. It is the season of the chanterelle, the region's reigning mushroom. The wild and wavy forest fungi taste like earth, smoke, and apricots. Chanterelles can vary somewhat in color and flavor, so you should smell them before buying and look for a characteristic earthy scent. When you find a good crop of the bronzed beauties, try this curiously delicious tart, which is made crisp and fragrant with caramelized walnuts and garlic. Serve with autumn's finest bounty: Comice pears, fresh figs, and crisp apples.

Serves 4 as a main course or 6 as a first course

For the pastry:

1 tablespoon chopped fresh tarragon, or 1 teaspoon dried tarragon

1 cup unbleached all-purpose flour

$\frac{1}{4}$ pound ($\frac{1}{2}$ cup) unsalted butter, chilled, cut into $\frac{1}{2}$-inch pieces

1 tablespoon water

1 large egg yolk, beaten

For the filling:

1 head garlic (about $\frac{1}{4}$ pound), separated into cloves and peeled

$\frac{1}{2}$ cup walnuts

1 tablespoon light brown sugar

6 tablespoons butter

6 ounces fresh chanterelles, sliced

4 tablespoons minced fresh tarragon

3 large eggs

1 cup heavy cream

$\frac{1}{2}$ cup half-and-half

2 tablespoons Dijon mustard

1. To make the pastry, combine the tarragon and flour in a food processor fitted with the steel blade. Process to mix using the on/off pulse. Add the butter and process just until the mixture resembles coarse meal. Add the water and process just until the dough comes together in a ball. Remove the ball from the processor and flatten the dough into a disk.

2. Lightly flour a work surface. Using a lightly floured rolling pin, gently roll the pastry from the center of the circle toward the outer rim, using short outward strokes. Roll the pastry into a round about $\frac{1}{8}$ inch thick. Drape the pastry over the rolling pin and transfer it to a 9-inch tart pan with a removable bottom. Undrape the pastry and gently press it onto the bottom and sides of the pan. Roll the pin over the top of the pan to cut away any excess dough. Prick the crust well, cover, and chill for 1 hour.

3. Preheat an oven to 350 degrees F.

4. Cover the pie shell with an extended sheet of aluminum foil. Weigh the foil down with dried beans or pie weights.

Place in the oven and bake for 10 minutes. Remove the weights and foil. Brush the shell with the egg yolk. Bake until the crust is brown, another 10 to 15 minutes. Remove from the oven and let cool. Raise the oven temperature to 375 degrees.

5. To make the filling, reserve 2 of the garlic cloves. Place the remaining garlic cloves and the walnuts in a lightly greased shallow baking pan. Sprinkle the brown sugar over the garlic and walnuts. Cut 2 tablespoons of the butter into small bits and use to dot the top evenly.

6. Place in the oven and roast until the butter and sugar have caramelized, 20 to 30 minutes. Remove the pan from the oven and let cool. Coarsely chop the cooled walnuts and garlic; set aside. Increase the oven temperature to 400 degrees.

7. Mince the reserved 2 cloves garlic. Heat the remaining 4 tablespoons butter in a large skillet over medium heat. When the foam subsides, add the chanterelles, minced garlic, and 2 tablespoons of the tarragon and sauté, stirring and tossing, until mushrooms are tender, about 3 minutes. Remove from the heat and set aside.

8. In a mixing bowl, whisk together the eggs, cream, half-and-half, Dijon mustard, and the remaining 2 tablespoons tarragon. Arrange the chanterelles in the cooled pie shell. Pour the egg-cream mixture over the mushrooms.

9. Place in the oven and bake for 15 minutes. Remove from the oven and sprinkle the reserved garlic and walnuts over the top. Return the tart to the oven and bake until the custard is set, another 20 minutes.

10. To serve, remove to a wire rack. Cool 10 minutes; cut into wedges and serve.

From Briggs and Crampton's Catering and Table for Two

CHAPTER THREE

OYSTER BISQUE, MUSSEL CHOWDER, AND OTHER SEASONAL SOUPS

Pacific Oyster and Spinach Bisque

Chef Pattie Hill of Portland's Bread and Ink Cafe said she didn't have oysters Rockefeller on her mind when she created the following recipe, but her creamy mingling of Northwest oysters, fresh spinach, and anise liqueur brings to mind that American classic. Tarragon gives the dish a clean, sharp edge, and the pale green soup plays up the richness of oysters beautifully. Serve with champagne and hot crusty bread.

Serves 6

1 pound spinach
$\frac{1}{4}$ cup unsalted butter
1 small onion, chopped
3 tablespoons unbleached
   all-purpose flour
3 cups Fish Stock (page 240),
   or 2 cups bottled clam
   juice mixed with 1 cup
   water
1$\frac{1}{2}$ pints shucked oysters,
   with their liquid
1 cup heavy cream

3 tablespoons Pernod
1 tablespoon chopped fresh
   tarragon or parsley
Salt and freshly ground
   pepper
Tabasco sauce
Fresh tarragon sprigs to
   garnish, optional
Sour cream or crème
   fraîche (page 236) for
   garnish

1. Discard any tough stems or blemished leaves from the spinach. Chop and set aside.

2. Melt the butter in a large saucepan over medium heat. Add the onion and sauté until soft and slightly colored. Add the flour and stir to incorporate thoroughly with the onion. Cook 2 to 3 minutes. Slowly stir in the fish stock or diluted clam juice, raise the heat, and bring the liquid to a boil, stirring constantly. Add the oysters with their liquid and then the spinach. Reduce the heat to low and simmer until the edges of the oysters begin to curl, about 10 minutes.

3. Transfer the soup to a blender or a food processor fitted with the steel blade and purée until smooth. Transfer the purée to a clean saucepan. Add the cream, Pernod, and tarragon or parsley. Season to taste with salt, pepper, and Tabasco sauce. Heat thoroughly without bringing the soup to a boil.

4. Serve immediately. Top each serving with a dollop of sour cream or crème fraîche. Garnish, if desired, with fresh tarragon.

From Bread and Ink Cafe

 # Oregon Mussel Chowder

Mussels can always be found clinging to craggy rocks along the Oregon coast. Among knowing scavengers of wild delights, they've become something of a regional culinary fashion. It's definitely an adventure to descend upon a vast stretch of sandy beach, shovel and bucket in hand, to hunt for the bearded bivalves. The best of them often find their way into a rich and powerful chowder, a local specialty. This chunky assemblage, mottled with red pepper and threaded with saffron, defines the genre. It's a signature dish at Portland's Cafe des Amis, a restaurant of casually elegant rusticity that mingles Mediterranean style with Northwest ingredients.

Serves 6

2 pounds mussels in the shell

3 cups bottled clam juice

l cup water

$\frac{1}{4}$ cup unsalted butter

2 onions, diced

1 carrot, peeled and diced

1 large potato, peeled and diced

Pinch of saffron threads

1 small red bell pepper, seeded, deribbed, and diced

$1\frac{1}{2}$ cups heavy cream

1. Place the mussels in a large pot. Add water to cover and a handful of cornmeal. Soak the mussels for 24 hours to loosen any sand or grit. Drain the water off and wash the mussels in 2 or 3 changes of cold water. Pick over the mussels, discarding any that are open or broken. Pull off and discard the beards on the remaining mussels.

2. Rinse the pot and add the clam juice and water to it. Bring the mixture to a boil. Add the mussels and cover tightly. Cook over high heat until the mussels open, 5 to 6 minutes, shaking the pot occasionally to distribute the mussels evenly. Remove the pot from the heat. Discard any mussels that did not open. Set aside to cool. Strain the mussel broth into a bowl and set aside. Remove the mussels from their shells. Set the mussels aside.

3. Melt the butter in a deep saucepan over medium heat. Add the onions and sauté until soft and translucent, about 5 to 10 minutes. Add the carrot, potato, mussel broth, and saffron. Bring the mixture to a boil and reduce the heat to low. Simmer until the vegetables are nearly cooked through, about 15 minutes. Add the red pepper and simmer until tender, 5 to 10 minutes longer.

4. Add the cream and the reserved mussels. Heat thoroughly, being careful not to let the mixture boil. Ladle into bowls and serve immediately.

From Cafe des Amis

 ## Sturgeon and Fennel Chowder

Caterers Nancy Briggs and Juanita Crampton have some electrifying notions about cooking. Working out of an old Portland house, they serve a three-course lunch in their dining

room once a day, for two people only. The menu is never repeated, and it features Oregon ingredients in original combinations that capture the season. This chowder, which captures the oily essence of Columbia River sturgeon and its salty jet-black roe, speaks of a hot Oregon evening in July. If sturgeon is not available, shark, marlin, or swordfish may be substituted.

Serves 8

$\frac{1}{2}$ **pound fennel bulbs**
$\frac{1}{4}$ **pound ($\frac{1}{2}$ cup) unsalted butter**
2 cups coarsely chopped onions
1 cup coarsely chopped celery
2 teaspoons fennel seeds
2 teaspoons salt
2 teaspoons freshly ground white pepper
$\frac{1}{4}$ **cup fresh lemon juice**
$\frac{1}{2}$ **pound turnips, parboiled, peeled, and diced (1 cup)**

1 pound new potatoes, parboiled and cut into eighths (2 cups)
6 cups half-and-half
2 cups milk
2 pounds skinless, boneless sturgeon, marlin, shark, or swordfish, cut into 1-inch pieces
$\frac{1}{2}$ **cup sour cream or crème fraîche (page 236)**
2 ounces Columbia River sturgeon caviar or other black caviar

1. Trim off the hard top stems and the base of each fennel bulb. Discard any tough outer leaves. Snip off 2 tablespoons of the feathery leaves and set aside for the garnish. Coarsely chop the remaining fennel bulbs and stems.

2. Melt the butter in a large, heavy pot over medium heat. Add the onions, celery, fennel seeds, and chopped fennel bulbs and stems and sauté until soft, about 20 minutes. Add the salt, pepper, lemon juice, turnips, potatoes, half-and-half, and milk. Simmer for 15 minutes. Add the sturgeon and continue to simmer until the fish and the vegetables are tender, about 10 minutes.

(continued)

3. Divide the chowder among 8 soup bowls. Add a dollop of crème fraîche to each bowl. Garnish with the caviar and the reserved fennel leaves. Serve immediately.

From Briggs and Crampton's Catering and Table for Two

 ## Asparagus Soup with Dill Cream

Asparagus is one of the Northwest's best-kept secrets. A wild variety—crisp, elegant, and sleek, with a frisky flavor—thrives in Oregon's fields, providing inspiration for exquisite soups and side dishes. And the rich soil of Washington's Yakima and Wenatchee valleys produces the superior stalks found in pro- duce aisles. This dill-scented cream soup comes from my friend and premier food source Lisa Shara Hall, who is known for her soup savvy and culinary smarts.

Serves 4

2 pounds asparagus
$\frac{1}{4}$ cup unsalted butter
4 cups chicken stock,
    preferably homemade
    (page 239)
2 fresh dill sprigs
$\frac{1}{4}$ cup fresh lemon juice
Salt and freshly ground
    pepper

1 cup heavy cream
$\frac{1}{4}$ cup sour cream or crème
    fraîche (page 236) for
    garnish
2 to 3 tablespoons minced
    fresh dill for garnish

1. Using a sharp knife, cut off the tough bottom ends of the asparagus stalks. Starting about 2 inches from the top of the tips, peel the asparagus stalks. Then cut the asparagus into 1-inch pieces, keeping the tips whole.

2. Melt the butter in a heavy skillet over very low heat. When the foam subsides, add the asparagus tips. Cover and cook until tender, 15 to 20 minutes. Remove from the heat and set aside.

3. Bring the stock to a boil in a medium saucepan. Add the cut asparagus stalks and the dill branches. Cover and cook until soft, about 20 minutes.

4. Using a slotted spoon, transfer the cooked stalks and dill to a blender or a food processor fitted with the steel blade. Purée the stalks and return the purée to the saucepan containing the stock. Add the lemon juice, salt and pepper to taste, and cream. Taste and adjust the seasonings.

5. Heat the soup until hot, being careful not to let it boil. Add the reserved asparagus tips. Ladle the soup into serving bowls. Lightly beat the sour cream or crème fraîche and flavor it with the minced dill and a little salt and pepper to taste. Place a dollop in each bowl and serve immediately.

From the kitchen of Lisa Shara Hall

 # Chanterelle Cream Soup

Mushrooms and cream have an affinity on the order of cheese and wine: they seem to need each other. Here, sweet, woodsy, trumpet-shaped chanterelles, among the Northwest's champion champignons, float proudly in a creamy broth rippled by an undercurrent of Marsala wine. The soup is a seasonal highlight on the menu at Portland's Genoa restaurant, known for seven-course dinners inspired by Northwest bounty and northern Italian tradition.

Serves 6

1¾ cups half-and-half
¼ pound (½ cup) unsalted
butter
¼ cup unbleached all-
purpose flour
½ cup heavy cream
1 pound fresh chanterelles,
sliced

2 large cloves garlic
½ cup dry Marsala wine
5 cups chicken stock,
preferably homemade
(page 239)
Salt and freshly ground
white pepper

1. Warm the half-and-half in a small, heavy saucepan over medium heat until small bubbles appear along the edge of the pan. Keep the half-and-half warm without letting it boil.

2. In another small, heavy saucepan of stainless steel or enamel, melt ¼ cup of the butter. Add the flour and whisk over moderate heat until the mixture foams without browning, about 2 minutes. Remove from the heat and pour in the warm half-and-half all at once, whisking rapidly and continuously until the mixture is smooth. Add the cream and return the saucepan to the burner over low heat. Whisk until the mixture is very smooth and not quite boiling. Remove from the heat and set aside.

3. Melt the remaining ¼ cup butter in a 2½-quart stainless-steel or enamel saucepan over high heat. Add the chanterelles and sauté until the mushrooms exude liquid. Push the garlic cloves through a garlic press into the saucepan. Sauté, stirring frequently, for 2 minutes. Pour in the Marsala and cook over moderate heat until the alcohol burns off (the vapors from the pan will no longer burn your nose), about 3 to 5 minutes. Add the stock and the reserved cream sauce. Cook for 5 minutes, stirring occasionally.

4. Season with salt and white pepper to taste. Ladle the soup into bowls and serve hot.

From Genoa

Three-Onion Cream Soup

This almond-colored soup is a tangy mélange of leeks, chives, and native Walla Walla Sweets, which originated in Washington near the turn of the century. Highly prized for their mild disposition and sugary character, Walla Wallas have a short season of usually about three months. They are more delicate when young and best cooked slowly over low heat. For a richer, more robust flavor, cook the onions until soft, then briefly raise the heat to caramelize them. If Walla Wallas aren't available, substitute sweet Vidalias.

Serves 8

$\frac{1}{4}$ **pound ($\frac{1}{2}$ cup) unsalted butter**

3 pounds Walla Walla Sweet onions, quartered and sliced

1 large leek, white and lightest green parts only, sliced

2 cloves garlic, chopped

4 cups milk

1 cup heavy cream or half-and-half

$\frac{3}{4}$ **teaspoon fresh grated nutmeg**

1 bay leaf

2 tablespoons unbleached all-purpose flour

Salt and freshly ground white pepper

Chopped fresh chives for garnish

1. Melt the butter in a large, heavy saucepan over very low heat. Add the onions, leek, and garlic and sauté, stirring frequently, until the onions are very soft and lightly golden, about 15–20 minutes. If desired, raise the heat and stir constantly until the onions are caramelized.

2. Meanwhile, combine the milk and cream or half-and-half with the grated nutmeg and bay leaf in a heavy saucepan. Warm over medium heat until small bubbles appear

(continued)

along the edge of the pan. Turn off the heat just before the liquid boils and let the nutmeg and bay leaf steep in the liquid until needed.

3. Sprinkle the flour over the onions, then stir in to incorporate thoroughly. Add just enough water to cover the onions. Raise the heat and bring the mixture to a boil. Reduce the heat to low and simmer for 10 minutes.

4. Working in batches if necessary, transfer the mixture to a blender or a food processor fitted with the steel blade and purée until smooth. Pour the purée into a clean saucepan. Strain the scalded milk mixture into the purée. Season with salt and white pepper to taste.

5. Heat thoroughly without bringing the mixture to a boil. Ladle the soup into individual bowls and garnish each serving with chopped chives.

From Bread and Ink Cafe

 # White Bean Soup with Fennel Pesto

Fennel is a Northwest mainstay. It can be found everywhere from along roadsides to pushing up through cracking sidewalks. Thus, it comes as no surprise that fennel should surface on local menus. This potage of fennel and white beans derives its spunky character from a unique pesto topping, fashioned from the plant's licorice-scented greens. It is the perfect antidote for the wet chill of a Northwest winter. Serve with hot baguettes, and if it's been a really nasty day, break out a bottle of Pinot Noir.

Serves 8

For the soup:

1 pound (2 cups) dried white beans such as white kidney beans or Great Northern beans

3 quarts water

1 bay leaf

A few fresh thyme sprigs, or pinch of dried thyme

2 small fennel bulbs

$\frac{1}{4}$ cup olive oil

1 onion, diced

2 small carrots, peeled and sliced

1 celery rib, sliced

Salt and freshly ground white pepper

For the pesto:

$\frac{1}{4}$ cup olive oil

2 cloves garlic, finely chopped

$\frac{1}{2}$ cup tightly packed chopped fennel greens, or $\frac{1}{2}$ cup chopped fresh parsley mixed with 2 teaspoons finely ground fennel seeds

1 small tomato, coarsely chopped

$\frac{1}{3}$ cup freshly grated Parmesan cheese

Salt and freshly ground white pepper

1. To prepare the soup, place the beans in a bowl and add cold water to cover by 1 inch. Soak for at least 8 hours, or as long as overnight. Drain and rinse under cold running water.

2. Place the beans in a kettle with the water, bay leaf, and thyme. Bring the water to a boil and reduce the heat to low. Simmer, uncovered, until the beans are almost tender, about 1 hour.

3. Meanwhile, trim off the leafy portions at the top of the fennel bulbs. Coarsely chop enough of the tops to measure $\frac{1}{2}$ cup tightly packed leaves. Set the leaves aside for making the fennel pesto. Trim off the hard top stem and the base of each fennel bulb. Discard any tough outer leaves. Cut the stalks and bulbs crosswise into thin slices.

(continued)

4. Warm the olive oil in a large soup pot over medium heat. Add the sliced fennel, onion, carrots, and celery. Sauté until the onion is translucent, about 5–10 minutes. Raise the heat and sauté until the vegetables are slightly colored. Add the beans and their cooking liquid. Continue cooking until the beans are tender, about 10 to 15 minutes.

5. To prepare the pesto, in a blender or a food processor fitted with the steel blade, combine the olive oil, garlic, reserved fennel greens or the parsley, tomato, and Parmesan cheese and blend until thick and smooth. Season with salt and white pepper to taste.

6. Season the cooked beans with salt and white pepper to taste. Ladle the hot soup into serving bowls. Garnish each portion with a generous dollop of fennel pesto and serve.

From Bread and Ink Cafe

 **Wild Sorrel Soup**

French sorrel, favored for its powerful and puckery taste, thrives in rain-soaked Northwest gardens. In backwoods and on shady riverbanks, foragers can also find abundant quantities of the wild species, which is even more flavorful than the domestic variety but with a slightly higher concentration of oxalic acid. Sorrel soup is a memorable affair—splendid in its sour character and thoroughly refreshing. The following dish was created by Pat Failing and Bob Sitton, Oregon art critics and culinary explorers. If sorrel is not available, substitute an equal amount of fresh spinach.

Serves 6

½ pound (1 cup) unsalted
   butter
1 large onion, grated
5 cups chicken stock,
   preferably homemade
   (page 239)
5 cups coarsely chopped
   wild sorrel leaves, or
   6 cups finely chopped
   garden sorrel leaves

Juice of ½ lemon, or more
   to taste
¾ cup crème fraîche
   (page 236)
Salt and freshly ground
   pepper

1. Melt ¼ pound of the butter in a heavy 4-quart saucepan
over medium heat. Add the onion and sauté until transparent, about 10 minutes. Add the remaining ¼ pound
butter and 1 cup of the stock.

2. Stir in the sorrel and continue cooking until the leaves
are soft and dark green, about 2 minutes. Pour in the
remaining 4 cups chicken stock along with the lemon
juice. Simmer for 10 minutes.

3. Stir in the crème fraîche and heat to just below the boiling point. Season with salt and pepper to taste. If desired,
add more lemon juice to taste. Serve immediately.

From the kitchen of Pat Failing and Bob Sitton

 # Chilled Cucumber and Watercress Soup

*When the dog days of summer strike, nothing caresses the
palate quite like a chilled soup. It's hard to find a more refreshing blend than this purée of cucumbers, crème fraîche, and
watercress—the crisp, peppery water herb that flourishes in
Oregon creeks as well as supermarket produce sections. Punctuated by green onions and parsley leaves, and thinned with*

cream just before serving, the mixture is at once cool, sour, and sassy. For a light lunch, serve with a bowl of fresh berries, a pitcher of iced mint tea, and sliced tea bread.

Serves 6

1 large cucumber
12 scallions, including 3
  inches of green tops, sliced
¾ pound cream cheese, at
  room temperature, cut
  into small pieces
1 cup watercress leaves
1 cup fresh parsley leaves

3 tablespoons sour cream or
  crème fraîche (page 236)
1 cup heavy cream, or as
  needed
Salt and freshly ground
  white pepper
Minced fresh chives for
  garnish

1. Peel the cucumber. Cut in half lengthwise and remove the seeds. Cut the cucumber halves crosswise into 1-inch-thick slices.

2. Place the cucumber, scallions, cream cheese, watercress, and parsley in a food processor fitted with the steel blade or in a blender. Add the crème fraîche and blend until smooth. Transfer the mixture to a glass or ceramic bowl. Cover and chill for at least 4 hours, or preferably overnight.

3. To serve, thin the mixture to the desired consistency with the heavy cream. Season with salt and white pepper to taste. Garnish with chives and serve cold.

From the kitchen of Lisa Shara Hall

 # Fruit Soup with Rhubarb, Berries, and Mint

Cold fruit soups are among the joys of summer. These polished purées, almost like liqueurs in their intense fruitiness, are ideal for a light brunch or as an opener to a three-course lunch. The

following recipe is vibrant with its sweet and sharp tastes of berries, rhubarb, and pomegranate juice. Honeydew melon and fresh mint are cooling undertones.

Serves 8

1 large rhubarb stalk (about 1 pound), cut into 1-inch pieces

$\frac{1}{4}$ cup sugar

1 tablespoon water

1 pint (2 cups) strawberries, hulled and roughly sliced

$\frac{1}{2}$ pint (1 cup) raspberries

2 cups cubed honeydew melon

12 large fresh mint leaves, chopped

2 cups pomegranate juice, unfiltered apple juice, or white grape juice

Sugar and fresh lemon juice as needed

1 cup sour cream, crème fraîche (page 236), or plain yogurt

8 fresh mint leaves for garnish

1. Place the rhubarb in a heavy, noncorrosive saucepan. Add the $\frac{1}{4}$ cup sugar and the water and simmer over low heat until the rhubarb breaks down to a soft texture, about 5 to 8 minutes. Remove from the heat and cool to room temperature.

2. Meanwhile, combine the strawberries, raspberries, honeydew melon, and chopped mint leaves in a large bowl. Stir in the stewed rhubarb. Transfer one third of the mixture to a blender or food processor fitted with the steel blade. Purée the mixture, adding just enough of the pomegranate or other juice to ensure smooth blending.

3. Transfer the purée to a large glass or ceramic serving bowl. Continue the process until all of the mixture has been puréed, adding all the remaining juice to the last batch. Taste the purée and adjust the sweetness and tartness with sugar and lemon juice. Cover and refrigerate until well-chilled.

(continued)

4. To serve, ladle the soup into chilled bowls. Place a generous dollop of crème fraîche in each bowl and garnish with a mint leaf.

From Bread and Ink Cafe

CHAPTER FOUR

GATHERED GREENS, FIELD FLOWERS, AND FRESH FRUIT SALADS

Blackberries with Mint, Zinnia Petals, and Lime

Brilliantly hued zinnia petals and cool green mint adorn this seasonal salad like jewels and feathers of edible color. Whether served as a precursor to the meal or a light finale, this fruity melange is a grabber. Use only flower petals that have been grown for edible purposes.

Serves 8

1 cantaloupe, peeled, seeded, and sliced
1 honeydew melon, peeled, seeded, and sliced
1 pint (2 cups) blackberries
2 tablespoons fresh lime juice

Fresh mint sprigs for garnish
Zinnia petals for garnish, optional
2 limes, cut into quarters

1. Combine the melons and blackberries in a serving bowl. Sprinkle the lime juice over all. Garnish with sprigs of mint and zinnia petals. Serve with lime wedges on the side.

From Briggs and Crampton's Catering and Table for Two

Red Pear, Purple Cabbage, and Toasted Walnut Salad

This is a typical Oregon salad concept—simple, pretty, and crunchy, with every ingredient holding its own and no one taste overwhelming the others.

Serves 8

3 cups gently torn red leaf lettuce	1 tablespoon fresh lemon juice
3 cups shredded red cabbage	1 cup coarsely broken toasted walnuts
2 cups watercress leaves	1 cup Oregon Blue Cheese Dressing (page 65)
4 Red Bartlett pears, peeled, cored, and sliced	

1. Toss the lettuce, cabbage, and watercress together in a bowl. Arrange the mixture on a serving platter and top with an attractive arrangement of sliced pears. Sprinkle the lemon juice over the pears.

2. Garnish with the toasted walnuts and pass the dressing at the table.

From Briggs and Crampton's Catering and Table for Two

 # Spring Greens, Asparagus, and Morels

To Oregon cooks spring offers countless opportunities for culinary invention. Two of the most celebrated feast makers—the marvelous forest morel and magnificent asparagus—inspire bold experimentation. In this improvisation, chilled asparagus spears play off warm sautéed morels and the whole is enlivened by a spunky tarragon vinaigrette. If morels are not available, substitute any mushroom of your choosing.

Serves 8

32 asparagus	$\frac{3}{4}$ pound fresh morels or other seasonal mushrooms, cut in half
8 cups loosely packed mixed seasonal salad greens such as red leaf lettuce, spinach, arugula, radish sprouts, limestone lettuce, and romaine in any combination	1 tablespoon chopped fresh tarragon, or 1 teaspoon dried tarragon
	1 teaspoon minced shallots
2 tablespoons unsalted butter	$1\frac{1}{2}$ cups Tarragon Vinaigrette (page 65)

1. Using a sharp knife, cut off the tough bottom ends of the asparagus stalks. Starting about 2 inches from the top of the tips, peel the asparagus. Place the spears in a skillet and add cold, lightly salted water to cover. Bring to a boil, reduce the heat, and simmer until the spears are crisp-tender, up to 5 minutes. Drain the asparagus and then rinse immediately under cold running water to stop the cooking process. Chill thoroughly before serving.

2. Divide the mixed greens among 8 chilled salad plates. Attractively arrange the chilled asparagus over the greens.

3. Melt the butter in a heavy skillet over medium heat. Add the morels, tarragon, and shallots and sauté for 1 minute. Divide the morels equally among the plates. Serve the salad immediately and pass the vinaigrette separately.

From Briggs and Crampton's Catering and Table for Two

 # Spinach Salad with Salmon, Strawberries, and Warm Honey-Bacon Dressing

Here, little red berries are beautiful over deep green leaves and pink hunks of salmon. Crisp bacon blades and red onion rings add textural dimension. For a winter variation, replace the strawberries with 3 Comice or Red Bartlett pears, cored and sliced.

Serves 6

For the salad:

1½ pounds spinach

6 slices bacon

1 pound cold poached salmon, broken into coarse pieces

1 small red onion, thinly sliced and separated into rings

1 pint (2 cups) strawberries, hulled and sliced

1 tablespoon fresh lemon juice

For the dressing:

Reserved bacon drippings

1 tablespoon red wine vinegar

1 tablespoon honey

¼ teaspoon Dijon mustard

¼ teaspoon salt

1. First, assemble the salad. Remove and discard the stems from the spinach and dry the leaves thoroughly.

2. Fry the bacon in a skillet over medium-high heat until crisp. Using a slotted utensil, drain on paper towels; reserve the drippings in the skillet.

3. In a salad bowl, combine the spinach, salmon, and onion rings. Crumble the bacon into pieces and add to the bowl. Sprinkle the strawberries with the lemon juice and add to the salad.

4. To make the dressing, reheat the reserved bacon drippings in the skillet. Stir in the vinegar, honey, mustard, and salt. Taste and adjust the seasoning. Bring the dressing to a boil, remove from the heat, and immediately pour over the salad. Toss lightly and serve immediately.

 # Gathered Greens and Field Flowers in Walnut Vinaigrette

With gardening now a major Northwest activity, edible flowers—from trumpet-shaped nasturtiums to johnny-jump-ups—are decorating the local salad bowl. The blooms enhance leafy greens

with their curious textures, unexpected colors, and totally unique flavors. Here, domestic greens and floral exotica are tossed with toasted walnuts for a touch of creative whimsy. Use only flower petals that have not been sprayed with pesticides.

Serves 6

8 cups loosely packed mixed seasonal greens and edible flowers such as red leaf lettuce, butter lettuce, dandelion leaves, watercress, sorrel, mustard greens, violets, nasturtiums, anise, hyssop, and johnny-jump-ups in any combination
$\frac{1}{2}$ cup grated imported Jarlsberg cheese
About $\frac{1}{2}$ cup Walnut Oil Dressing (page 64)
$\frac{1}{2}$ to 1 cup toasted walnut pieces

1. In a salad bowl, combine the greens, flowers, and cheese. Toss the salad with just enough of the dressing to coat the greens lightly.

2. Divide the greens among 6 chilled salad plates. Garnish each portion with toasted walnuts and serve.

From Cafe des Amis

 # Warm Goat Cheese Salad with Winter Greens

L'Auberge was the first establishment on the Oregon restaurant scene to express a genuine personal style without self-conscious-ness. Twenty years later, the Oregon-meets-country-French food of this venerable institution remains as distinctive as the ambi-ence—a split-level dining room with a rustic stone hearth and

contemporary art. The following is a specialty of chef James Beals. His hazelnut-coated goat cheese rounds emerge from the oven hot and creamy, fragrant with the aroma of roasted nuts. Arrange them on fans of vinaigrette-dressed winter greens, and serve with hot, crusty baguettes and a robust wine.

Serves 6

$\frac{1}{2}$ **cup roasted hazelnuts (page 236)**
1 firm goat cheese log (8 ounces), cut into 6 equal rounds
6 tablespoons hazelnut oil
5 teaspoons balsamic vinegar

Salt and freshly ground pepper
6 curly endive leaves
6 Belgian endive leaves
6 escarole leaves
6 radicchio leaves

1. Preheat an oven to 350 degrees F.

2. Finely chop the roasted hazelnuts and place in a shallow bowl. Place the goat cheese rounds in the bowl and turn to coat both sides with the nuts. Line a baking sheet with aluminum foil. Place the rounds on the baking sheet and set aside.

3. Make a vinaigrette by whisking together the oil, vinegar, and salt and pepper to taste. Place all the salad leaves in a bowl, add the vinaigrette, and toss to coat evenly. Arrange the leaves, one of each kind to a plate, in a fan pattern.

4. Place the baking sheet in the preheated oven until the cheese becomes soft and warm but still holds its shape, 3 to 5 minutes.

5. Place one round of warmed cheese at the base of each fan. Serve immediately.

From L'Auberge

Orange Salad with Shredded Beets, Blue Cheese, and Raspberry Vinaigrette

Portland textile artist Larry Kirkland is one of those rare culinary innovators who can turn a simple meal into an electrifying personal vision, full of unexpected flavors and striking colors. Vivid, moist, and crunchy, this composition is ideal for entertaining or winter holiday tables.

Serves 8

For the salad:
4 navel oranges
1 pound beets, trimmed
$\frac{1}{4}$ cup fresh orange juice
**6 ounces Oregon blue
   cheese or any good-
   quality blue cheese ($\frac{3}{4}$ cup
   crumbled)**
**1 cup coarsely chopped
   roasted hazelnuts
   (page 236)**
Bibb lettuce

For the dressing:
1 cup extra-virgin olive oil
**2 tablespoons raspberry
   vinegar**
**2 tablespoons balsamic
   vinegar**
**2 tablespoons fresh orange
   juice**
**Salt and freshly ground
   pepper**

1. To make the salad, using a sharp paring knife, peel the oranges, removing all the white membrane. Cut the oranges in half crosswise and remove the center core. Place the oranges cut side down on a clean work surface and cut them vertically into neat $\frac{1}{4}$-inch-thick slices. Place the orange slices in a bowl, cover with plastic wrap, and refrigerate.

2. Place the beets in a large saucepan and add water to cover. Bring to a boil, reduce the heat to medium-low, and simmer until the beets can be pierced easily with a fork. Drain and set aside. When cool, remove the skins; they will peel off easily. Shred the skinned beets. Place in a bowl and pour in the orange juice. Cover the bowl with plastic wrap and refrigerate.

3. To make the dressing, in a small bowl whisk together the oil, raspberry vinegar, balsamic vinegar, orange juice, and salt and pepper to taste. Set aside.

4. To assemble the salad, line each of the chilled salad plates with lettuce. Arrange a mound of shredded beets on one side and a row of orange slices on the other side. Crumble 2 tablespoons of the blue cheese down the middle of each salad. Sprinkle 2 tablespoons of the hazelnuts over the top. Drizzle a little dressing over each salad and serve immediately.

From the kitchen of Larry Kirkland

 # Hood River Anjou Salad with Lime Mayonnaise

Although Harry and David, the Northwest mail-order tycoons, have made Oregon's Rogue River Valley famous for its succulent Comice pears, the Hood River Valley is unrivaled for its Bartlett, Anjou, and Bosc pears. The following salad is a regional take on the classic Waldorf theme. It was created by one of Portland's top culinary observers, Sara Perry, author of The Timberline Cookbook *(Graphic Arts),* The Complete Coffee Book *(Chronicle Books), and* The Chocolate Book *(Chronicle Books). If you don't want to make your own mayonnaise, substitute a good-quality brand and season to taste with fresh lime juice.*

Serves 8

For the salad:

**2 tablespoons fresh lemon
  juice**
$\frac{1}{2}$ cup water
2 ripe but firm Anjou pears
2 tart green apples
**1 cup coarsely chopped
  roasted hazelnuts
  (page 236)**
**1 celery rib, cut into $\frac{1}{2}$-inch
  lengths**
2 carrots, peeled and grated
**1 cup dried black currants
  or golden raisins**

For the mayonnaise:

2 limes
2 medium eggs
**2 tablespoons Dijon
  mustard**
1 cup safflower oil
$\frac{3}{4}$ cup light olive oil
Freshly ground pepper
**1 tablespoon chopped fresh
  mint leaves for garnish**

1. To prepare the salad, combine the lemon juice and water in a large bowl. Core the pears and apples and cut into $\frac{1}{2}$-inch pieces. Place the pear and apple pieces in the lemon water for 5 minutes to retard the browning of the fruit. Drain the fruit pieces, then pat them dry with paper towels.

2. Set aside 1 tablespoon of the hazelnuts for a garnish. Toss the remaining hazelnuts in a salad bowl with the fruit pieces. Fold in the celery, carrots, and currants or raisins.

3. To make the mayonnaise, bring a small saucepan filled with water to a boil. Using a swivel-bladed vegetable peeler or a zester, remove the zest (colored portion) from the limes. Trim away any of the bitter white skin that may have been removed with the zest. Drop the zest briefly into the boiling water. Drain and cut the zest into very fine shreds. Set aside.

4. Place the eggs and mustard in a food processor fitted with the steel or plastic blade. Process for a few seconds. Then, with the machine running, slowly add the safflower and olive oils, pouring in a steady stream. When the mixture forms a mayonnaise consistency, transfer it to a small bowl. Fold in the lime zest and season with pepper.

5. To assemble the salad, toss the salad with enough of the mayonnaise to coat. Cover and chill thoroughly. Garnish with the mint and the reserved hazelnuts and serve.

From the kitchen of Sara Perry

 # Ron Paul's Smoked Chicken Salad

This salad, a specialty of Ron Paul's exquisite Portland cafe, is a feisty blend of Oregon nuts, backyard garden vegetables, and southwestern influences. A smoked-chili mayonnaise gives the whole production a sultry edge. The chipotle chilies are sold in 6-ounce cans at well-stocked grocery stores and Latin American markets. Their flavor is strong, so only a small amount is needed. Some come with seeds, some without. The former is definitely more piquant and can be used in smaller amounts. Any leftover chilies can be covered and stored in the refrigerator. This salad is a wonderful luncheon entrée, made all the better with a chilled bottle of Oregon Riesling.

Serves 6

For the salad:
- **4 boneless, skinless smoked chicken breast halves**
- **2 broccoli stalks**
- **1 large red bell pepper, seeded, deribbed, and thinly sliced**
- **1 jicama, peeled and sliced**
- **1 small red onion, thinly sliced**
- **½ cup roasted hazelnuts (page 236)**

For the dressing:
- **1 cup good-quality mayonnaise**
- **1 tablespoon mashed smoked chipotle chilies**
- **1 tablespoon fresh lemon juice**

1. Slice the smoked chicken breasts into long, thin strips. Set aside.

2. Cut the broccoli florets from the stems. Bring a saucepan filled with water to a boil. Add the florets and boil for a few seconds. Scoop them out with a slotted utensil and plunge them immediately into a cold-water bath to stop the cooking process. Drain well and set aside. Blanch the stems in the same boiling water for about 1 minute and plunge them into a cold-water bath. Using a sharp paring knife, start at the base of the stems and trim away the tough outer skin. Thinly slice the stems on the diagonal. Set aside.

3. Combine the sliced chicken, broccoli florets, and stems in a bowl. Add the bell pepper, jicama, onion, and nuts.

4. Combine the dressing ingredients in a small bowl and stir to mix. Add to the chicken mixture and toss well. Cover and chill before serving.

From Ron Paul Restaurant and Charcuterie

 # Dungeness Crab Salad with Warm Apple Dressing

From autumn to winter, when regional waters begin to cool, Dungeness crab shows up with the sweet, plump meat for which it is famous. During warmer months, however, the crab can be heavy with roe and lean on meat. Try the following salad recipe in the fall when apples are crisp, crab is sweet, and cabbage leaves are splendidly purple. This is a handsome dish and, when combined with a warm dressing of baked apples, sharp mustard, crème fraîche, and apple brandy, it holds a wealth of uncommon flavors.

Serves 8

For the dressing:

1 pound good-quality baking apples such as Rome Beauty (about 2 large)

$\frac{1}{2}$ teaspoon each ground cinnamon, freshly grated nutmeg, paprika, and freshly ground pepper

$\frac{1}{2}$ cup apple brandy or Calvados

$\frac{3}{4}$ cup crème fraîche (page 236) or sour cream

2 teaspoons fresh lemon juice

1 teaspoon Dijon mustard

For the salad:

3 pounds tart apples such as Granny Smith (about 6 large)

Fresh lemon juice

2 cups finely shredded red cabbage

2 cups finely shredded arugula or watercress leaves

1 pound cooked Dungeness crab meat or other sweet crab meat

1. Preheat an oven to 350 degrees F.

2. To make the dressing, peel and core the apples. Cut them in half lengthwise. Place the apple halves in a roasting pan, cut side down. Combine the cinnamon, nutmeg, paprika, pepper, and apple brandy and pour over the apples. Place in the oven and bake until the apples are soft, 45 to 60 minutes. Remove from the oven and set aside to cool. Transfer the cooled apples and any pan juices to a food processor fitted with the steel blade. Add the crème fraîche, lemon juice, and mustard. Process until smooth, about 1 minute. The dressing can be used immediately or covered and refrigerated for up to 1 week.

3. To make the salad, core and slice the apples. Place the slices in a large bowl. Sprinkle with 3 tablespoons lemon juice and add enough water to cover to retard the browning of the fruit. Divide the red cabbage and arugula among 8 salad plates.

(continued)

4. Warm the dressing in a saucepan over medium heat. Drain the apple slices and arrange the crab meat and apple slices attractively over the top. Lace some of the warm apple dressing over each portion and serve immediately.

From Briggs and Crampton's Catering and Table for Two

 # Walnut Oil Dressing

The power of this dressing lies in its warm, nutty flavor, the trademark of walnut oil. Due to its increasing popularity with adventurous cooks, it it readily available in upscale markets and health-food stores. Little else, save a full-bodied vinegar, a bit of garlic, and a blast of fresh pepper, is needed to dress a salad properly. If you like a more pronounced flavor, add a teaspoon of Dijon mustard.

Makes about $1\frac{1}{3}$ cups

6 tablespoons good-quality
  red wine vinegar
1 clove garlic, minced
$\frac{1}{2}$ teaspoon salt
$\frac{1}{4}$ teaspoon freshly ground
  black pepper

6 tablespoons walnut oil
$\frac{1}{2}$ cup plus 2 tablespoons
  safflower oil

1. In a small bowl, whisk together the vinegar, garlic, salt, and pepper. Add the oils and whisk until creamy. Taste and adjust the seasonings. Serve at room temperature. The dressing will keep in a tightly covered jar in the refrigerator for $1\frac{1}{2}$ to 2 weeks.

From Cafe des Amis

Tarragon Vinaigrette

Given the region's vast berry population, it makes sense that fruit vinegars are staples of the Northwest kitchen. Good commercial berry vinegars can usually be found at specialty-food stores. Here, fresh tarragon and sharp mustard combine with the vinegar to make a dressing capable of resurrecting the most mundane salad greens.

Makes 1$\frac{1}{2}$ cups

$\frac{1}{2}$ cup berry vinegar

2 tablespoons Dijon
   mustard

2 tablespoons chopped fresh
   tarragon, or 2 teaspoons
   dried tarragon

$\frac{1}{2}$ cup good-quality olive oil

$\frac{1}{2}$ cup canola oil or safflower
   oil

l. In a small bowl, whisk together all the ingredients until creamy and thoroughly blended. Taste and adjust the seasonings. Serve at room temperature. The dressing will keep in a tightly covered jar in the refrigerator for 1$\frac{1}{2}$ to 2 weeks.

From Briggs and Crampton's Catering and Table for Two

 # Oregon Blue Cheese Dressing

Local blue cheese has a deserved reputation for its complex flavor. When properly aged, it's as rich as thick cream, with a sensuous tang and a faint suggestion of wood smoke—quite unlike any other blue. The following is one of the fabulous

dressings enterprising cooks can fashion using the superb blue cheese.

Makes about 2 cups

$1\frac{1}{2}$ cups crème fraîche
  (page 236) or sour cream
6 ounces Oregon blue
  cheese ($1\frac{1}{2}$ cups
  crumbled)

1 teaspoon freshly ground
  white pepper
1 tablespoon Dijon mustard
1 tablespoon fresh lemon
  juice

1. In a small bowl, stir together all the ingredients. Taste and adjust the amount of pepper and lemon juice. Cover and refrigerate until serving time.

From Briggs and Crampton's Catering and Table for Two

CHAPTER FIVE

SEAFOOD WITH FRUIT BUTTERS, FENNEL GREENS, AND OTHER FRESH IDEAS

Grilled Salmon with Mint Pesto

*Although culinary inventions are always alluring, the wise
cook balances adventure with restraint. With this in mind, the
following creation plays an innovative pesto against the classic
simplicity of grilled salmon fillets. If you wish to dress things
up further, roast a few red bell peppers (page 238) and purée
them in a food processor. Spoon a little of the roasted pepper
purée on one side of each fillet and the mint pesto on the other.*

Serves 6

$2\frac{1}{2}$ **pounds salmon fillets, cut**
  into 6 equal pieces of even
  thickness
Salt and freshly ground
  pepper

$\frac{2}{3}$ **cup unsalted butter,**
  melted
$\frac{3}{4}$ **cup Mint Pesto (page 232)**

1. Light a charcoal grill or preheat a broiler. Check the
salmon for bones and remove any you find with a pair of
tweezers. Sprinkle the fillets with salt and pepper to taste
and brush them lightly with some of the melted butter.

2. Place the salmon fillets with a grill rack set 4 inches above
the hot coals and grill for 4 to 5 minutes on each side per
inch of thickness. While the fillets are grilling, baste them
with the melted butter. Or arrange the fillets on a baking
sheet and place under the preheated broiler about 4
inches from the heat source. Broil for approximately 4
minutes on each side per inch of thickness, basting them
with melted butter.

3. Spread about 2 tablespoons of the pesto on the bottom of
each serving plate. Place the fish on top of the pesto and
serve immediately.

From Ron Paul Restaurant and Charcuterie

Sweet-and-Sour Salmon with Fennel Greens

There's always a touch of genuis in the fish course at Portland's Genoa restaurant. For this dish, the kitchen was inspired by a recipe for marinated salmon with dill from Joseph Famularo's The Festive Famularo Kitchen *(Atheneum). Fennel, an Oregon favorite, is lovely with salmon. One of the virtues of the marinade is that when the salmon is on the grill, the sugar caramelizes and forms a light crust around the fillets, sealing in their juice.*

Serves 6

$2\frac{1}{2}$ pounds Chinook salmon fillets, cut into 6 equal pieces of even thickness

2 tablespoons fresh lemon juice

3 tablespoons Dijon mustard

3 tablespoons sugar

1 teaspoon salt

1 tablespoon finely chopped fresh fennel greens

$\frac{1}{2}$ teaspoon finely ground fennel seeds

Chopped fresh fennel greens for garnish

Lemon wedges for serving

1. Check the salmon pieces for bones and remove any you find with a pair of tweezers. In a small bowl, stir together all the remaining ingredients, except the fennel greens garnish and lemon wedges. Place the salmon pieces in a glass or stainless-steel container just large enough to hold all the pieces in one layer. Coat the salmon pieces with the mixture. Cover the salmon with plastic wrap and place a plate on top. Add a sizable weight to the plate. Cover and refrigerate overnight.

2. Light a charcoal fire or preheat a broiler.

3. Place a grill rack 2 to 3 inches above the fire. When the coals are ready, place the salmon on the rack and grill

(continued)

quickly, 2 to 3 minutes on each side, being careful not to let it dry out. When done, the fish should be opaque and starting to flake near the skin but dark pink in the center and crispy on the outside. Or arrange the fillets on a baking sheet and place under the preheated broiler 2 to 3 inches from the heat source. Broil for 2 to 3 minutes on each side.

4. Garnish the salmon with fennel greens and serve with lemon wedges.

From Genoa

 # Parchment-Baked Chinook Salmon with Peach Chutney

When Portland artist Larry Kirkland turns his creative energy to cooking, the results are invariably daring and distinctive. In the following recipe, salmon fillets slathered with peach chutney are packaged in parchment paper. The bundles are then baked to encourage a gentle steaming. It's a simple process that encourages a natural blending of flavors, with no escape route. The true surprise comes at the table, when each guest opens a package and the captured fragrance is released.

Cooking parchment can be found in many cookware shops and restaurant supply houses. A sealed tent of aluminum foil or a plastic oven baking bag may be used instead, but should not be presented at the table. Simply unwrap the fillets in the kitchen and transfer to a serving platter.

Serves 8

1 Chinook salmon fillet, about $2\frac{1}{2}$ pounds, cut into 8 equal pieces of even thickness

1 cup Oregon Peach Chutney (page 225) or other fruit chutney

1. Preheat the oven to 425 degrees F.

2. To make the cooking envelopes, cut 8 circles of parchment paper, each the size of a 12-inch plate. Lightly oil or butter one side of each circle. Fold each circle in half, greased side in, to make a crease and then reopen the circle. Place 1 portion of salmon above the crease on the greased side. Cover it with a heaping tablespoon of chutney. Fold the other side of the circle over the salmon, lining up the 2 edges of the paper. Starting at one end, make a fold $\frac{1}{2}$ inch wide and $1\frac{1}{2}$ inches long. Crease the fold firmly. Begin the next fold near the end of the already folded section. This will prevent gaps between folds. Crease firmly each time. Continue to form overlapping folds all the way around the edge of the circle. Twist the ends to ensure a tight seal. Continue the process with the remaining salmon and parchment paper.

3. Place the sealed circles on 2 baking sheets. Bake for 10 minutes for every 1 inch of thickness of fish measured at its thickest point. Place each bag on an individual serving plate and serve immediately.

From the kitchen of Larry Kirkland

 # Poached Silver Salmon with Rhubarb Compote

Here the superior Silver or Coho salmon is accented by another Northwest classic—fresh rhubarb. Piquant and inviting, the compote complements the salmon's subtle personality.

Serves 6

2 lemon slices
1 bay leaf
8 peppercorns
8 coriander seeds
6 Coho or Chinook salmon
   fillets or steaks, about
   6 ounces each
$1\frac{1}{2}$ pounds rhubarb stalks,
   trimmed and cut into
   $\frac{1}{2}$-inch-thick slices (3 cups)

1 cup plus $1\frac{1}{2}$ tablespoons
   sugar
1 tablespoon fresh lemon
   juice, optional
1 cup sour cream or crème
   fraîche (page 236)
Fresh mint leaves for
   garnish

1. Fill a fish poacher or deep roasting pan with enough water to cover the salmon fillets in a single layer—the water will need to be about 3 inches deep. Add the lemon slices, bay leaf, peppercorns, and coriander seeds and bring to a boil. Reduce the heat to low and lower the fillets into the liquid. Simmer until the fillets are just tender when pierced with a fork, 7 to 8 minutes. Using a wide spatula, gently remove the fillets from the liquid and arrange them side by side on a baking sheet. When completely cooled, carefully remove the skin from the fish and discard. Cover the fish with plastic wrap and chill overnight.

2. Combine the rhubarb and sugar in a noncorrosive saucepan. Cook over medium heat, stirring frequently, until the rhubarb is soft, 5 to 8 minutes. Add a little water to the pan if the rhubarb is not juicy enough to release some liquid after a few minutes. Taste and adjust the sweetness, adding some lemon juice if necessary. Remove the pan from the heat and set the mixture aside to cool. Cover and chill before serving.

3. To serve, place a fillet on each serving plate. Place a generous dollop of rhubarb compote and sour cream or crème fraîche over each portion. Garnish with mint leaves and serve.

From Bread and Ink Cafe

McKenzie Creek Trout
with Fennel Pear Butter

Oregon is a trout fisherman's paradise. Rainbow, brook, and German brown are just a few of the species found in local streams. The McKenzie River Valley in the Oregon Cascades, with its seductive green waters and transparent lakes, has long been celebrated as a trout haven. If you catch your own, clean them right away, but don't let them sit in a bucket of water; that common mistake renders the flesh mushy and tasteless. Place your catch in a creel basket (a fisherman's wicker case) on a bed of moistened grass. If you want the flavor of truly fresh trout, cook the fish within three hours.

Serves 4

$\frac{1}{4}$ **cup unsalted butter, at room temperature**
$\frac{1}{4}$ **cup chopped fennel leaves**

$\frac{1}{4}$ **cup minced, peeled pear**
1 tablespoon pear brandy
4 trout, cleaned

1. Light a charcoal grill or preheat an oven to 325 degrees F.

2. Stir together the butter, fennel leaves, pear, and pear brandy in a mixing bowl. Stuff the cavity of each fish with one fourth of the mixture. Tightly wrap each trout in a double layer of foil.

3. Grill on a rack set 4 inches above the hot coals, turning once, until done, 8 to 9 minutes per side. Alternatively, place the wrapped trout in a baking dish and bake until done, about 30 minutes.

4. Unwrap and serve immediately.

Ginger Mussels

These are Northwest mussels at their finest—steamed in a peppery sauce accented by powerful Asian flavors. Originated by Portland restaurant critic and food scholar Roger Porter and culinary adventuress Joan Strouse, it took top honors at the annual Penn Cove Mussel Festival at Captain Whidbey's Inn, a restaurant located on Washington's Whidbey Island. Fashioned from logs in the early 1900s, the inn is perched above Penn Cove, one of the world's finest mussel-growing areas.

Serves 4

4 dozen mussels in the shell

1 tablespoon chopped, peeled fresh ginger

1 cup chopped scallions

2 garlic cloves, minced

1 teaspoon freshly ground black pepper

2 small, fresh hot chili peppers, seeded and finely diced

5 tablespoons peanut oil

1 tablespoon Asian sesame oil

$\frac{1}{4}$ cup rice vinegar

2 tablespoons soy sauce

$\frac{1}{2}$ cup rice wine

1. Wash the mussels. Pull and discard the beards that protrude from the shells. Discard any broken or open ones. Place the mussels in a bowl. Cover with cold water and let stand for one hour. Change the water several times as they render their sand.

2. Combine all the ingredients in a stainless-steel or enamel pot large enough to hold the mussels easily. Cover the pot tightly and cook over medium-high heat until the mussels open, 5 to 6 minutes.

3. Remove the pot from the heat and swirl the mussels in the cooking sauce. Divide the mussels and sauce among

four individual bowls; discard any mussels that didn't open. Serve immediately.

From the kitchens of Roger Porter and Joan Strouse

 # Dungeness Crab Curry with Roasted Hazelnuts, Currants, and Lime

A chilled beer is the required complement to this Oregon-style curry, a creation of food wizard Pat Vidor. The dish is best served with plenty of hot rice and an uncommon assortment of condiments: roasted hazelnuts, lime wedges, dried currants, finely chopped scallions, slivered jalapeños, chopped fresh cilantro leaves. Let the diners pick and choose among the goodies and flavor the curry to taste. Be sure to include an interesting chutney, a dab of which will provide the essential sweet-hot undertone to the meal.

While it is always best to combine your own seasonings, you can successfully substitute 2 to 3 tablespoons good-quality commercial curry powder.

Serves 6

For the spice powder:
1 tablespoon coriander seeds
1½ teaspoons cumin seeds
1 teaspoon each cardamom seeds, peppercorns, and ground cinnamon
1 to 2 teaspoons dried red chili peppers, optional

For the curry:
3 cups dried, shredded, or flaked sweetened coconut
3 cups milk
6 ounces (¾ cup) unsalted butter

½ cup finely chopped onion
¾ cup unbleached all-purpose flour
2 tablespoons finely chopped, peeled fresh ginger
3 tablespoons fresh lemon juice
1 tablespoon salt, or to taste
2 pounds cooked Dungeness crab meat or other sweet crab meat

1. To prepare the spice powder, combine the coriander, cumin, and cardamom seeds in a dry skillet and roast over low heat. The spices are ready when they release a characteristic aroma. Combine the roasted spices with all the remaining spices in a blender, in a food processor fitted with the steel blade, or in a spice mill and reduce to a powder.

2. To prepare the curry, combine the shredded coconut and milk in a saucepan. Let stand at room temperature for 20 minutes. Bring the mixture to a boil, reduce the heat to low, and simmer, uncovered, for 10 minutes. Using a fine-mesh strainer, strain the milk into a bowl; press against the coconut with the back of a spoon to extract all the milk, then discard the coconut.

3. Melt the butter in a large saucepan over medium heat. Add the onion and sauté until transparent, about 3–5 minutes. Stir in the flour, ginger, lemon juice, salt, and reserved spice powder. Cook for a few minutes to blend the flavors. Add the coconut milk and stir to combine. Cook over low heat, stirring constantly, until thickened, about 5 minutes. Simmer, uncovered, for 30 minutes. Add the crab meat and heat through. Taste and adjust the seasonings. Transfer the curry to a serving bowl. Serve hot.

From the kitchen of Pat Vidor

 ## Oregon Shrimp and Scallop Enchiladas

A mundane meal at Portland's Indigine restaurant is difficult to imagine. The midweek "simple supper" is actually a three-course extravaganza beginning with a salad basket that looks like one of the hanging gardens of Babylon. Entrées often include fabulous enchiladas featuring local seafood and presented Sonora style, which means the tortillas are layered

rather than rolled. Hence no frying is required, meaning less preparation time and fewer calories.

The following recipe serves 4 for dinner, or 8 as an appetizer if you halve the tortillas and use smaller baking dishes. Either way, the sauce is best when made a day in advance. If serving as a main course, accompany with black beans and rice, if desired.

Serves 4

For the sauce:
1 tablespoon cumin seeds
2 tablespoons unsalted butter
1½ cups coarsely chopped onion
3 cloves garlic, finely chopped
1 cup sour cream
1½ cups heavy cream
1 cup diced, canned green chili peppers
3 tablespoons chopped fresh oregano, or 1 tablespoon dried oregano
1 teaspoon coarsely ground black pepper

1 small dried red chili pepper, pulverized
1 teaspoon salt

For the enchiladas:
1½ cups coarsely grated jack cheese
1½ cups coarsely grated provolone cheese or crumbled goat cheese
12 corn tortillas
½ pound sea scallops (1 cup)
1 cup bay shrimp
8 large shrimp, peeled and deveined
2 ripe tomatoes, quartered

1. To make the sauce, first roast the cumin seeds. Place them in a small dry skillet over medium-low heat and cook for a few minutes, until they release their characteristic aroma. Remove from the heat and pulverize in a blender or spice mill.

2. Melt the butter in a large saucepan over medium heat. Add the onion and garlic and sauté until wilted, about 5 minutes. Stir in all the remaining sauce ingredients, including the cumin. Whisking gently with a wire whisk,

(continued)

slowly bring the mixture to a boil. Reduce the heat and simmer for 15 minutes, stirring occasionally.

3. Preheat an oven to 500 degrees F.

4. To assemble the enchiladas, very lightly grease 4 oven-proof dishes at least $3\frac{1}{2}$ inches deep and about 10 inches in diameter. Combine the cheeses. For each serving, cover a dish bottom with a tortilla. Add $\frac{1}{4}$ cup of the sauce and smooth it over the tortilla. Evenly distribute $\frac{1}{4}$ cup of the scallops and $\frac{1}{4}$ cup of the cheese over the top. Then add another tortilla, cover with $\frac{1}{4}$ cup of the sauce, and smooth it. Add $\frac{1}{4}$ cup of the shrimp meat and $\frac{1}{4}$ cup of the cheese. Add another tortilla, another $\frac{1}{4}$ cup sauce, and smooth it. Add another $\frac{1}{4}$ of the cheese and top with 2 of the large shrimp. Place 2 tomato quarters on either side of dish. Repeat with the remaining ingredients.

5. Bake until the enchiladas are heated through and the cheese has melted, about 15 minutes. Serve immediately.

From Indigine

 # White Sturgeon with Hot Chili Condiment

The sturgeon is one of Oregon's great treasures. This legendary creature can live well over a century. Old tintypes show fish 15 feet long and weighing close to a ton, hauled ashore by horse teams. Today state law prohibits catching any sturgeon over six feet long, which still makes this the Northwest's most challenging trophy, as well as one of its tastiest. These fish are bottom feeders, lurking in deep pools of the Snake and Colum-

bia rivers. They're also holdovers from prehistoric times, wearing their skeleton on the outside as hard plates. That means the mild, white flesh won't have any sneaky bones waiting to snag your throat halfway down. In this simple recipe the topping of yellow peppers and fresh tomatoes is pretty against the pale meat, and the lively condiment of hot chilies, mint, and green olives adds an unexpected jolt of flavors.

Serves 6

3 tablespoons olive oil
1 shallot or scallion, chopped
1 small onion, chopped
1 yellow bell pepper,
   seeded, deribbed, and
   diced
2 tomatoes, peeled, seeded,
   and chopped
2 tablespoons dry white
   wine

6 white sturgeon, marlin,
   shark, or swordfish
   steaks, about 6 ounces
   each
Salt and freshly ground
   pepper
Fresh lemon juice
Hot Chili Condiment
   (page 228)

1. Preheat an oven to 350 degrees F.

2. Warm the oil in a heavy skillet over medium heat. Add the shallot or scallion, onion, and bell pepper and sauté until they start to brown—8 to 10 minutes. Add the tomatoes and wine and cook until the tomatoes are tender, about 5 minutes.

3. Grease a baking dish. Sprinkle the sturgeon steaks with salt, pepper, and lemon juice to taste. Place the steaks in the prepared dish. Gently spoon the tomato mixture over the top. Bake, uncovered, until fish flakes easily, 20 to 25 minutes.

4. Remove from the oven and spoon a few tablespoons of the Hot Chili Condiment over each steak. Serve immediately.

Petrale Sole with Champagne Sauce

Chef Karl Schaefer's recipes can be summed up in a word: sublime. He's not a wild experimenter or a trend seeker, but he's obsessive when it comes to combining regional ingredients and classic cooking techniques to produce simple dishes of exceptional flavor. For this dish, the fish is lightly dusted with flour before it's sautéed, giving the flesh an exquisitely browned exterior. The interior falls into perfect flakes, and the whole sparkles in a champagne sauce that bristles with crème fraîche, fresh tarragon, and citrus juices. Bite for bite, this is an exceedingly gratifying dish. Petrale sole is a favored regional variety, but any firm-fleshed fresh white fish, such as flounder or Atlantic turbot, is fine. Even salmon works beautifully with this sauce.

Serves 4

For the sauce:
- **1 cup Fish Stock (page 240) or bottled clam juice**
- **1 cup brut champagne**
- **2 scallions or shallots, chopped**
- **1 cup crème fraîche (page 236) or heavy cream**
- **Salt and freshly ground pepper**
- **Juice of $\frac{1}{4}$ lemon**

For the fish:
- **Salt and unbleached all-purpose flour for dusting**
- **2 pounds petrale sole or other firm-fleshed fish fillets**
- **3 tablespoons extra-virgin olive oil**
- **1 tablespoon chopped fresh tarragon**

1. Preheat an oven to 400 degrees F.

2. To make the sauce, place the stock or clam juice in a heavy saucepan over medium heat. Add $\frac{2}{3}$ cup of the champagne and the scallions or shallots. Turn up the heat to high and reduce the mixture by four fifths of its volume, skimming the surface occasionally. This will take about 15 minutes. Add the crème fraîche or cream and reduce by half of its volume. This will take about 5 to 7 minutes. At this point the liquid should be very thick; if not, reduce it a bit more. Season with salt and pepper to taste and the lemon juice. Remove from the heat and set aside.

3. To assemble the dish, salt the fillets and then dust them with flour. Heat two 10-inch sauté pans over high heat. Add 1½ tablespoons of the oil to each hot pan. Divide the fillets between the 2 skillets and sauté them for 30 seconds. Turn the fillets over and place the pans in the preheated oven for 2 minutes.

4. Remove the pans from the oven, cover with tight-fitting lids, and let stand for 3 minutes. Remove the lids and gently pour any liquid collected in the pan bottoms into the reserved sauce. Cover the pans again and set aside.

5. Bring the reserved sauce to a boil and reduce the heat to low so the sauce simmers. Return the sauté pans to the stove and remove the lids. Divide the chopped tarragon and the remaining ⅓ cup champagne evenly between the pans. Divide the sauce evenly between the pans and bring the mixture to serving temperature, about 1 minute at a simmer. Spoon one-fourth of the sauce onto the bottom of each of 4 plates. Top each portion with a fillet. Serve immediately.

From Le Cuisinier

 # Halibut with Hot Mint Relish

Oregon fishermen call the halibut "white steak," referring to its meaty, full-flavored flesh. Local cooks do simple but marvelous things with the catch, as demonstrated in this recipe, in which

the fish is baked with a creamy sauce and then lavished with a piquant relish.

Serves 4

4 halibut steaks, about 6
  ounces each
Salt and freshly ground
  pepper

1 cup sour cream
Juice of $\frac{1}{2}$ lime
$\frac{3}{4}$ cup Hot Mint Relish
  (page 230)

1. Preheat the oven to 350 degrees F.

2. Lightly grease a baking dish large enough to hold the steaks without overlapping and place the fish in the dish. Season with salt and pepper to taste. In a small bowl stir together the sour cream and lime juice. Spoon the mixture evenly over the fish. Cover with aluminum foil. Place in the oven and bake until the fish flakes easily when tested with a fork, about 25 minutes.

3. Remove the fish from the oven and garnish each portion with Hot Mint Relish. Serve immediately.

 ## Scallops and Forest Mushrooms

A quick sauté of sea scallops and wild mushrooms created by artful party hostess Chris Maranze comes to the table in a garlicky sauce set against a field of rice. Serve with a tossed green salad garnished with toasted walnuts and crumbled Oregon blue cheese. Whole-Wheat Walnut Baguettes (page 170) or a loaf of warm, crusty sourdough and a bottle of good regional Riesling would fit in nicely.

Serves 4

1 pound sea scallops
¼ cup unbleached all-
   purpose flour
2 tablespoons olive oil
2 tablespoons unsalted
   butter
4 cloves garlic, minced
⅓ cup chopped scallions, or
   4 shallots, minced
1 pound fresh seasonal
   mushrooms such as
   chanterelles or morels,
   sliced

½ cup dry vermouth or dry
   sherry
⅛ teaspoon freshly grated
   nutmeg
⅛ teaspoon cayenne pepper
Salt and freshly ground
   white pepper

1. Pat the scallops dry. Lightly coat them with the flour. Heat the olive oil in a skillet over medium high heat. Add the scallops and sauté, stirring frequently, until the scallops are opaque, 4 to 5 minutes. Transfer the scallops to a bowl and set aside.

2. Add the butter, garlic, and scallions or shallots to the skillet and sauté over medium heat for 3 minutes. Add the mushrooms and continue to sauté for 3 to 5 minutes. Add the vermouth or sherry, nutmeg, cayenne, and salt and white pepper to taste. Raise the heat to high and stir until the liquid reduces and thickens, 3 to 5 minutes.

3. Return the scallops and any accumulated juices to the skillet. Cook just until the mixture is heated through. Adjust the seasonings and serve.

From the kitchen of Chris Maranze

CHAPTER SIX

GAME BIRDS WITH GOOSEBERRIES, STUFFED FIGS, AND OTHER INSPIRATIONS

Lemon Chicken with Stuffed Figs

Chicken figures prominently in just about every cuisine in the world, and new Northwest cooking is no exception. Oregon birds, frequently free-roaming residents of the barnyard, are tastier and plumper than the assembly-line competition imported on ice. Here the entourage of flavors, the celebration of aromas, and the textural interplay of tender meat, crisp nuts, and succulent figs is ideal for warming a wintry evening.

Serves 6

1 roasting chicken,
  4 to 5 pounds
6 lemons
2 cloves garlic, finely
  minced
2 cups Chardonnay or other
  dry white wine
1 tablespoon olive oil
4 fresh thyme sprigs, or
  1 teaspoon dried thyme
Salt and freshly ground
  white pepper

$\frac{3}{4}$ cup chicken stock,
  preferably homemade
  (page 239)
24 large and supple
  Calimyrna figs, each
  stuffed with 1 skinned
  whole hazelnut
$\frac{1}{4}$ cup heavy cream
Fresh thyme sprigs for
  garnish, optional

1. Dry the chicken thoroughly. Squeeze the juice of 4 of the lemons into a large mixing bowl. Add the garlic, wine, olive oil, thyme, and salt and white pepper to taste and stir well. Add the chicken, turning to coat all sides. Cover and refrigerate for 3 to 4 hours, turning occasionally.

2. Preheat an oven to 450 degrees F.

3. Drain the chicken, reserving the marinade but discarding the thyme sprigs, if using. Place the chicken, breast side up, in a roasting pan and pour the stock over the top. Place in the oven and immediately reduce the heat to

350 degrees F. Roast for approximately 20 minutes per pound, basting occasionally during the first hour of cooking and every 10 minutes thereafter.

4. While the chicken is roasting, pour the marinade into an enamel saucepan over medium-high heat. Reduce the liquid by half of its volume. This will take about 10 to 15 minutes. Remove from the heat and set aside. Cut the remaining 2 lemons crosswise into slices and set aside.

5. When the chicken is almost done, remove it from the oven. Skim off the fat from the pan juices. Add the stuffed figs to the pan. Pour the reserved marinade over all and stir the cream into the pan juices. Return the pan to the oven and continue baking until the chicken is done and the figs are hot, about 10 minutes.

6. Remove the chicken from the oven. Carve the bird and arrange on a large serving platter with the figs. Spoon a little of the pan juices over all and garnish with the reserved lemon slices and fresh thyme sprigs. Pour any remaining pan juices into a serving bowl and pass at the table.

 # Chicken with Blackberries, Limes, and Fresh Herbs

Lena Lencek created this dish at her summer home in Neah-kahnie, an Oregon coast town where wild blackberry brambles grow freely near the Pacific surf. Lencek, who has a deserved reputation for her fabulous dinner parties, serves the chicken with a warm mushroom risotto, zucchini sautéed with minced garlic and fresh parsley, and a salad perfumed with purple basil. Dessert might be strawberries macerated in red wine and

sugar or ripe pears with a plate of Oregon blue cheese. A bottle of red wine, rustic bread, coffee, and a shot of pear brandy complete the feast.

Serves 4

1 roasting chicken,
  4 to 5 pounds
$\frac{1}{4}$ cup unsalted butter, at
  room temperature
2 tablespoons fresh sage
  leaves, or 2 teaspoons
  dried sage
3 tablespoons fresh thyme
  leaves, or 2 teaspoons
  dried thyme
2 tablespoons fresh rosemary
  leaves, or 2 teaspoons
  dried rosemary
Zest of 2 lemons, minced

6 cloves garlic, minced, plus
  6 whole cloves
3 tablespoons blackberry
  preserves
1 tablespoon Dijon mustard
2 tablespoons honey
4 tablespoons soy sauce
Salt and freshly ground
  pepper
2 limes
Fresh sage, thyme, and
  rosemary for garnish
$\frac{1}{2}$ cup fresh blackberries for
  garnish

1. Preheat an oven to 400 degrees F. Position a rack on the lowest rungs in the oven.

2. Dry the chicken thoroughly inside and out with paper towels. Set aside.

3. In a food processor fitted with the steel blade or in a blender, combine the butter, sage, thyme, rosemary, lemon zest, minced garlic, blackberry preserves, mustard, honey, and 2 tablespoons of the soy sauce. Blend well and set aside.

4. Sprinkle the chicken cavity with the remaining 2 tablespoons soy sauce. Then sprinkle the interior with salt and pepper to taste. Prick the limes all over with a fork. Slip the limes and whole garlic cloves inside the chicken cavity. Pull the skin at the neck over the opening and skewer or sew closed with heavy kitchen thread. Tie the legs together with string.

5. Rub the skin of the chicken with salt and pepper to taste. Then brush with the reserved blackberry-herb mixture. Place on a rack in a roasting pan and place in the oven. Immediately reduce the temperature to 375 degrees F. Roast the chicken, uncovered, for 10 minutes. Then reduce the heat to 350 degrees F. Cook, basting every 15 minutes or so with the pan juices, until the juices run clear when the thigh is pierced, approximately 20 minutes per pound of chicken.

6. Remove the skewer, if using, and string from the chicken. Remove the limes and garlic from the cavity and discard. Serve the chicken on a platter surrounded by fresh sage, thyme, and rosemary and fresh blackberries, and carve at the table. Pour the pan juices into a small pot. Let stand 1 or 2 minutes and spoon off the grease that rises to the top. Reheat the remaining juice. Pour into a serving bowl and pass at the table.

From the kitchen of Lena Lencek

 # Chicken, Mushroom, and Spicy Sausage Stew

Here is a recipe for the quintessential Oregon stew—succulent chicken on the bone, nippy sausages, and tender carrots simmered in local Chardonnay. Like many stews, this one is even better the day after it's cooked. If wild mushrooms aren't in season, cultivated ones can be substituted. Serve with steaming rice, a salad of winter greens, and perhaps an apple crisp for dessert.

Serves 4

4 chicken thighs
4 chicken legs
Salt and freshly ground
   pepper
2 tablespoons olive oil
4 hot Italian sausages, about
   4 ounces each
1 onion, chopped
2 cloves garlic, minced
1 cup quartered seasonal
   wild mushrooms, such as
   morels or chanterelles, or
   cultivated mushrooms
1 can (16 ounces) Italian
   plum tomatoes, drained
   and chopped
2 cups chicken stock,
   preferably homemade
   (page 239)

1 cup Chardonnay or other
   dry white wine
1$\frac{1}{2}$ cups sliced, peeled
   carrots
1 tablespoon chopped fresh
   marjoram, or 1 teaspoon
   dried marjoram
1 tablespoon chopped fresh
   oregano, or 1 teaspoon
   dried oregano
1$\frac{1}{2}$ teaspoons chopped fresh
   thyme, or $\frac{1}{2}$ teaspoon
   dried thyme
Pinch of hot-pepper flakes

1. Season the chicken thighs and legs with salt and pepper to taste. Warm the oil in a flameproof, noncorrosive casserole dish over medium-high heat. Add the chicken and cook, turning every minute or two until browned on both sides, about 10 minutes total time. Remove the chicken from the dish and set aside.

2. Prick the sausages with a fork. Add them to the pan and cook over high heat, turning frequently, until browned on all sides, about 10–15 minutes. Remove the sausages from the pan and set aside.

3. Add the onion and garlic to the casserole and sauté over medium heat until soft and transparent but not brown, about 5–10 minutes. Add the mushrooms and sauté for 2 minutes. Then add the tomatoes, chicken stock, wine, and carrots. Bring to a simmer. Return the chicken to the dish and add the marjoram, oregano, thyme, and hot-pepper flakes.

4. Cover the stew and simmer for 30 minutes. Slice the reserved sausages and add them to the stew. Simmer until the chicken is tender, 30 minutes longer. Add salt and pepper to taste and serve immediately, or let cool, and cover, refrigerate and then reheat the next day.

From Cafe des Amis

 # Chicken with Morels and Cream

Available fresh for a limited time each spring, morels are one of the stars of the new Oregon cuisine. "They are horribly expensive," admits Dennis Baker of Portland's Cafe des Amis, "but definitely worth the splurge." Although small, the spongy-looking fungi go the distance in flavor. Each one packs enormous punch, with a taste and smell that is at once earthy and exquisite. Morels are at their finest when mingled with cream, as Baker's recipe demonstrates.

Serves 4

4 chicken breast halves,
   boned and skinned
Unbleached all-purpose
   flour seasoned with salt
   and freshly ground
   pepper
5 tablespoons clarified
   butter (page 239)
2 tablespoons chopped
   shallots

$\frac{1}{4}$ pound fresh morels or
   other seasonal
   mushrooms
$\frac{2}{3}$ cup dry vermouth
2 cups chicken stock,
   preferably homemade
   (page 239)
2 cups heavy cream
Salt and freshly ground
   white pepper

1. Place the chicken breasts between 2 sheets of waxed paper. Using a wooden mallet, pound to a uniform $\frac{3}{4}$-inch thickness. Dust the breasts lightly with the seasoned flour.

(continued)

2. Melt 3 tablespoons of the clarified butter in a large, heavy, noncorrosive sauté pan over medium heat. Add the chicken breasts and sauté until almost done (the breasts should be a little springy to the touch), about 3 minutes on each side. Remove the breasts from the pan and set them aside.

3. Heat the remaining 2 tablespoons clarified butter in the pan. Add the shallots and morels and sauté over medium heat until the mushrooms have softened, about 2 minutes. Add the vermouth and chicken stock. Bring to a boil over high heat, gradually adding 1 cup of the cream to prevent the sauce from boiling over the pot edge. Reduce the mixture by half of its volume. This will take 20 to 25 minutes.

4. Add the remaining cup of cream and reduce the volume again by half, another 10 to 15 minutes. Watch carefully to prevent the sauce from boiling over. When the sauce is ready, it should have the consistency of heavy cream and coat the back of a spoon.

5. Season with salt and white pepper to taste. Add the chicken breasts to the sauce and simmer to heat through. Serve immediately.

From Cafe des Amis

 # Hazelnut Chicken in Hell's Fire

This nut-dusted dish will fire up the blood on a rainy night and possibly inspire you to dance on tabletops. At least that's the word from its creator, my good friend Lisa Shara Hall. The sauce here says it all — a rich, steamy brew of orange, garlic, jalapeños, and cream. Serve with plenty of hot rice to soak it up.

Serves 8

For the sauce:

2 tablespoons unsalted butter

3 cloves garlic, minced

$\frac{1}{2}$ cup thinly sliced scallions

3 fresh jalapeño peppers, seeded and minced

$\frac{1}{4}$ cup fresh orange juice

$\frac{1}{4}$ cup chicken stock, preferably homemade (page 239)

$\frac{3}{4}$ cup heavy cream

For the chicken:

2 large eggs, beaten

$\frac{1}{2}$ cup milk

$\frac{1}{4}$ cup roasted and skinned hazelnuts, ground

$\frac{1}{4}$ cup unbleached all-purpose flour

4 whole chicken breasts, halved, boned, and skinned

4 tablespoons unsalted butter

4 tablespoons peanut oil

1. To prepare the sauce, melt the butter in a heavy skillet or saucepan over medium heat. Add the garlic, scallions, and jalapeño peppers and sauté until softened, about 3 minutes. Add the orange juice and chicken stock. Bring to a boil and reduce the liquid by a little more than half of its volume. This will take 10 to 20 minutes. Add the cream and reduce the heat to low. Simmer until thick enough to coat the back of a spoon, 3 to 4 minutes. Remove the pan from the heat and set aside.

2. To prepare the chicken, combine the eggs and milk in a deep, shallow bowl. In another wide, shallow bowl, combine the hazelnuts and flour. Dip the chicken breasts first in the egg mixture and then in the flour mixture, coating thoroughly and shaking off any excess flour.

3. Heat 2 tablespoons of the butter and 2 tablespoons of the oil in each of 2 skillets. Divide the chicken breasts between the skillets. Sauté, turning once, until cooked through but moist inside, 4 to 6 minutes on each side.

4. While the breasts are cooking, reheat the sauce. Transfer the cooked breasts to a warm platter. Pour the sauce over the chicken and serve.

From the kitchen of Lisa Shara Hall

Sweet-and-Savory Grilled Chicken

When the weather permits, Oregonians show their enthusiasm for that favorite American pastime, the summer barbecue. Here's a wonderful summer recipe for grilled chicken that features the outstanding Pinot Noir produced in Oregon's wine country.

Serves 8

4 whole chicken breasts, halved

2 cups seedless red flame grapes

3 tablespoons drained capers

$\frac{1}{2}$ cup pitted, chopped, Kalamata olives

1 tablespoon Dijon mustard

1 cup Pinot Noir or other dry red wine

1. Place the chicken breasts in a single layer in a glass baking dish. Combine all the remaining ingredients in a blender or in a food processor fitted with the steel blade and blend until smooth. Pour the marinade over the chicken breasts. Cover and refrigerate at least 2 hours, or as long as overnight.

2. Light a charcoal grill or preheat an oven to 350 degrees F. Meanwhile, allow the chicken breasts to come to room temperature.

3. Remove the chicken from the marinade, reserving the marinade. Place the breasts on a rack set about 5 inches above hot coals and grill, turning once and basting occasionally with the marinade, until cooked through but still moist inside, about 10 minutes on each side. Or place the breasts in a shallow roasting pan and bake, without turning and basting occasionally with the marinade, 30 to 45 minutes until cooked through but still moist inside. Serve immediately.

From Briggs and Crampton's Catering and Table for Two

Roast Duck with Gooseberry Compote

In the '30s and '40s, gooseberry pie could be found in most neighborhood diners in Oregon. The small, yellow green fruit, native to the western part of the state, had little of the sweetness of Oregon's darker berries, but nothing could touch it for tang. The new Oregon chef, however, has taken the gooseberry out of the pie, blending its walloping tartness with rich meats. My friend Lena Lencek, a leading-edge recreational cook, transforms gooseberries into a liquored compote that is a smashing finish to stuffed and glazed duck.

Serves 4

For the duck:
1 duck, about 4 pounds
Kosher salt and freshly ground pepper
1 navel orange, cut into wedges
1 Golden Delicious apple, peeled, cored, and cut into wedges
1 small Walla Walla Sweet onion, cut into wedges
$\frac{1}{2}$ cup water, boiling

For the compote:
$\frac{1}{4}$ cup light corn syrup
$\frac{1}{4}$ cup sugar
2 tablespoons unsalted butter

1 pint (2 cups) gooseberries, stems and tendrils removed; or substitute rhubarb, raspberries, huckleberries, marionberries, blackberries, boysenberries, or blueberries
$\frac{1}{3}$ cup Cointreau

For the glaze:
Juice and grated zest of 1 orange
1 cup gooseberry jelly or currant jelly
1 tablespoon Dijon mustard
$\frac{1}{4}$ cup Cointreau

1. To prepare the duck, dry thoroughly with paper towels and then season the duck inside and out with salt to taste and plenty of pepper.

2. Preheat an oven to 400 degrees F.

(continued)

3. Combine the orange, apple, and onion wedges. Stuff the mixture inside the cavity. Tie the legs together and turn the wings under the body. Position a rack inside an aluminum foil–lined roasting pan. Set the duck on the rack, breast side up, and prick the skin all over with a fork. Pour the boiling water over the duck. Place in the oven for 20 minutes. Reduce the heat to 350 degrees F and roast for about 2 hours, pricking the skin occasionally to allow the fat to drain from the meat.

4. Prepare the compote while the duck is roasting. Combine the corn syrup, sugar, and butter in a large, heavy skillet over medium-high heat. Stir until the butter and sugar melt. Add the gooseberries or other berries or rhubarb, stir with a wooden spoon, and reduce the heat to a medium simmer. Cook, stirring occasionally, until the gooseberries are opaque and tender but the skins are not broken, about 15 to 20 minutes. Remove the skillet from the heat and stir in the Cointreau. Set aside; the compote will thicken as it cools.

5. About 40 minutes before the duck is done, make the glaze. Combine all the glaze ingredients in a small, heavy saucepan. Heat over medium-high heat until bubbly and smooth, about 15 minutes.

6. About 25 minutes before the duck is cooked, remove it from the oven and spoon the glaze over it. Return it to the oven for 10 minutes and then repeat the glazing. Repeat the glazing one or two more times. When the duck is finished, it should have a shiny, deep golden, candylike coating.

7. Transfer the duck to a large platter. Spoon any remaining glaze over it. Let stand for 15 minutes before carving. Serve the stuffing and the gooseberry compote on the side.

From the kitchen of Lena Lencek

Duck with Wild Blackberry Sauce

Here is a dish that brings together native bounty and classical genius. The duck is roasted and bathed in a luxurious pool of berry purée sharpened with fresh ginger and orange zest. Serve with wild rice and something interesting from the vegetable family, perhaps a sauté of fresh kale or fennel.

Serves 8

2 ducklings, 4 to 5 pounds each

Salt and freshly ground pepper

8 or 9 Valencia oranges

2 cups sugar

2 cups red wine vinegar

1½ cups ruby port

3 cups beef stock or canned beef bouillon

2 tablespoons minced, peeled fresh ginger

2 pints (4 cups) fresh or frozen dry-packed blackberries

Salt and cayenne pepper to taste

1 teaspoon cornstarch, optional

1. Preheat an oven to 350 degrees F.

2. Dry the ducks thoroughly. Remove and discard the wing tips from the ducks. Season the ducks inside and out with salt and pepper, then truss them. Save the giblets for another use or discard. Place a large rack in a roasting pan. Set the ducks breast sides up on the rack and prick the thighs with a fork. Place in the oven and roast for 2 hours.

3. While the ducks are roasting, using a swivel-bladed vegetable peeler or a zester, remove the zest from 2 of the oranges. Cut the zest into very fine shreds and set aside. Squeeze enough juice from the remaining oranges to measure 2 cups. Set aside.

(continued)

4. Stir together the sugar and vinegar in a large enamel or stainless-steel saucepan and cook over medium-high heat until the mixture is syrupy, about 10 minutes. Add the port, orange juice, stock or bouillon, ginger, three fourths of the orange zest and half of the berries. Raise the temperature to high and reduce the mixture by about two thirds of its volume. This will take 10 to 20 minutes. Season, if desired, with a little salt and a pinch of cayenne pepper. The sauce is usually on the thin side. For a thicker sauce, blend the cornstarch with 1 tablespoon water and stir the mixture into the sauce. Set aside.

5. When the ducks are ready, remove from the oven (do not turn off the oven) and cut into quarters with poultry shears. Add the remaining berries to the sauce and heat until the berries are hot. Spoon a little sauce over each portion and garnish the portions with the remaining orange zest. Just before serving, warm the ducks through in the hot oven.

From Cafe des Amis

 # Quail with Chestnut Stuffing and Warm Pears

This recipe is an excellent example of the heights to which Oregon cookery can reach. The quail are stuffed with brandied chestnut purée, then arranged over warm pear slices and swathed in a sauce of pear brandy and crème fraîche. Little is needed alongside this dish, but something with a rich color would be nice. Think cranberries, perhaps, or winter vegetables with deep green hues. Ask your butcher to bone the quail. The chestnut purée is imported from France and is available in markets that sell fine foods.

Serves 4

For the stuffing:
1 tablespoon unsalted
   butter
5 ounces ($\frac{2}{3}$ cup)
   unsweetened chestnut
   purée
$\frac{1}{2}$ cup finely chopped day-
   old French bread
2 large egg yolks
1$\frac{1}{2}$ tablespoons pear brandy
Pinch of ground allspice
Salt and freshly ground
   white pepper

For the sautéed pears:
3 ripe pears, peeled, cored,
   and sliced lengthwise $\frac{1}{4}$
   inch thick

1 tablespoon fresh lemon
   juice
2 to 3 tablespoons unsalted
   butter

For the quail:
8 quail, boned
3 to 4 tablespoons clarified
   butter (page 239) or
   vegetable oil
1 cup crème fraîche
   (page 236) or sour cream
$\frac{1}{4}$ cup pear brandy
Salt and freshly ground
   white pepper

1. To make the stuffing, place the butter and chestnut purée in a bowl and beat with an electric mixer until creamy. Add the bread, egg yolks, pear brandy, and allspice and mix until the ingredients are thoroughly incorporated. Season with salt and white pepper to taste. Set aside.

2. To sauté the pears, sprinkle them with the lemon juice. Melt the butter in a skillet over medium-low heat. Add the pears and sauté until tender and translucent, 5 to 10 minutes, depending upon the ripeness of the pears. Remove from the heat and set aside.

3. Preheat an oven to 375 degrees F.

4. To cook the quail, stuff them with the reserved stuffing. Heat the butter in a 12- to 14-inch ovenproof skillet over medium-high heat. When the pan is hot, add the stuffed quail, shaking constantly to prevent the quail from sticking.

(continued)

Brown for 1 to 2 minutes on each side. Place the skillet in the preheated oven and roast the quail for 15 minutes.

5. To serve, reheat the sautéed pears. Divide the warmed slices among 4 dinner plates. Remove the quail from the oven and place 2 on each plate.

6. Pour off any butter remaining in the skillet. Add the crème fraîche or sour cream and pear brandy to the skillet. Cook over high heat until the mixture is reduced by half of its volume, or until thick enough to coat the back of a spoon. This will take 5 to 7 minutes. Season with salt and white pepper to taste. Spoon a little sauce over each quail and serve immediately.

From L'Auberge

 # Braised Pheasant with Juniper Cream

The gamy character of Oregon-raised pheasant stands up perfectly to the pungent and slightly resinous flavor of the juniper berry, which grows east of the Cascade Mountains. Here the purple berries are blended into a bold peppercorn purée seasoned with garlic and shallots. Serve with a rice pilaf or grilled polenta and a colorful vegetable or wild mushroom sauté.

Serves 4

4 cups unsalted chicken
  stock, preferably
  homemade (page 239)
2 teaspoons peppercorns
1 teaspoon juniper berries
2 large cloves garlic
1 large whole shallot plus
  2 tablespoons minced
  shallot
10 fresh thyme sprigs

1 pheasant, preferably
  fresh, 3 to 4 pounds
2 tablespoons clarified
  butter (page 239)
$\frac{1}{4}$ cup gin
Scant $\frac{1}{2}$ cup heavy cream,
  plus extra cream as
  needed
Pinch of salt

1. Place the chicken stock in a saucepan. Simmer over medium heat until the liquid is reduced to half of its volume (2 cups). This will take 15 to 20 minutes. Set aside.

2. In a blender or food processor fitted with the steel blade, combine the peppercorns, juniper berries, garlic, whole shallot, and 2 thyme sprigs. Purée coarsely. Set aside.

3. Melt the clarified butter over medium heat in a sauté pan large enough to hold the quartered pheasant. Add the quarters and brown on both sides, about 10–15 minutes on each side. Pour in the gin, averting your face from the flame. Ignite the pan juices with a long-handled match. Shake the pan for a few seconds, until the flames subside. Transfer the pheasant quarters to a plate.

4. Swirl the gin in the pan and use a metal spatula to scrape up any bits that cling to the bottom. Add the minced shallots and reserved chicken stock. Reduce the heat to a low simmer. Add the cream and the reserved peppercorn purée. Simmer until the mixture is reduced by half of its volume. This should take 10 to 12 minutes.

5. Return the pheasant quarters and any juices that have accumulated on the plate to the sauté pan. Cover and braise over low heat until the pheasant is fork-tender, about 45 minutes.

6. Transfer the pheasant to a heated platter, saving the liquid in the pan. To make a sauce, reduce the pan liquid over medium heat, lightly whisking frequently and adding additional cream as necessary to keep the sauce from separating. Season with the salt. Pour the sauce over the pheasant and garnish with the remaining thyme.

From Ron Paul Restaurant and Charcuterie

Roast Game Hens with Corn Bread, Sausage, and Apple Brandy Stuffing

This classic Oregon winter production can transform any evening's repast into a warm and cheery feast. The secret here is a stuffing brought to life with prunes plumped in a heady infusion of local apple brandy. It's my variation on an original recipe from Millie Howe, chef at the innovative Indigine restaurant. Howe roasts the hens on a dense bed of coarsely chopped garlic, using about 1 head for each hen. This is the ultimate experience for garlic aficionados, but the garlic can be omitted by the nonenthusiast.

Serves 6

2 cups chopped, pitted
  prunes
Apple brandy or Calvados as
  needed
6 Cornish game hens
Salt and freshly ground
  pepper
¼ pound (½ cup) unsalted
  butter
6 heads garlic

For the corn bread:
¾ cup coarse-grind cornmeal
1 cup unbleached all-
  purpose white flour
2 tablespoons sugar
½ teaspoon salt
2 teaspoons baking powder

1 teaspoon baking soda
1 large egg, lightly beaten
1 cup buttermilk
2 tablespoons bacon
  drippings or unsalted
  butter, melted

For the stuffing:
½ pound spicy bulk pork
  sausage meat
1 tablespoon bacon
  drippings or unsalted
  butter
2 onions, finely chopped
2 large eggs, lightly beaten
Salt and freshly ground
  black pepper

1. Place the prunes in a bowl and add apple brandy or Calvados to cover. Let stand for several hours or overnight. These prunes will be used in the stuffing.

2. Dry the game hens thoroughly and rub them inside and out with salt and pepper to taste. Set aside the butter at room temperature to soften. Separate the garlic into cloves, peel and coarsely chop. Scatter the garlic over the bottom of a shallow baking pan.

3. Preheat an oven to 425 degrees F. Position a rack in the middle of the oven.

4. To make the corn bread, grease a 9-inch round cake pan. Sift the cornmeal, flour, sugar, salt, baking powder, and baking soda together into a mixing bowl. Stir in the egg, buttermilk, and bacon drippings or butter until well mixed.

5. Pour the batter into the prepared pan and bake until nicely browned, about 25 minutes. Remove to a wire rack to cool completely, then crumble the corn bread into a mixing bowl.

6. Increase the oven temperature to 450 degrees F.

7. To make the stuffing, fry the sausage in a dry skillet over low heat, breaking it up with a fork, until lightly browned. Add the corn bread and mix well with the sausage. Remove from the heat and transfer the sausage mixture to a mixing bowl.

8. Heat the bacon drippings in the same skillet over medium heat. Add the onions and cook until transparent, about 5–10 minutes. Add to the corn bread mixture and mix well.

9. Drain the apple brandy from the prunes, reserving the brandy. Toss the prunes with the corn bread mixture and add a few tablespoons of the brandy, or to taste. Stir in the beaten eggs and season the mixture with salt and pepper to taste.

(continued)

10. To roast the hens, stuff them with the corn bread stuffing, then close the cavities with small skewers or toothpicks. Tie the legs with string and place the birds atop the bed of garlic, breast sides up, in the baking pan. Rub the hens generously with the reserved butter. Roast for about 1 hour, basting occasionally with the pan juices.

11. To serve, remove the skewers and clip the strings. Serve hot.

CHAPTER SEVEN

GRILLED MEATS WITH SWEET ONIONS, ORCHARD FRUITS, AND OREGON WINES

Lamb Braised with Quince, Cinnamon, and Apples

Oregon-raised lamb has developed a well-deserved reputation as the next best thing to those grazing in the French countryside. Try this dish in the fall, when local quince are at their peak. Serve with plenty of hot rice on the side.

Serves 8

2 tablespoons fresh lemon
  juice, or apple cider or
  white wine vinegar
2 large ripe quinces, peeled,
  cored, and dried
2½ pounds boneless lamb
  shoulder or any cut
  suitable for stewing
1 cup unbleached all-
  purpose flour
2 teaspoons salt
1 teaspoon freshly ground
  pepper

¼ cup olive oil
2 tablespoons vegetable oil
2 onions, diced
2 cinnamon sticks
3 large tart green apples,
  peeled, cored, and diced
1 small head green cabbage,
  cored and shredded
  (4 cups)
Chopped fresh parsley

1. Fill a bowl with water and add the lemon juice or vinegar. Place the cut quinces in the bowl and set aside.

2. Trim the excess fat and gristle from the lamb. Cut the lamb into 1-inch chunks.

3. Combine the flour, salt, and pepper in a shallow bowl. Measure out 2 tablespoons of the seasoned flour and set aside. Coat the lamb pieces with the remaining seasoned flour.

4. Combine the oils in a large, heavy noncorrosive pot over medium heat. When the pan is hot, add the lamb in

106

batches, without crowding the pan, and sauté until the pieces turn a rich brown, about 25 to 30 minutes in total. As the pieces are browned, using a slotted spoon, remove them to a bowl and set aside. When all the pieces have been browned, pour half of the oil out of the pan. Add the onions to the remaining oil and sauté over medium heat until the onions are translucent, about 15 minutes, scraping up any brown bits from the pan bottom.

5. Return the lamb to the pot. Sprinkle the reserved 2 tablespoons seasoned flour into the pan, stirring quickly to coat the lamb and onions. Drain the quince and add to the pot along with the cinnamon sticks and enough water to cover. Bring to a boil over high heat. Reduce the heat to low, cover, and simmer, stirring occasionally for 45 minutes.

6. Add the apples and the cabbage. Continue simmering until the lamb is tender enough to pierce with a fork, about 15 minutes.

7. Stir in the chopped parsley. Taste and adjust the seasonings. Serve hot.

From Bread and Ink Cafe

 # Grilled Leg of Lamb with Apricot-Mint Sauce

Oregon lamb roasts — a springtime ritual involving friends, family, and serious feasting — make generous use of the mint that grows in backyards and borders the edges of swollen creeks that snake throughout the state. Marinated in a ginger-honey blend spiked with garlic, the meat is grilled over coals and anointed with a sauce perfumed with apricot and bourbon.

Serves 8 to 10

1 leg of lamb, 8 to 9 pounds
Apricot-Mint Sauce
  (page 231)

For the ginger marinade:
$1\frac{1}{2}$ cups canola oil or
  safflower oil
$\frac{1}{2}$ cup soy sauce
$\frac{1}{4}$ cup red wine vinegar
$\frac{1}{4}$ cup fresh lemon juice
$\frac{1}{4}$ cup Worcestershire
  sauce

$\frac{1}{4}$ cup dry white wine
2 scallions, chopped
2 teaspoons minced, peeled
  fresh ginger
2 teaspoons crushed garlic
2 tablespoons dry mustard
2 teaspoons salt
1 tablespoon freshly ground
  pepper

1. To prepare the lamb, ask your butcher to butterfly the lamb, or cut the meat at home, leaving it in one piece so that it will lie flat on a grill. Carefully trim away any fat or gristle. Using a sharp knife, pierce the flesh in various spots on both sides of the lamb. Place the lamb in a rectangular, glass or enamel dish large enough to hold it easily. Set aside.

2. To make the marinade, combine all the marinade ingredients in a food processor fitted with the steel blade or in a blender. Blend until liquefied, about 30 seconds.

3. Pour the marinade over the lamb and rub the mixture well into the meat. Cover and refrigerate for 24 hours, turning occasionally.

4. To grill the lamb, light a fire in a charcoal grill. Place the meat on a grill rack about 5 inches above the hot coals and grill until the meat is dark on the exterior but still slightly pink inside, about 45 minutes.

5. Transfer the lamb to a warm platter. Slice and serve hot. Pass the Apricot-Mint Sauce on the side.

Roast Rack of Lamb with Hazelnut Hollandaise

Here is a rack of lamb like no other — that special-occasion dish that is as handsome as it is original. Baked to a rosy finish and garnished with roasted hazelnuts, this regional dish features a rich, nutty hollandaise distinguished by an infusion of hazelnut oil. Ask the butcher to french or trim the lamb.

Serves 8

For the hollandaise sauce:
6 large egg yolks
2 tablespoons water
2 cups clarified butter, melted (page 239)
Juice of 2 to 3 lemons, or to taste
Salt

Pinch of cayenne pepper
2 to 3 tablespoons hazelnut oil
4 racks of lamb, 6 to 8 chops each
$\frac{1}{4}$ cup chopped roasted hazelnuts (page 236)

1. Preheat an oven to 450 degrees F.

2. To make the sauce, combine the egg yolks and water in a stainless-steel bowl. Fill a sauté pan with 1 to 2 inches of water and bring to a simmer. Set the bowl of egg yolks in the simmering water. Whisk the yolks until they begin to thicken, removing the bowl from the simmering water occasionally to prevent the yolks from scrambling. When the yolks look like thick cream, remove the bowl from the heat. Lift the whisk from the bowl. If a drop falls and stands on the surface briefly, the eggs are ready. Again, do not let the eggs get too hot.

3. Slowly drizzle the butter into the yolks, whisking constantly. Add the lemon juice to taste. Season with salt to

(continued)

taste and cayenne pepper. Then beat in enough of the hazelnut oil to make a smooth and glossy sauce. Set the hollandaise sauce over a pan of warm water until ready to use.

4. To roast the lamb, position a roasting rack inside a shallow pan. Place the lamb on the rack and roast for 15 to 20 minutes or until an instant-read meat thermometer reads 135 to 140 degrees F for medium-rare.

5. To serve, cut each rack in half; 3 or 4 chops should be plenty for each person. Top the halved racks with the hazelnut hollandaise and garnish with the hazelnuts.

From Cafe des Amis

 # Pork Chops with Prunes, Sweet Onions, and Apple Brandy

The short season of the Walla Walla Sweet—spring and early summer—is motivation to strike when the onion is hot. Here it works with a trio of Oregon specialties, apple brandy, tart apples, and prunes, to create a splendid topping for pork.

Serves 6

6 loin pork chops, each cut
$\frac{1}{2}$ inch thick

Unbleached all-purpose
flour for dusting

Salt and freshly ground
pepper

4 tablespoons vegetable oil,
or as needed

1 large Walla Walla Sweet
onion or Vidalia onion,
halved and sliced

1 large Granny Smith apple,
cored and sliced

12 large pitted prunes,
halved

1$\frac{1}{4}$ cups water, or as needed

$\frac{1}{2}$ cup apple brandy or
Calvados

1. Coat the chops lightly with the flour, shaking off any excess. Season both sides with salt and pepper to taste.

2. Heat 3 tablespoons of the oil in a large skillet over medium-high heat. Add the chops and brown on both sides, about 5 minutes on each side. Transfer the chops to a heavy casserole dish or dutch oven and set aside.

3. Add the remaining 1 tablespoon oil to the skillet over medium heat. Add the onions and sauté until golden, about 15–20 minutes, adding a little more oil if necessary. Add the apple and sauté for 3 minutes longer. Spoon the onion and apple slices over the tops of the chops and arrange the prunes around the sides.

4. Add the water to the skillet and bring to a boil, scraping up any brown pieces that cling to the pan bottom. Stir in the apple brandy or Calvados. Pour the mixture over the chops. Cover with a tight-fitting lid and simmer over low heat until the chops are tender, 45 to 60 minutes. Check occasionally and add a little water if the liquid cooks down too rapidly. You should have enough sauce left at the end of the cooking time to pour over the ingredients just before serving.

Roast Pork Loin with Raspberry-Prune Compote

Italian plums are among the Willamette Valley's great unheralded treasures. This variety is a full-flavored fruit with a tart undertone. In this recipe, the plums, dried into prunes, are softened in sherry and then transformed into a crimson compote made with another Oregon classic, fresh raspberries. You

*will need to plan ahead to make this dish. Both the compote
ingredients and the pork must sit overnight.*

Serves 4 to 6

For the compote:
$\frac{3}{4}$ **pound pitted Italian
   prunes (about 2 cups)**
1 cup dry sherry
**1$\frac{1}{2}$ cups Pinot Noir or other
   dry red wine**
1$\frac{1}{4}$ cups raspberries
Zest of $\frac{1}{2}$ orange
Zest of $\frac{1}{2}$ lemon
**1 tablespoon raspberry
   vinegar**

1 lemon
$\frac{1}{2}$ **onion**
1$\frac{1}{2}$ cups dry sherry
**1$\frac{1}{2}$ cups Pinot Noir or other
   dry red wine**
**1 tablespoon white
   peppercorns**
**Olive oil for rubbing on
   meat**
**Watercress sprigs for
   garnish**

For the pork:
**2 pounds center-cut
   boneless pork loin**

1. To make the compote, in a bowl soak the prunes in the
sherry and Pinot Noir overnight. The next day, pour the
prunes and soaking liquid into an enamel saucepan.
Purée the raspberries in a blender or in a food processor
fitted with the steel blade and then pass the purée
through a fine-mesh sieve to remove the seeds. Add the
strained purée to the saucepan. Tie the orange and lemon
zests in a piece of cheesecloth and place the bundle in the
saucepan.

2. Bring the compote mixture to a simmer and cook until
the fruit is cooked and the liquid is syrupy, about 20 minutes. Remove the saucepan from the heat and let cool to
room temperature.

3. Discard the cheesecloth bundle. Stir in the raspberry
vinegar. Transfer the mixture to a container with a tight-
fitting lid and refrigerate until ready to use. The compote
tastes better with time and will keep for several weeks.

4. To marinate the pork, roughly chop the lemon, onion, and garlic in a food processor fitted with the steel blade. Mix in the sherry and wine. Place the pork in a bowl and pour the wine marinade over the top. Cover and marinate in the refrigerator overnight, turning the meat once or twice.

5. Preheat an oven to 475 degrees F.

6. Remove the pork loin from the marinade and dry with paper towels; discard the marinade. Press the peppercorns into the loin. Rub the loin with olive oil and place in a roasting pan. Roast, basting frequently with the pan juices, for 20 minutes, or until an instant-read thermometer inserted into the center of the meat reads 140 degrees F. Let rest for 5 to 10 minutes before slicing.

7. To serve, heat the compote. Spoon the warm compote over the sliced meat. Serve garnished with watercress sprigs.

From L'Auberge

Grilled Venison with Cranberry-Pepper Sauce

This dish is a good introduction to the menagerie of wildlife in the Northwest wilderness. Here, a bold cranberry-pepper sauce serves as a wonderful counterpart to the strongly-flavored venison. The meat may be grilled or panfried. In either case, be careful not to overcook the meat; game is low in natural fats and dries out easily. Serve on the rare side.

Serves 4

$\frac{1}{4}$ cup olive oil

6 cloves garlic, slightly crushed

15 peppercorns

1 tablespoon fresh thyme, or 1 teaspoon dried thyme

4 bay leaves

8 venison loin medallions, 2 to 3 ounces each

2 teaspoons vegetable oil plus 3 tablespoons, if panfrying

1 cup dry red wine

$\frac{1}{2}$ cup red wine vinegar

3 tablespoons currant jelly

4 cups beef stock or canned beef bouillon

1 cup cranberries

3 tablespoons unsalted butter, if panfrying

1. Combine the olive oil, garlic, peppercorns, thyme, and bay leaves in a shallow baking dish. Add the venison medallions and turn them in the marinade to coat both sides. Cover and refrigerate for at least 3 to 4 hours, or preferably overnight.

2. Remove the steaks from the marinade a few hours before serving. Strain the marinade, reserving the garlic and herbs. Heat the 2 teaspoons vegetable oil in a heavy 2-quart saucepan over medium heat. Add the reserved garlic and herbs and sauté until the cloves are golden brown. Add the wine, vinegar, and currant jelly. Bring the mixture to a boil and reduce until only a few table-spoons of liquid remain in the pan. Add the stock or bouillon and cranberries. Simmer at a low boil until the cranberries are tender and the sauce is thick enough to coat a spoon, about 1 hour. Reduce the heat to low to keep the sauce warm while you cook the venison steaks.

3. To grill the venison, light a fire in a charcoal grill. Place the medallions on a grill rack 3 inches above the hot coals and grill, turning once, 3 to 5 minutes on each side, depending upon the desired degree of doneness. Alterna-tively, heat $1\frac{1}{2}$ tablespoons of the butter and $1\frac{1}{2}$ table-spoons of vegetable oil in each of 2 heavy skillets over high heat. Add the steaks and sauté for 3 minutes or longer on each side, depending upon the desired degree of doneness.

4. Serve the venison medallions hot with the cranberry-pepper sauce on the side.

From The Heathman Hotel

 ## Veal Scallops with Morels

In this dish tender veal scallops are merged with an earthy sauce that brings together the wild and woodsy flavor of Oregon's morels and the smoky, oaky character of a Northwest Pinot Noir. Steamed stalks of spring asparagus and a dish of roasted new potatoes with a touch of fresh rosemary would be nice on the side.

Serves 4

16 veal scallops, approximately 1 ounce each
Salt and freshly ground pepper
2 tablespoons unbleached all-purpose flour
4 to 6 tablespoons clarified butter (page 239)
1 cup sliced fresh morels or other seasonal mushrooms
$\frac{1}{2}$ teaspoon minced garlic

1 teaspoon minced shallot
$\frac{1}{2}$ cup **Pinot Noir** or other dry red wine
1 cup veal stock or canned beef bouillon
$\frac{1}{4}$ cup heavy cream
3 tablespoons unsalted butter, at room temperature
Chopped watercress or fresh parsley for garnish

1. Using a flat mallet, pound the veal scallops between two sheets of waxed paper until $\frac{1}{4}$ inch thick. Sprinkle with salt and pepper to taste. Coat lightly with the flour, shaking off any excess.

(continued)

2. Heat 2 to 3 tablespoons of the clarified butter in a large, heavy skillet over medium heat. Working in batches, add the veal and sauté until cooked through and browned on both sides, about 1 minute on each side. As they are cooked, transfer the scallops to a warm serving platter. Add more butter to the skillet as needed to keep the pan moist.

3. Heat the remaining 2 to 3 tablespoons clarified butter in the skillet over medium heat. Add the morels and sauté until tender, about 3 minutes. Toss in the garlic and shallot and cook for about 30 seconds without browning. Add the wine and reduce the liquid by half of its volume, about 10 to 12 minutes. Add the stock or bouillon and the cream. Reduce until slightly thickened.

4. Remove from the heat and whisk in the 3 tablespoons of unsalted butter. Season with salt and pepper to taste. Pour the sauce over the veal, garnish with watercress or parsley, and serve.

From L'Auberge

 # Flank Steak in Ginger– Pinot Noir Marinade

In the following, thin strips of marinated beef, rolled into coils of haunting flavor, are seared and set against a field of watercress leaves. It's a sprightly production and a strong expression of Oregon Pinot Noir, a fine regional wine that figures prominently in Northwest marinades.

Serves 6

For the marinade:
$\frac{1}{4}$ **cup olive oil**
$\frac{1}{2}$ **onion, chopped**
5 cloves garlic, minced

1 tablespoon chopped, peeled fresh ginger
1$\frac{1}{2}$ cups beef stock or canned beef bouillon

$1\frac{1}{2}$ cups **Pinot Noir or other dry red wine**
5 whole cloves
2 cinnamon sticks
2 tablespoons honey

For the steaks:
2 flank steaks, about 2 pounds each
Freshly ground pepper
3 bunches watercress, picked over (about 3 cups leaves)

1. To make the marinade, heat the oil in a large, heavy skillet. Add the onion, garlic, and ginger and sauté until the onion is transparent, about 5 minutes. Add the stock or bouillon, raise the heat to high, and reduce the mixture by half of its volume, 5 to 7 minutes. Add the wine, cloves, cinnamon, and honey. Reduce the mixture again over high heat by about half of its volume, 5 to 7 minutes. Set aside to cool completely.

2. While the marinade cools, place the flank steaks in the freezer for 30 minutes.

3. Remove the steaks from the freezer and place on a clean cutting board. Using a sharp knife, cut the steaks vertically across the grain into strips $\frac{1}{8}$ inch thick. Place the strips in a bowl with the reserved marinade. Cover and refrigerate for at least 12 hours, or preferably overnight.

4. To cook the steak, remove from the marinade, reserving the marinade. Discard the cinnamon and cloves from the marinade. Roll one of the beef strips into a tight coil. Roll 3 or 4 more strips around the coil. When finished, the coils should measure about 3 inches across. Continue the process to make 15 more rolls. Butter a flameproof baking pan large enough to hold the rolls and place the rolls in the dish. Grind a little pepper over the rolls. Set aside.

5. Place the reserved marinade in a saucepan and reduce it over high heat to about 1 cup. This will take 3 to 5 minutes. Meanwhile, preheat a broiler.

(continued)

6. Make a bed of watercress leaves on 8 dinner plates.

7. Place the baking pan under the broiler about 4 inches away from the heat source. Broil for 7 minutes for rare and 10 minutes for medium-rare.

8. Remove from the broiler and place 2 rolls on each bed of watercress. Spoon a little of the pan juices into the reduced marinade and whisk to make a sauce. Spoon a little sauce over each roll. Serve immediately.

From the kitchen of Larry Kirkland

 # Willowdale Flank Steak

In Willowdale, a small eastern Oregon community, cattle ranchers like to show off another side of their profession—good cooking with good-quality ranch beef. A bunkhouse favorite using flank steak calls for rubbing the meat with mustard paste and then grilling it over hot coals in a barbecue pit. In winter the ranchers broil the meat to a deep brown finish, which is how it is prepared here. Just before serving, the beef is basted with hot butter that has been mingled with fresh cilantro, pepper, and lemon juice.

Serves 4

1 flank steak, about
  $2\frac{1}{2}$ pounds
2 tablespoons Dijon
  mustard
1 teaspoon dry mustard
$1\frac{1}{2}$ teaspoons kosher salt, or
  to taste
1 clove garlic, put through a
  press
$\frac{1}{2}$ teaspoon onion powder

3 tablespoons unsalted
  butter, at room
  temperature
1 tablespoon finely minced
  fresh cilantro or parsley
$\frac{1}{2}$ teaspoon freshly ground
  pepper
2 teaspoons fresh lemon
  juice

1. Preheat a broiler.

2. Place the flank steak on a flat surface. Holding a sharp knife diagonally to the beef, score it lightly on both sides, making the cuts about 1 inch apart. In a small bowl, make a paste of the Dijon mustard, dry mustard, salt, garlic, and onion powder. Rub the paste over the top of the meat.

3. Place the steak on a baking sheet and place it under the broiler about 4 inches from the heat source. Broil for 5 minutes on each side, or until the steak is cooked as desired. While the meat is broiling, combine the butter, cilantro, pepper, and lemon juice in a bowl.

4. Remove the meat from the broiler and place it on a cutting platter. Place dollops of the butter mixture over the surface of the cooked meat. Using a sharp knife, cut the steak into thin slices on the bias. Serve immediately.

From the kitchen of Sara Perry

 ## Stuffed Sirloin Steaks

Although red meat took something of a culture beating during the cholesterol-conscious 1980s, the popularity of a well-turned sirloin never waned. A fine cut of beef, after all, lends itself to experimentation. In that spirit, the following entrée, which comes from Nick's Italian Cafe near the vineyards of Yamhill County, blends bold packaging with unquestioned carnivorous lust—perfect with a bottle of Oregon Pinot Noir. Owner-chef Nick Pierano brought the concept of wine-country cuisine to Oregon 16 years ago, and his vision can be seen in other restaurants that mix local wines and casual style with smart, accessible menus and regional ingredients. Ask your butcher to cut the steaks from the large end of the sirloin to secure the necessary weight and thickness.

Serves 2

2 boneless sirloin steaks,
  each about 1¼ pounds and
  cut ¾ inch thick

For the garlic-mustard paste:
2 cloves garlic
½ cup fresh parsley leaves
1 teaspoon olive oil
1 teaspoon dry mustard
1½ teaspoons Dijon mustard,
  or to taste

For the stuffing:
2 slices prosciutto
2 slices jack cheese

To finish the steaks:
Olive oil as needed
1¾ cups dry Marsala wine
1 tablespoon unbleached
  all-purpose flour mixed
  with 2 tablespoons butter,
  optional
1 tablespoon unsalted
  butter, optional

1. To butterfly the steaks, trim the fat from each steak and discard. Slice each steak in half by putting one hand flat on top of the steak and, using a sharp knife, slicing horizontally three fourths of the way through the steak. Flatten the steak out like an opened book. Pound the steaks very thin with a mallet between 2 sheets of waxed paper. Trim to make the steaks an even shape and save the meat trimmings.

2. To prepare the garlic-mustard paste, combine all the ingredients in a blender. Process until the mixture is reduced to a creamy paste. Taste and adjust the seasonings, adding more Dijon mustard if necessary. The paste should have a sharp, pungent flavor.

3. To stuff the steaks, spread a thin layer of the garlic mustard paste on the inside of each steak. Cover one half of the paste with a slice of prosciutto and a slice of cheese. Fold the steak in half to enclose the filling and press gently to seal. Then coat the entire outside of each steak with a thin layer of the paste.

4. To finish the steaks, warm a little olive oil in a large, heavy skillet over high heat. Add the reserved meat trim-

mings and brown in the hot oil. Add the Marsala and bring the mixture to a boil over medium heat. Reduce the mixture by one third of its volume, watching carefully to make sure the sauce does not boil over. This will take about 15 minutes. Use a metal spatula to scrape up any bits stuck to the bottom of the skillet. If you want a thicker sauce, stir the flour-butter paste into the reduced Marsala sauce. Or, for a richer taste, stir the melted butter into the reduced sauce.

5. Heat a little olive oil in a heavy skillet or dutch oven. Turn the heat to high and add the stuffed steaks. Fry until browned, turning once, on both sides, about 2 minutes on each side for medium-rare. Pour the Marsala sauce over the steaks and serve immediately.

From Nick's Italian Cafe

CHAPTER EIGHT

FANCIFUL VEGETABLES, FOREST MUSHROOMS, AND OTHER SMART SIDE DISHES

Asparagus with Black Morel Butter

*This dish testifies to the power of simplicity. Northwest aspara-
gus spears, known for their superior flavor, are steamed to
snappy perfection and embellished with an earthy mingling of
wild mushrooms, lemon zest, and shallots, all moistened with
butter. The recipe is often a showcase at the dinner parties
hosted by Portland textile artist Larry Kirkland.*

Serves 8

Zest of 1 lemon
6 tablespoons unsalted
  butter
2 tablespoons finely
  chopped shallots

$\frac{1}{2}$ pound fresh morels, finely
  chopped
2 tablespoons fresh lemon
  juice
$1\frac{1}{2}$ pounds asparagus

1. Using a zester or a swivel bladed vegetable peeler, remove
the zest (colored portion) from the lemon. Trim away any
of the bitter white skin that may have been removed with
the zest. Drop the zest briefly in boiling water. Drain. If
you don't have a zester, cut the zest into very fine shreds.

2. Using a sharp knife, cut off the tough ends of the asparagus stalks. Starting about 2 inches from the top of the
tips, peel the stalks.

3. Melt the butter in a large skillet over medium heat. Add
the shallots and sauté for 3 minutes. Add the chopped
morels, reduce the heat and sauté over low heat until the
morels are very dark in color, about 7 minutes.

4. Combine the lemon zest and lemon juice with the morels.
Meanwhile place the asparagus in a skillet and add lightly
salted water to cover. Bring to a boil, reduce the heat,
and simmer until the spears are tender but crisp to the

bite, about 5 minutes. Drain the asparagus, then run them under cold running water to stop the cooking process.

5. Place the cooked asparagus on a serving platter. Spoon the morel butter over the top and serve immediately.

From the kitchen of Larry Kirkland

 # Broccoli with Toasted Walnut Butter

Broccoli has long been a favorite Oregon staple. Here it is emboldened by toasted walnuts and plumped currants.

Serves 6

$\frac{1}{2}$ **cup dried black currants**
$\frac{1}{2}$ **cup water, boiling**
$\frac{1}{2}$ **cup coarsely broken walnuts**
3 pounds broccoli, trimmed and cut into large sprigs with florets

6 tablespoons unsalted butter
2 tablespoons currant jelly
$\frac{1}{4}$ **teaspoon freshly ground white pepper**
2 tablespoons fresh lemon juice

1. Place the currants in a bowl and pour in the boiling water. Let steep until plump, about 30 minutes. Drain, discarding the water. Set the currants aside.

2. Preheat an oven to 350 degrees F.

3. Spread the walnuts on a baking sheet. Place them in the oven, shaking the sheet occasionally to ensure the nuts toast evenly until golden, about 10 minutes. Set aside to cool.

(continued)

4. Place the broccoli on a steamer rack over boiling water, cover, and steam until crisp-tender, about 5 to 7 minutes. Alternatively, fill a saucepan with salted water, bring to a boil, and add the broccoli. Cook until crisp-tender, about 8 minutes.

5. While the broccoli is cooking, melt the butter in a large saucepan over medium-high heat. Add the reserved currants, currant jelly, white pepper, and lemon juice. Stir to blend. Then add the toasted walnuts and heat through.

6. As soon as the broccoli is ready, place it under cold running water for a few seconds to prevent further cooking. Transfer to a serving bowl. Pour the walnut-currant butter over the broccoli and serve immediately.

Cauliflower with Caramelized Onions and Fresh Herb Chutney

The culinary world has not been overly generous to the cauliflower. But Oregon cauliflower, which is among the country's best, inspires cooks to experiment. Oregon's moist air and cool days and nights result in a supercrisp head that is delicious raw, or mingled with local herbs and Indian spices as in the following recipe. If using as a main dish, serve over a mound of hot rice.

Serves 4 as a main course, or 8 as a side dish

1 tablespoon cumin seeds
$\frac{1}{4}$ cup unsalted butter
2 cups chopped onion
2 cups nonfat yogurt
1 tablespoon minced garlic
2 teaspoons ground tumeric
2 teaspoons kosher salt, or
   to taste

4 cups cauliflower florets
1 cup julienned red or green
   bell pepper
1 cup Fresh Herb Chutney
   (page 226)

1. Preheat an oven to 350 degrees F. Place the cumin seeds in a small pan in the oven and toast lightly, about 15 minutes. Watch carefully to prevent burning. Set aside.

2. Melt the butter in a large, heavy skillet over low heat. Add the onion and sauté, stirring occasionally, until tender and slightly caramelized, about 30 minutes.

3. Meanwhile, combine the cumin seeds and all the remaining ingredients, except the chutney, in a glass or enamel bowl. Transfer the mixture to a $2\frac{1}{2}$ quart saucepan. Add the onions. Cover and cook over low heat, stirring occasionally, until the cauliflower is tender, about 15 minutes.

4. Serve immediately. Place the chutney in a bowl and pass on the side.

From Indigine

 # Chanterelle Sauté with Basil and Shredded Leeks

This dish speaks of fall. Try it with hearty meats or serve alongside a simple roast duck or chicken.

Serves 6

1 tablespoon olive oil
1 tablespoon minced garlic
2 tablespoons minced
  shallots
1 cup dry Marsala wine
2 tablespoons fresh lemon
  juice
1 cup chicken stock, preferably homemade (page 239)
1 pound fresh chanterelles
  or other seasonal
  mushrooms, sliced

1 cup very finely shredded
  leeks, white part only
Salt and freshly ground
  pepper
1 cup loosely packed fresh
  basil leaves
2 tablespoons unsalted
  butter
Lemon wedges for garnish

1. In a large sauté pan, heat the oil over medium-high heat. Add the garlic and shallots, reduce the heat to medium, and sauté, stirring briskly and constantly. When the shallots and garlic turn golden brown, add the Marsala wine, lemon juice, and chicken stock. Simmer until the mixture is reduced by half of its volume. This will take about 7 to 10 minutes. Add the chanterelles or other mushrooms and leeks. Continue to reduce the mixture until the mushrooms and leeks are cooked through, 3 to 5 minutes. Season with salt and pepper to taste.

2. Transfer the chanterelle-leek mixture to a warm serving dish. Arrange the basil leaves over the top. Whisk the softened butter into the sauté pan over medium heat. When the butter is hot, pour it over the basil leaves. Serve immediately with lemon wedges.

From The Heathman Hotel

 # Braised Fennel with Blue Cheese

Garden vegetables of all varieties flourish in the Northwest and fennel is no exception. The sweet licorice flavor of fennel bulbs complements the authoritative flavor of an Oregon blue cheese. Here, braised in chicken stock and accented with crumbled cheese and walnuts, the bulbs are a lusty accompaniment to roast lamb or beef as well as grilled trout or salmon.

Serves 6

3 large fennel bulbs
¾ cup chicken stock, preferably homemade (page 239)
Salt and freshly ground pepper

3 to 4 tablespoons unsalted butter, cut into small bits
½ cup crumbled blue cheese, at room temperature
2 tablespoons finely chopped walnuts

1. Preheat an oven to 325 degrees F.

2. Cut off the tops of the fennel bulbs. Discard or save for another use. Trim off the base of the core and tough outer leaves. Cut the bulbs in half lengthwise. Fill a saucepan with water, bring to a boil, add the fennel, and parboil for 5 minutes. Drain well.

3. Butter a baking dish large enough to hold the fennel in a single layer. Arrange the blanched fennel cut side down in the dish. Add the stock and season with salt and pepper to taste. Dot with the butter. Cover and bake for 30 minutes.

4. Combine the blue cheese and walnuts. Remove the cover from the baking dish. Sprinkle the cheese-walnut mixture over the fennel and bake for 30 minutes longer. Serve hot.

 ## Ramekins of Fresh Fennel and Parsnips

Thick, white, and creamy, with a sultry licorice perfume, this intriguing purée brings to mind mashed potatoes with a high IQ. Try it alongside such wintry inspirations as dishes featuring duck, pumpkin, cranberries, wild mushrooms, and so on. Or serve it on the holiday table alongside roast goose or a stuffed turkey. For a variation, substitute pears for the parsnips; the fennel is fabulous with the juicy fruit.

Serves 8

2 teaspoons fresh lemon
   juice
6 small parsnips
1 cup heavy cream
$\frac{1}{4}$ cup white rice
2 cups water, or more
   as needed
3 small fennel bulbs
$\frac{1}{4}$ pound ($\frac{1}{2}$ cup) unsalted
   butter

$\frac{1}{4}$ cup minced shallots
Salt and freshly ground
   pepper
2 tablespoons Pernod or
   Ricard
3 tablespoons chopped
   fresh tarragon, or
1$\frac{1}{2}$ tablespoons dried
   tarragon

1. Fill a large bowl with water and add the lemon juice. Peel
   the parsnips. Cut them in half lengthwise and then into
   quarters. Immediately place the parsnips in the bowl of
   water once they are cut; parsnips brown quickly when
   exposed to air.

2. Drain the parsnips and place in a 4-quart saucepan. Add
   the cream, rice, and 1$\frac{1}{2}$ cups of the water. Bring to a boil,
   reduce the heat to low, and cover with a tight-fitting lid.
   Simmer, stirring occasionally, until the parsnips are
   cooked through and almost soft, about 20 minutes. Be
   careful not to let the mixture boil.

3. Cut off the tops of the fennel bulbs. Discard or save for
   another use. Cut the bulbs into quarters lengthwise. Cut
   out the core from each quarter and remove any tough
   outer leaves. Coarsely chop the quarters.

4. Melt half of the butter in a heavy skillet over medium-
   high heat. Add the shallots and the fennel. Sauté, stirring
   constantly. When the fennel is almost limp, after about
   7 minutes, add the remaining $\frac{1}{2}$ cup of water and reduce
   the heat to low. Simmer until the fennel is cooked
   through, about 15 minutes, adding more water if necessary to prevent sticking. Meanwhile, melt the remaining
   butter and set aside. When the fennel is done, drain off
   any liquid remaining in the skillet.

5. Add the parsnip mixture to the skillet with the fennel. Season with salt and pepper to taste. Add the reserved melted butter along with the Pernod or Ricard and tarragon. Remove from the heat and set aside to cool to room temperature.

6. Preheat an oven to 350 degrees F. Butter 8 ramekins or a 1½-quart soufflé dish.

7. Working in batches, place the cooled fennel-parsnip mixture in a food processor fitted with the steel blade and purée. Spoon the puréed mixture into the prepared ramekins. Place the ramekins in a large baking pan and pour in enough hot water to reach halfway up the sides of the ramekins. Bake for 10 to 12 minutes.

8. Remove the ramekins from the oven and grind a little fresh pepper over the tops. Serve immediately.

From the kitchen of Larry Kirkland

 Pears with Brandied Currants

This is it. Here is the side dish you're always searching for when nothing else seems quite right. Fresh pear halves are scooped out and filled with tiny dark currants and pear brandy. The results may be the last word in elegant simplicity. You can serve it with just about anything you can imagine, from roast fowl to baked salmon to a wild mushroom tart.

Serves 8

2 tablespoons fresh lemon
  juice
2 cups water
4 ripe but firm and
  unblemished Anjou pears

½ cup pear brandy
1 cup dried black currants
Freshly ground pepper
½ cup unsalted butter

1. Combine the lemon juice and water in a bowl. Cut the pears in half lengthwise. Cut a quarter-size slice off the back side of each half at the roundest part of the pear. This will allow the pear halves to stand firmly upright on the plate. With a melon scooper, scoop out the core and enough of the center of each pear half to make a well. As the pears are cut, place them in the lemon water to prevent them from browning.

2. Place the pear brandy and the currants in a small saucepan. Bring to a simmer and cook for 10 minutes to plump the currants.

3. Preheat an oven to 350 degrees F.

4. Melt the butter in a small pan. Lightly butter a baking dish and place the pear halves in it cut side up. Grind a little pepper over the tops. Spoon a few tablespoons of the plumped currants and pear brandy into each pear well. Drizzle the melted butter evenly over the tops.

5. Place in the oven and bake until the pears can be easily pierced with a fork, 25 to 30 minutes. Serve hot.

From the kitchen of Larry Kirkland

 # Mashed Pumpkin with Cider Raisins and Cinnamon Crème Fraîche

It's unfortunate that pumpkins have been relegated to Thanksgiving desserts and Halloween porch art. The big orange beauties are the sweetest North American squash and the greatest native source of vitamin A. Although you can get pumpkin canned any time of year, it's best right from the field. Oregon

crops mature throughout the fall, and natives make good use of the U-pick pumpkin patches that dot the landscape. The following side dish is an example. Try it as a companion to Lemon Chicken with Stuffed Figs (page 86) or serve with roast duck, lamb, or grilled venison.

Serves 4 to 6

1 pumpkin, about 3 pounds
1 cup raisins
3 tablespoons apple brandy
  or Calvados
2 tablespoons apple cider
1 cup crème fraîche
  (page 236) or sour cream

1 tablespoon ground
  cinnamon
4 to 6 tablespoons dark
  brown sugar

1. Preheat an oven to 350 degrees F.

2. Cut the pumpkin in half crosswise. Scoop out the seeds and stringy portions. Place in a pan, cut side up, and bake in the oven until the pumpkin meat can be pricked easily with a fork and the shell begins to fall apart, about 1 hour.

3. While the pumpkin is baking, place the raisins in a small bowl. Combine the apple brandy and apple cider. Pour the mixture over the raisins and set aside.

4. Combine the crème fraîche or sour cream, cinnamon, and brown sugar. Set aside.

5. Scrape the pumpkin pulp from the shell and put it through a ricer or strainer. Alternatively, purée it in a blender or in a food processor fitted with the steel blade. Transfer the pulp to a mixing bowl.

6. Fold in the crème fraîche mixture and stir to blend thoroughly. Add the raisins and their soaking liquid. Serve immediately or reheat in a double boiler over hot water.

Sauté of Spinach, Shiitake Mushrooms, and Comice Pears

Ginger and shiitake mushrooms were once the province of the Asian cook. Today both ingredients are cultivated by Northwest growers. It's no surprise then that they should show up together in the following recipe, which goes beautifully with grilled meat, fish, or fowl.

Serves 8

6 tablespoons unsalted butter

1 tablespoon minced shallots

1 pound fresh shiitake or other seasonal mushrooms, sliced

12 cups torn fresh spinach leaves, (about 3 pounds untrimmed)

1 tablespoon thinly sliced crystallized ginger

$\frac{1}{2}$ cup pear brandy

$\frac{3}{4}$ cup heavy cream

2 teaspoons Dijon mustard

4 Comice pears

1. Heat 3 tablespoons of the butter in a large, heavy skillet over medium heat. Add the shallots and sauté until soft. Add the remaining 3 tablespoons of butter and allow to melt. Then add the mushrooms and sauté for 2 to 3 minutes. Using a slotted spoon, remove the shallots and mushrooms from the pan and set aside.

2. Add the spinach leaves to the same skillet and wilt them over medium heat for 1 minute. Transfer the spinach leaves to a warm serving platter, forming a bed. Set aside.

3. Combine the ginger, brandy, cream, and Dijon mustard in the same skillet over high heat. Cook to reduce the amount by one third of its volume, about 5 minutes.

4. While the sauce is reducing, quarter the pears lengthwise and core them. Arrange the mushrooms, shallots, and pears over the spinach bed. Drizzle the reduced sauce over the dish and serve immediately.

From Briggs and Crampton's Catering and Table for Two

 ## Summer Garden Ragout with Dark Greens and Fresh Herbs

With its bright jade colors and warm gold hues, this richly aromatic stew is a wonderful dish to make in the summer, when good garden vegetables and fresh herbs abound. Serve it as a colorful sidekick to grilled meats or fish. As a meatless main course, top it with plenty of freshly grated Parmesan cheese and serve with crusty French bread on the side.

Serves 4 as a main course or 8 as a side dish

$\frac{1}{3}$ **cup olive oil**

1 large onion, quartered and cut into thin slices

4 to 6 cloves garlic, minced

2 large russet or Finnish yellow potatoes, unpeeled, cut into 1-inch pieces

5 mixed small summer squash, cut into $\frac{1}{2}$-inch-thick slices

$\frac{1}{4}$ **cup green beans, cut into 1-inch lengths**

$\frac{1}{4}$ **cup shelled young green peas**

$\frac{1}{2}$ **cup green or purple broccoli florets**

2 or 3 large ripe red or yellow tomatoes, peeled, seeded, and diced

4 cups mixed shredded dark seasonal greens such as Swiss chard, sorrel, spinach, dandelion, mustard, or beet greens, and so on

$\frac{1}{2}$ **cup water**

Juice of 1 lemon

Salt and freshly ground pepper

2 handfuls of fresh herbs such as basil, lemon thyme, oregano, and chives, coarsely chopped

1. Heat the olive oil in a large pot over medium heat. Add the onion and garlic and sauté until the onion is translucent, about 10 minutes; be careful not to brown. Add the potatoes and stir to coat the pieces with the oil. Cover and cook for about 5 minutes, giving the pot a shake from time to time.

2. Add all the remaining ingredients, except the herbs. Cover and cook until the vegetables are tender but firm, about 10 minutes. Stir in the herbs. Taste and adjust the seasonings, then serve.

From Bread and Ink Cafe

 # Zucchini with Wine and Shallots

Zucchini grows everywhere in Oregon, from the damp loam of the forests of the Coast Ranges to the high desert sand of the Oregon Cascades. The squash grows and grows and grows; a single bush can keep a family of four eaters satisfied all summer. This sauté is a flavorful way of dealing with the inevitable surplus.

Serves 4

3 tablespoons olive oil
1 tablespoon unsalted
   butter
6 shallots, minced, or 3
   scallions, chopped
1 clove garlic, finely minced
2 zucchini, sliced crosswise
   $\frac{1}{2}$ inch thick
1$\frac{1}{2}$ teaspoons minced fresh
   basil, or 1 teaspoon dried
   basil

1$\frac{1}{2}$ teaspoons minced fresh
   thyme, or 1 teaspoon
   dried thyme
$\frac{1}{4}$ cup Chardonnay or other
   dry white wine
$\frac{1}{4}$ cup chicken stock,
   preferably homemade
   (page 239)
$\frac{1}{2}$ cup crumbled blue cheese
Freshly ground pepper

1. Warm the oil and butter in a heavy saucepan over medium heat. Add the shallots or scallions and garlic and sauté until soft, $1\frac{1}{2}$ to 2 minutes. Add the zucchini, basil, thyme, wine, and stock. Cook over medium heat, stirring occasionally, until the zucchini are tender, about 15 minutes.

2. Transfer the zucchini to a serving bowl. Sprinkle the cheese over the top. Add a few grinds of fresh pepper and serve immediately.

 # Roasted Potatoes with Red Pepper Salsa

Oregon spuds, while not enjoying the fame of their Idaho kin, give away nothing in quality. Herb-scented new potatoes are an ideal accompaniment to eggs or just about anything off the barbecue grill. The peppery salsa adds a colorful jolt. If you don't want to make your own salsa, good commercial tomato salsas can be found in most grocery stores.

Serves 4

$1\frac{1}{2}$ pounds small new
  potatoes
$\frac{1}{4}$ cup olive oil
1 tablespoon unsalted
  butter
2 large eggs
2 large cloves garlic, finely
  minced, optional
2 tablespoons finely minced
  fresh chives
1 tablespoon snipped fresh
  thyme, or 1 teaspoon
  dried thyme

1 tablespoon snipped fresh
  tarragon, or 1 teaspoon
  dried tarragon
Salt and freshly ground
  white pepper
Red Pepper Salsa (page 231)
  or any good-quality
  tomato salsa, optional

1. Peel the potatoes, if desired. Cut the potatoes into rounds $\frac{1}{8}$ inch thick. Wash in several changes of cold water to remove the starch. Dry well with paper towels.

2. Preheat an oven to 400 degrees F. Lightly butter a 1-quart casserole.

3. Heat the oil and butter in a large heavy skillet over medium heat. Add the potatoes and sauté for 5 minutes. Remove from the heat and set aside.

4. In a bowl beat the eggs until well mixed. Add the garlic, if using, chives, thyme, and tarragon. Season with salt and white pepper to taste.

5. Place the potatoes in the prepared dish. Pour the beaten eggs evenly over the top. Cover, place in the oven, and bake until the potatoes are tender when pierced with a fork, about 30 minutes.

6. Serve hot. If desired, pass a bowl of salsa on the side.

From Briggs and Crampton's Catering and Table for Two

 # Potato Gratin with Thyme Leaves and Goat Cream Cheese

Goat cream cheese, full of high flavor and tart undertones, is a rising star on the local culinary horizon. Produced in Canby, Oregon, by the Tall Talk Dairy, it has been showcased in Bloomingdale's in New York and Neiman-Marcus in Texas. Here the cheese is layered with slivered garlic and fresh thyme in a potato gratin that is browned and finished with cream. This is a rich dish, so serve it with a simple entrée. Or try it

for brunch, alongside poached eggs and fresh fruit. If goat cream cheese is not available, substitute regular cream cheese.

Serves 6

6 tablespoons unsalted
  butter
3 or 4 cloves garlic, thinly
  sliced
6 potatoes, peeled and
  thinly sliced
3 tablespoons chopped fresh
  thyme, or 1 tablespoon
  dried thyme

Salt and freshly ground
  white pepper
$\frac{1}{4}$ pound goat cream cheese,
  cut into $\frac{1}{2}$-inch cubes
2 tablespoons freshly grated
  Parmesan cheese
$\frac{3}{4}$ cup heavy cream
Fresh thyme leaves for
  garnish

1. Preheat an oven to 375 degrees F.

2. Melt the butter in a heavy skillet over low heat. Add the garlic and sauté until it softens, $1\frac{1}{2}$ to 2 minutes; be careful not to brown. Remove the pan from the heat.

3. Using a pastry brush, brush the bottom of a gratin dish with a little of the butter in the skillet. Cover with one third of the sliced potatoes. Sprinkle with 1 tablespoon of the chopped fresh thyme leaves or 1 teaspoon of the dried, salt and white pepper to taste, and one third of the cream cheese. Drizzle one third of the garlic butter over the cheese. Repeat the layers two more times, seasoning each layer with salt and white pepper to taste. Sprinkle the Parmesan cheese over the top layer and then pour the cream evenly over the entire dish.

4. Place in the oven and bake, uncovered, until most of the cream has been absorbed and a golden crust forms on top, 45 minutes to 1 hour. Garnish with thyme leaves and serve.

Lemon Rice Pilaf with Forest Mushrooms

The following is a worthy companion for roasted meats or grilled fish. A pronounced citrus flavor cuts through the grains, pretoasted rice lends a nutty flavor, and the wild mushrooms add an unexpected woodsy note.

Serves 4

1 cup long-grain brown rice	**$\frac{1}{2}$ cup sliced fresh chanterelles, morels, or other seasonal mushrooms**
2 cups water	
Juice of 2 lemons	
3 tablespoons unsalted butter	**Salt and freshly ground pepper**

1. Wash the rice well and place in a dry skillet over medium heat. Stir constantly until the rice "pops," or is lightly browned, about 3 to 4 minutes. Remove from the heat.

2. Combine the rice, water, lemon juice, and 1 tablespoon of the butter in a heavy 2-quart saucepan. Bring to a boil and boil for 5 minutes. Reduce the heat to low, cover with a tight-fitting lid, and simmer until the liquid is absorbed and the rice is tender, about 45 minutes.

3. Meanwhile, melt the remaining 2 tablespoons butter in a heavy skillet, over medium heat. Add the mushrooms and sauté until tender, about 5 minutes; keep warm.

4. Remove the rice from the heat and let stand for 2 minutes to steam-dry. Season with salt and pepper to taste and fluff with a fork. Stir in the sautéed mushrooms and serve.

Wild Rice with Apricots, Fennel, and Hazelnuts

This is a simply prepared side dish made of intriguing ingredients. It is moist and crunchy and is a fine accompaniment to pork or just about any bird, from duck to quail to chicken. Or try it as a stuffing.

Serves 8

3 tablespoons butter
½ bulb fresh fennel, chopped
½ cup wild rice
4 cups chicken stock, preferably homemade (page 239)
½ cup long-grain brown rice
1 cup chopped dried apricots

½ cup coarsely chopped roasted hazelnuts (page 236)
2 teaspoons ground ginger
1 tablespoon grated orange zest
Salt and freshly ground pepper

1. Thoroughly wash the wild rice in cold water. Place in a bowl and add water to cover. Soak for at least 2 hours. Drain off any remaining water.

2. Melt the butter in a heavy skillet over medium heat. Sauté the fennel until tender, about 20 minutes. Set aside.

3. Bring the stock to a boil in a 3-quart saucepan. Add the wild rice and boil for 20 minutes. Add the brown rice and continue boiling for 5 minutes. Reduce the heat to low, cover with a tight-fitting lid, and simmer for 40 minutes. Drain off any remaining liquid.

4. Preheat an oven to 350 degrees F. Lightly grease a 2½-quart baking dish.

(continued)

5. Mix the fennel, apricots, nuts, ginger, and orange zest into the cooked rice. Season with salt and pepper to taste. Transfer to the prepared dish. Place in the oven and bake, uncovered, until the rice is hot and tender, about 30 minutes. Fluff the mixture with a fork and serve immediately.

CHAPTER NINE

PASTA WITH WILD BERRIES, WALNUT PESTO, AND OTHER WHIMSICAL NOTIONS

Fettuccine with Clams, Mussels, and Spicy Sausage

In this dish Oregon mussels and clams merge with sweet red peppers and tomatoes in a rousing sauce. The dish gains intensity from chorizo, a fiery Spanish sausage with a near cult following in the Northwest. If chorizo is unavailable, consider garlic sausage or hot Italian sausage. Upscale food markets and ethnic markets are good sources for interesting sausages.

Serves 4 generously

For the sauce:

1 pound steamer clams in the shell, preferably manila

1 pound mussels in the shell

¼ cup olive oil

2 large cloves garlic, chopped

1 onion, diced

½ pound chorizos, casings removed

1 red bell pepper, seeded, deribbed, and diced

1 cup peeled, seeded, and chopped tomatoes

2 cups Fish Stock (page 240) or bottled clam juice

¾ cup Chardonnay or other dry white wine

½ teaspoon hot-pepper flakes

Salt and freshly ground pepper

For the pasta:

3 quarts water

Salt

¾ pound fresh fettuccine

2 tablespoons chopped fresh cilantro for garnish

1. To make the sauce, wash the clams and mussels to remove any sand. Pull off and discard the beards that protrude from the mussel shells. Discard any broken or open clams or mussels. Place the shellfish in a bowl, covered by an inch of water and let stand for one hour. Change the water several times as they render their sand. Set aside.

2. Heat the olive oil in a heavy skillet over medium heat. Add the garlic and onion and sauté until tender, about 3 minutes. Add the chorizo and cook, stirring frequently, until the meat loses its color, 3 to 4 minutes. Add the bell pepper and sauté until softened, about 2 minutes. Stir in the tomatoes, fish stock or clam juice, wine, and hot-pepper flakes. Season with salt and pepper to taste. Bring to a simmer and cook for about 5 minutes to blend the flavors. Just before serving, add the clams and mussels and cook just until they open, 3 to 5 minutes. Discard any clams or mussels that do not open.

3. To cook the pasta, bring the water to a rolling boil in a large pot. Season generously with salt. Drop the fettuccine into the water and cook, stirring occasionally, until *al dente*, about 2 to 3 minutes. Drain immediately.

4. Transfer the pasta to a warm serving dish, pour on the sauce, and toss. Garnish with cilantro and serve.

From Cafe des Amis

 # Fettuccine with Blue Cheese, Walnuts, and Sun-Dried Tomatoes

Veronique Vitt is a family friend who uses adventurous instincts for inspired home cooking. This creation is the sheerest indulgence, but rest assured that every forkful is worth tomorrow's guilt. Serve with a salad of winter greens and a bottle of Oregon Chardonnay or a good dry white wine.

Serves 6 to 8

6 quarts water	**Salt**
$\frac{1}{4}$ pound ($\frac{1}{2}$ cup) unsalted butter	**1 pound fettuccine, preferably fresh**
2 cups heavy cream	**4 sun-dried tomatoes, cut into coarse slivers, for garnish**
$\frac{1}{2}$ pound Oregon blue cheese	
$\frac{1}{2}$ cup chopped fresh parsley	
2 cups walnut pieces	

1. Bring the water to a rapid boil in a large pot. Meanwhile, in a small saucepan, melt the butter in the cream over medium-high heat. Lower the heat to keep the mixture hot but not boiling.

2. Crumble the cheese into a large mixing bowl. Add the parsley and nuts. Mix together.

3. Season the boiling water generously with salt. Drop the fettuccine into the water and cook, stirring occasionally, until *al dente,* about 2 to 3 minutes for fresh pasta; for dried fettuccine, follow the directions on the package. Drain immediately.

4. In a warm serving bowl, quickly mix together the pasta and the cheese mixture. Add the hot cream and toss well. Garnish with the sun-dried tomatoes and serve at once.

From the kitchen of Veronique Vitt

 # Pasta with Nehalem Bay Crab and Blackberries

The most interesting dishes often use ingredients in unexpected combinations. The following, for example, from artist and pop culture writer Lena Lencek, unites corkscrew pasta and steamed garden vegetables with crushed walnuts, fresh dill, walnut oil, and vinegar. Lencek then folds fresh crab from Oregon's most popular crab pot, Nehalem Bay, into the mix and scatters wild blackberries on top.

Serves 6

1 small red bell pepper,
   seeded and deribbed
1 small yellow bell pepper,
   seeded and deribbed
1 cup broccoli florets
$\frac{1}{2}$ cup julienned zucchini
3 quarts water
Salt
1 pound dried corkscrew
   pasta

$\frac{1}{3}$ cup chopped shelled
   walnuts
$\frac{1}{3}$ cup chopped fresh dill
$\frac{1}{2}$ cup walnut oil
2 tablespoons balsamic
   vinegar, or to taste
Freshly ground pepper
$\frac{1}{2}$ pound cooked crab meat
Blackberries for garnish
Fresh dill sprigs for garnish

1. Using a very sharp knife, cut the red and yellow pepper into julienne strips about $\frac{1}{8}$ inch wide and 2 inches long. Place on a steamer rack set over boiling water. Cover and steam until crisp-tender, 2 to 3 minutes. Transfer to a bowl and set aside.

2. Repeat the steaming process, first with the broccoli and then with the zucchini, allowing approximately 2 to 3 minutes for the broccoli and 30 seconds to 1 minute for the zucchini. Transfer the crisp-tender broccoli and zucchini to the bowl with the peppers and set aside.

3. Bring the water to a rolling boil in a large deep pot. Season generously with salt. Drop the pasta into the boiling water and cook, stirring occasionally, until *al dente,* 10 to 12 minutes, or according to package directions. Drain the pasta in a colander and rinse with cold water. Drain well and transfer to a large serving bowl.

4. Toss the pasta with the chopped walnuts and chopped dill. Combine the walnut oil and vinegar. Toss with the pasta. Season with salt and pepper to taste. Gently stir in the crab meat and steamed vegetables. Garnish with the blackberries and dill sprigs. Serve immediately or cool to room temperature and chill for later use.

From the kitchen of Lena Lencek

Pasta with Mussel Sauce

Just about every Oregon cook has a repertoire of recipes featuring the voluptuous, coral-hued mollusks from the Oregon coast. This one comes from an old Portland restaurant known as Genoa, an elegant little eatery where Northwest cooking meets northern Italian tradition. It is the kind of festive affair that can readily be emulated at home.

Serves 4 as a main course or 6 as a first course

24 small mussels in the shell
¾ cup dry white wine
6 ounces (¾ cup) unsalted butter
2 tablespoons finely minced shallot
2 large cloves garlic, finely minced
1 tablespoon finely minced fresh thyme leaves

Pinch of hot-pepper flakes
Salt and freshly ground pepper
4 quarts water
1 pound fresh pasta such as linguine or fettuccine
6 tablespoons finely minced flat-leaf parsley

1. Wash the mussels to remove any sand and pull off and discard the beards that protrude from the shells. Discard any broken or open mussels. Place the mussels in a bowl. Cover with cold water and let stand for one hour. Change the water several times as they render their sand.

2. Place the mussels in a stainless-steel or an enamel saucepan large enough to hold them easily. Add the wine, cover tightly, and cook over medium-high heat until the mussels open, 3 to 5 minutes (they won't open very wide). Discard any mussels that do not open. Using a slotted utensil, transfer the mussels to a bowl and cover to keep warm. Line a strainer with a double thickness of cheesecloth and strain the mussel juices into a separate bowl; reserve.

3. In another small stainless-steel or enamel saucepan, melt the butter over medium heat. Add the shallot, garlic, thyme, and pepper flakes and sauté until the shallot and garlic are soft but not browned, 2 to 3 minutes. Add the reserved mussel juices and, over high heat, boil the liquid down to about one third of its original volume. This will take 5 to 7 minutes. Reduce the heat and season the mixture generously with salt and pepper to taste. Keep warm over very low heat.

4. Bring the water to a rolling boil in a large deep pot. Season generously with salt. Drop in the fresh pasta and cook, stirring occasionally, until *al dente,* about 2 to 3 minutes. Drain immediately.

5. Transfer the pasta to a warm bowl or pan, pour on the sauce, and toss. Season with salt and pepper to taste, then add half of the parsley. Divide the pasta evenly among warm serving plates. Arrange 4 to 6 mussels in their shells over the top of each serving. Garnish each plate with some of the remaining parsley and serve immediately.

From Genoa

 # Linguine with Scallops and Saffron Cream Sauce

This colorful dish, a nest of noodles brushed with an amber sauce and punctuated with stripes of red pepper, celebrates the region's exquisitely tender sea scallops. Local Chardonnay adds levity to the rich sauce, and nippy watercress sprigs provide a lively contrast to the sweet peppers. This is the perfect dish for summertime al fresco dining. It was created by my friends Pat Failing and Bob Sitton, who have earned a reputation for their

intimate dinner parties — handcrafted affairs generously complemented with regional wines and brandy.

Serves 4

4 tablespoons unsalted
   butter
1 red bell pepper, seeded,
   deribbed, and cut into
   1-inch-wide julienne
   strips
$\frac{1}{2}$ cup water
$\frac{3}{4}$ cup Chardonnay or other
   dry white wine
1 pound sea scallops, cut
   into quarters

2 cups heavy cream
$\frac{1}{2}$ teaspoon plus 2
   tablespoons salt
$\frac{1}{4}$ teaspoon powdered
   Spanish saffron
$\frac{3}{4}$ cup freshly grated
   Parmesan cheese
4 quarts water
1 pound fresh linguine
Watercress sprigs for
   garnish

1. In a small skillet, melt 1 tablespoon of the butter over medium heat. Add the pepper strips and sauté until softened, about 5 minutes. Remove from the heat and set aside.

2. In a medium saucepan, bring the water and $\frac{1}{2}$ cup of the Chardonnay to a simmer. Add the scallops and poach until tender, 2 to 3 minutes; be careful not to overcook them. Drain the scallops, reserving $\frac{1}{4}$ cup of the poaching liquid. Set aside.

3. Meanwhile, in a large, deep frying pan, bring the cream and the remaining 3 tablespoons butter to a simmer. Add the $\frac{1}{2}$ teaspoon salt. Continue to simmer over medium-high heat until the cream is thickened and reduced to one third of its volume. This will take 5 to 10 minutes.

4. When the cream is thickened, stir in the saffron. Add the reserved poaching liquid, the remaining $\frac{1}{4}$ cup Chardonnay, and $\frac{1}{2}$ cup of the cheese.

5. Bring the water to a rolling boil in a large pot. Add the 2 tablespoons salt and the linguine and cook, stirring occasionally, until *al dente*, 2 to 3 minutes.

6. Meanwhile, add the scallops and the reserved red pepper to the thickened cream sauce. Drain the linguine and divide it among 4 warm serving plates. Top each portion with one fourth of the scallop sauce. Garnish with the remaining ¼ cup cheese and the watercress. Serve immediately.

From the kitchen of Pat Failing and Bob Sitton

 # Linguine with Feta Cheese Sauce

Cool winters, hot summers, and a rich river basin make Oregon's Willamette Valley particularly lush turf for growing almost every kind of vegetable. The following recipe, created by my friend Chris Maranze, utilizes some of the bounty: broccoli, juicy red tomatoes, and aromatic herbs joined in a garden topping for fresh pasta. If you're lucky to obtain some of the goat feta cheese made at the Tall Talk Dairy in Canby, Oregon, this dish will be all the better. The farm is turning out one of the finest fetas found this side of Athens; it is moist and full of good flavor without being dry or too salty. Otherwise, choose a nice feta from your favorite cheese department.

Serves 4 to 6

1 large bunch broccoli, about 1½ pounds
2 tablespoons olive oil
1 small onion, chopped
4 cloves garlic, minced
1 large red or yellow bell pepper, seeded, deribbed, and chopped
1 can (28 ounces) Italian plum tomatoes, chopped, with juice reserved
1 tablespoon chopped fresh oregano, or 1 teaspoon dried oregano

1 teaspoon chopped fresh rosemary, or ½ teaspoon dried rosemary
1 teaspoon chopped fresh thyme, or ½ teaspoon dried thyme
Freshly ground pepper
¾ pound goat feta cheese or other Greek-style feta cheese
4 quarts water
Salt
½ pound fresh linguine

1. Separate the broccoli into florets and stems. Cut the stems into 1-inch pieces and place on a steamer rack over boiling water. Cover and steam for 3 minutes. Add the florets, cover, and steam for 3 to 4 minutes longer, or until crisp-tender. Remove from the steamer and place under cold running water to stop the cooking process. Set aside.

2. Heat the oil in a heavy skillet over medium-low heat. Add the onion and garlic and sauté until golden, about 15 minutes. Add the bell peppers and sauté for 2 minutes. Stir in the tomatoes and their juice. Season with the herbs and ground pepper to taste and simmer for 15 to 20 minutes.

3. Bring the water to a rolling boil in a large pot. Season generously with salt. Drop in the linguine and cook, stirring occasionally, until *al dente,* 2 to 3 minutes.

4. Meanwhile, add the broccoli to the skillet and cook, stirring, until heated through. Taste and adjust the seasonings. Crumble the cheese into the mixture and stir to melt.

5. Drain the linguine and place in a warm bowl. Spoon the sauce over the top and serve.

From the kitchen of Chris Maranze

 # Linguine with Bay Shrimp and Roasted Walnut Pesto

Neahkahnie, a laid-back Oregon coastal community of weathered homes, undulating dunes, bleached grass, and a 1,000-foot monolith of basalt, offers its own culinary specialties. With few restaurants nearby, residents have been turning out some interesting dishes that take advantage of the local catch.

The following pesto, from the Neahkahnie kitchen of physician and pop culture writer Gideon Bosker, uses roasted Oregon walnuts in place of the more traditional pine nuts. Bosker's blend is terrific with fresh pasta, especially when mingled with Oregon bay shrimp, fresh herbs, and wine. Complete this lively ensemble with a green salad and hunks of hot garlic bread.

Serves 4

For the pesto:

$\frac{1}{2}$ **cup coarsely chopped shelled walnuts**

2 cups fresh basil leaves

3 or 4 cloves garlic, chopped

$\frac{1}{2}$ **cup olive oil**

$\frac{1}{4}$ **cup freshly grated Parmesan cheese**

Salt

2 to 3 tablespoons heavy cream, optional

For the linguine:

4 quarts water

$\frac{1}{4}$ **cup olive oil**

$\frac{1}{2}$ **to $\frac{3}{4}$ pound bay shrimp or other small shelled shrimp**

1 tablespoon chopped fresh rosemary, or 1 teaspoon dried rosemary

1 tablespoon chopped fresh thyme, or 1 teaspoon dried thyme

1 tablespoon chopped fresh tarragon, or 1 teaspoon dried tarragon

1$\frac{1}{2}$ teaspoons chopped fresh oregano, or $\frac{1}{2}$ teaspoon dried oregano

2 tablespoons Chardonnay or other dry white wine

Fresh lemon juice

Salt

$\frac{3}{4}$ **pound fresh linguine**

Freshly grated Parmesan cheese for serving

1. Preheat an oven to 350 degrees F.

2. To make the pesto, place the walnuts in a small pan. Roast the nuts in the oven until toasted, about 5 minutes.

3. Combine the toasted walnuts, basil leaves, garlic, oil, and cheese in a blender or in a food processor fitted with the steel blade. Process until smooth. Season to taste with

(continued)

salt. Transfer to a serving bowl and stir in the cream, if desired. Set aside.

4. To prepare the linguine, bring the water to a rolling boil in a large pot. Meanwhile, heat the oil in a large, heavy skillet over medium heat. Add the shrimp, herbs, and wine and sauté until the shrimp are warmed through. Season with lemon juice to taste and keep warm over low heat.

5. Season the boiling water generously with salt. Drop the linguine into the water and cook, stirring occasionally, until *al dente,* 2 to 3 minutes. Drain the pasta in a colander, shaking off any excess moisture.

6. Turn the noodles immediately into the skillet and toss briskly with the sautéed shrimp. Transfer to a warm serving bowl. Using 2 forks or wooden spoons, add the pesto to taste and toss vigorously. Serve immediately. Pass a bowl of Parmesan at the table. Any leftover pesto can be stored in a container and coated with a thin layer of olive oil. Cover with a lid. Pesto will keep up to 4 months.

From the kitchen of Gideon Bosker

 # Hazelnut Lasagne with Oyster Mushrooms

Italy is a long way from the Pacific Northwest, but the culinary distance seems insignificant in this marriage of Tuscan pasta and Oregon bounty. The recipe is a specialty of Nick's Italian Cafe, a bastion of good food, high spirits, and cool jazz in the heart of Oregon's wine country. The delicate wild oyster mushroom, also known as the angel wing or hedgehog, lends a

woodsy note to the lasagne filling. And a topping of roasted hazelnuts is an unexpected touch. If oyster mushrooms aren't available, substitute any good seasonal mushrooms.

Serves 12

For the pesto:
1 cup fresh parsley leaves
1 cup fresh basil leaves
6 cloves garlic, or more to taste
$\frac{1}{8}$ teaspoon salt
$\frac{1}{4}$ cup olive oil
2 tablespoons pine nuts
$\frac{1}{2}$ to 1 cup freshly grated Parmesan cheese or part Parmesan and part pecorino romano
Salt

For the béchamel sauce:
6 ounces ($\frac{3}{4}$ cup) butter
1 cup unbleached all-purpose flour
7 cups milk, heated

For the lasagne:
2 tablespoons butter

$\frac{1}{2}$ pound fresh oyster mushrooms or other seasonal mushrooms, stemmed
6 quarts water
2 teaspoons salt
1 pound lasagne noodles, preferably fresh
$\frac{1}{2}$ pound ricotta cheese
$\frac{1}{2}$ cup freshly grated Parmesan cheese
$\frac{1}{2}$ cup freshly grated pecorino romano cheese
1 cup coarsely chopped roasted and skinned hazelnuts (page 236)

1. To make the pesto, place the parsley and basil leaves in a food processor fitted with the steel blade or in a blender and process to chop. Add the garlic, salt, oil, and pine nuts and process until the garlic and pine nuts are finely minced. Whirl in enough cheese to form a thick paste. Taste and adjust the amount of salt and garlic. Transfer the pesto to a bowl and set aside.

2. To make the béchamel sauce, melt the butter in a heavy 3-quart saucepan. Whisk in the flour to combine thoroughly

(continued)

and cook over low heat, stirring constantly, for 3 minutes. Add the milk, one third at a time, whisking rapidly and constantly after each addition. When the mixture is smooth and thickened, remove the pan from the heat.

3. Melt the butter in a large heavy skillet over medium-high heat. Sauté the whole mushrooms until just tender, about 5 minutes. Set aside.

4. To cook the noodles, bring the water and salt to a boil in a large pot. If you are using fresh noodles, drop in a few at a time and cook until barely tender, 1 to 2 minutes. Immediately transfer them to a pot of cold water and repeat with the remaining noodles. If using dried noodles, drop them into the boiling water all at once and cook until almost tender; follow the cooking directions on the package. Drain and plunge the noodles immediately into a pot of cold water. When the noodles have cooled, drain and transfer to a baking sheet lined with a cloth towel to cool.

5. Meanwhile, stir the ricotta cheese into the reserved pesto, then blend in $\frac{1}{2}$ cup of the béchamel sauce. Add more béchamel, a little at a time, to make the mixture barely spreadable.

6. Preheat an oven to 400 degrees F. Heavily butter a 9-by-13-inch baking dish.

7. To assemble the lasagne, using about one third of the noodles, form a layer of noodles in the bottom of the dish. Spread on the pesto mixture in a smooth layer. Add half of the remaining noodles, forming another layer. Top with the mushrooms. Cover the mushrooms with half of the remaining béchamel sauce. Combine the cheeses and sprinkle half of the mixture over the sauce layer. Top with a layer of the remaining noodles. Cover with the remaining béchamel sauce. Sprinkle the remaining cheese mixture on top and finish with a layer of hazelnuts.

8. Bake until the top is browned and bubbling, 20 to 30 minutes. Remove the lasagne from the oven and let stand for 10 minutes before cutting and serving.

From Nick's Italian Cafe

 # Chanterelle Lasagne

Between the sheets of pasta in this dish lies a cream sauce scented with smoky ham and woodsy mushrooms. It's a specialty of my good friend Chris Maranze, known for hosting grand regional food celebrations in her art-filled Portland home. This is a rich dish, so you won't need much with it. Just a nice green salad, perhaps, and a robust bottle of wine.

Serves 6

For the sauce:
- $\frac{1}{4}$ **cup unsalted butter**
- **1 pound fresh chanterelles, finely chopped**
- **3 cloves garlic, minced**
- $\frac{3}{4}$ **cup minced scallions, or 1 onion, minced**
- $\frac{1}{4}$ **cup unbleached all-purpose flour**
- **2$\frac{1}{2}$ cups milk, heated**
- $\frac{1}{4}$ **teaspoon freshly grated nutmeg**
- $\frac{1}{4}$ **teaspoon cayenne pepper**
- $\frac{1}{2}$ **teaspoon ground coriander**
- $\frac{1}{2}$ **teaspoon paprika**

- $\frac{1}{4}$ **cup dry sherry**
- $\frac{1}{2}$ **pound triple crème cheese, such as St. André, or cream cheese**
- $\frac{1}{2}$ **pound good-quality country ham or smoked turkey, chopped**

For the pasta:
- **4 quarts water**
- **Salt**
- **1 pound lasagne noodles, preferably fresh**
- $\frac{3}{4}$ **cup freshly grated Parmesan cheese**

1. To make the sauce, melt the butter in a heavy skillet over medium heat. Add the chanterelles, garlic, and scallions or onion and sauté about 5 minutes. Mushrooms should

(continued)

be just tender and the juice released. Sprinkle the flour into the skillet and stir to incorporate it into the mixture. Cook 1 to 2 minutes longer. Slowly pour the hot milk into the skillet, stirring constantly until thoroughly absorbed into the ingredients. Add the nutmeg, cayenne, coriander, paprika, and sherry and simmer for 10 minutes.

2. Break up the triple crème or cream cheese by hand. Add the pieces to the pan, stirring until the cheese is melted. Taste and adjust the seasonings; the sauce should be highly seasoned. Remove from the heat and stir in the ham or turkey.

3. To cook the noodles, bring the water to a boil in a large pot. Season lightly with salt. If you are using fresh noodles, drop in a few at a time and cook until barely tender, about 2 minutes. Immediately transfer them to a pot of cold water and repeat with the remaining noodles. If using dried noodles, drop them into the boiling water all at once and cook until barely tender; follow the cooking directions on the package. When the noodles have cooled, drain and transfer to a baking sheet lined with a cotton towel to cool.

4. Preheat an oven to 400 degrees F. Lightly butter a 9-by-13-inch baking dish.

5. To assemble the lasagne, put a ladleful of sauce on the dish bottom. Top with a layer of noodles. Add another layer of sauce and a sprinkling of Parmesan cheese. Repeat the process until all the noodles and sauce have been used, ending with the sauce. Sprinkle the top with the remaining Parmesan cheese.

6. Place in the oven and bake until the lasagne is bubbling and golden brown, 15 to 20 minutes. Remove the pan from the oven and let the lasagne rest for 10 minutes. Cut into squares and serve hot. Pass a bowl of freshly grated Parmesan on the side.

From the kitchen of Chris Maranze

White Lasagne with Scallops

This is pure comfort food — a cream-colored lasagne made with delicate seafood and béchamel sauce instead of the traditional ground meat and tomato sauce. If you must have fire in your food, spice up the production with a touch of Tabasco. For a variation, replace the sliced scallops with salmon.

Serves 6

For the béchamel sauce:
$\frac{1}{4}$ **cup unsalted butter**
$\frac{1}{4}$ **cup unbleached all-**
  purpose flour
2 cups half-and-half
$\frac{1}{2}$ **cup finely chopped**
  scallions
1 teaspoon kosher salt
1 teaspoon freshly ground
  pepper
$\frac{3}{4}$ **cup dry vermouth**

For the lasagne:
4 quarts water

Salt
8 fresh lasagne noodles
1 pound ricotta cheese
$\frac{1}{4}$ **cup hot water**
2 tablespoons unsalted
  butter
$\frac{1}{2}$ **pound wild or cultivated**
  fresh mushrooms, sliced
1 pound fresh scallops,
  sliced
3 cups coarsely grated
  imported Jarlsberg cheese

1. To make the sauce, melt the butter in a saucepan over medium heat. Whisk in the flour until bubbly. Add the half-and-half, scallions, salt, and pepper. Continue whisking until the mixture is boiling and thickened. Add the vermouth and bring to a boil, whisking constantly. Remove the saucepan from the heat until you are ready to assemble the lasagne. The sauce can be made a day in advance, in which case it should be refrigerated and reheated just before it is needed.

2. Bring the water to a rolling boil in a large pot. Generously salt the water. Add the lasagne noodles, one at a time. Cook until barely tender, 1 to 2 minutes. Drain the noodles and spread on a damp cotton cloth to cool.

(continued)

3. Preheat an oven to 450 degrees F. Lightly grease a 2½-quart terrine or loaf pan.

4. In a small bowl, beat the ricotta with the hot water to make it spreadable. Set aside.

5. Melt the butter in a skillet over medium heat. Add the mushrooms and sauté until just tender, about 5 minutes. Remove from the heat and set aside.

6. To assemble the lasagne, layer 2 of the lasagne noodles in the bottom of the prepared pan. Cover with the ricotta cheese and half of the scallops. Add another 2 lasagne noodles. Cover with 1 cup of the Jarlsberg cheese, the sautéed mushrooms, and half of the reserved sauce. Add another 2 lasagne noodles and cover with the remaining scallops and another cup of the Jarlsberg cheese. Add the last layer of 2 lasagne strips. Cover with the remaining sauce and sprinkle the remaining 1 cup of cheese over the top.

7. Place in the oven and bake until the lasagne is piping hot and bubbling throughout, about 30 minutes. Cut into squares and serve immediately.

From Indigine

 CHAPTER TEN

EARTHY BREADS AND ETHEREAL MUFFINS

Blueberry Corn Bread

Wedges of this hot amber bread, mottled with local blueberries and lavished with creamy butter and warm honey, are hard to match for down-home goodness. Other berries can be substituted, especially raspberries, which are marvelous against earthy cornmeal.

Makes 9 servings

6 ounces ($\frac{3}{4}$ cup) butter, at room temperature

1 cup sugar

3 large eggs

1$\frac{1}{2}$ cups coarse-grind yellow cornmeal

2 cups unbleached all-purpose flour

1 tablespoon baking powder

$\frac{1}{2}$ teaspoon salt

2 cups milk

1 cup blueberries

1. Preheat an oven to 375 degrees F. Position a rack in the middle of the oven. Grease a 9- or 10-inch square baking pan.

2. Combine the butter and sugar in a mixing bowl. Using an electric mixer, cream together until smooth and fluffy. Beat in the eggs until thoroughly blended, then beat in the cornmeal.

3. Sift together the flour, baking powder, and salt into a bowl. Alternately mix the dry ingredients and the milk into the creamed ingredients. Gently fold in the blueberries.

4. Turn the mixture into the prepared pan. Place in the oven and bake until lightly browned and a cake tester inserted in the center comes out clean, 40 to 50 minutes. Cool slightly on a wire rack before serving.

Apple-Cheddar Bread

This autumn sweet bread, imbued with local apples and sharp Oregon Cheddar, is as easy to make as it is to eat. Several excellent Cheddars are made in the Northwest. You might try Rogue Gold or an extra-aged variety of Tillamook's Cheddar. (Both creameries are on the Oregon coast.) Or, if these are unavailable, substitute your favorite Cheddar.

Makes one 9-inch loaf

$\frac{1}{4}$ **pound ($\frac{1}{2}$ cup) unsalted butter, at room temperature**

$\frac{1}{2}$ **cup granulated sugar**

$\frac{1}{4}$ **cup firmly packed dark brown sugar**

2 large eggs

2 cups unbleached all-purpose flour

1 teaspoon baking powder

$\frac{1}{2}$ **teaspoon baking soda**

$\frac{1}{2}$ **teaspoon salt**

$\frac{1}{2}$ **teaspoon ground ginger**

1 teaspoon ground cinnamon

1 cup finely chopped, unpeeled tart apples such as Gravenstein or Newton Pippin

$\frac{3}{4}$ **cup grated sharp Oregon Cheddar cheese**

$\frac{1}{4}$ **cup dried black currants**

$\frac{1}{4}$ **cup chopped hazelnuts or walnuts**

1. Preheat an oven to 350 degrees F. Position a rack in the middle of the oven. Grease a 5-by-9-inch loaf pan.

2. Combine the butter and sugars in a mixing bowl. Using an electric mixer, cream together until smooth and fluffy. Beat in the eggs until thoroughly blended.

3. Sift together the flour, baking powder, baking soda, salt, ginger, and cinnamon into a bowl. Mix one third of the flour mixture into the butter mixture. Stir in the apples, cheese, currants, and nuts. Mix in the remaining flour mixture.

(continued)

4. Pour the batter into the prepared pan. Place in the oven and bake until a cake tester inserted in the center comes out clean, about 1 hour. Cool completely on a wire rack before removing from the pan.

 # Strawberry Applesauce Bread with Black Currants and Golden Raisins

Northwest cooks are constantly devising new ways to show-case local fruit. Here, Oregon's famed strawberries are folded into a chunky applesauce batter, powerfully scented with cloves. You can't have too many of these loaves on hand: They freeze well and make lovely gifts to bring to friends.

Makes four 8-inch loaves

$5\frac{1}{3}$ cups cake flour

4 cups sugar

$1\frac{1}{2}$ tablespoons baking powder

$1\frac{1}{2}$ tablespoons baking soda

1 tablespoon salt

1 tablespoon ground cinnamon

$1\frac{1}{2}$ tablespoons ground cloves

3 cups chunky applesauce

1 cup coarsely chopped strawberries

$\frac{1}{4}$ cup unsalted butter, melted

5 large eggs

1 cup dried black currants

$\frac{3}{4}$ cup golden raisins

$\frac{3}{4}$ cup roughly broken walnuts

1. Preheat an oven to 350 degrees F. Position a rack in the middle of the oven. Grease four 4-by-8-inch loaf pans.

2. In a large mixing bowl, combine the flour, sugar, baking powder, baking soda, salt, cinnamon, and cloves. Make a well in the center and add the applesauce, strawberries, melted butter, and eggs. Stir with a large wooden spoon or beat on the lowest speed of an electric mixer, blending just until the ingredients are thoroughly combined. Be careful not to overmix. Carefully fold in the currants, raisins, and walnuts.

3. Divide the batter among the prepared pans. Each should be a little more than half full. Smooth the tops. Bake until a cake tester inserted in the center comes out clean, 50 to 60 minutes. Cool on wire racks before removing from the pans.

 # Bran Muffins with Pear Brandy Glaze

Bran muffins don't come better than these big, dark beauties. The batter, fueled by buttermilk and strong hot coffee, has an outgoing personality. When baked, it emerges from the oven moist and dense, not too sweet, and full of character. The pear brandy glaze is a celestial notion, especially first thing in the morning.

Makes 12 muffins

For the muffins:
$\frac{1}{2}$ **cup sugar**
$\frac{1}{4}$ **cup unsalted butter, at**
  room temperature
1 large egg
$\frac{1}{2}$ **cup strong brewed coffee,**
  heated
1 cup buttermilk
$\frac{3}{4}$ **cup unbleached all-**
  purpose flour
$\frac{1}{4}$ **teaspoon salt**

$1\frac{1}{2}$ **teaspoons baking soda**
$1\frac{1}{2}$ **cups bran**

For the glaze:
$\frac{1}{2}$ **cup firmly packed dark**
  brown sugar
$\frac{1}{4}$ **cup unsalted butter**
5 tablespoons heavy cream
  or whipping cream
1 tablespoon pear brandy

1. Preheat an oven to 350 degrees F. Position a rack in the middle of the oven. Line a 12-cup muffin pan with paper liners or butter the wells.

2. To make the muffins, in a large mixing bowl combine the sugar and butter. Using an electric mixer, cream together until smooth and fluffy. Beat in the eggs until thoroughly blended, then quickly beat in the coffee and buttermilk.

3. Sift together the flour, salt, and baking soda into a bowl. Add the dry mixture to the batter, being careful not to overmix. Then add the bran, again being careful not to overmix.

4. Fill the prepared pan wells two-thirds full. Wipe off any batter that spills on the sides of the cups. Place in the oven and bake until a tester inserted in the center of a muffin comes out clean, about 20 minutes. When the muffins are almost done, make the glaze.

5. Combine the brown sugar and butter in a small saucepan over low heat. Heat, stirring frequently, until the butter melts. Then stir in the cream and pear brandy and keep warm.

6. Remove the muffin pans to a wire rack. Loosen the muffins with an icing spatula and transfer them to the wire rack to cool. When slightly cooled, dip the top of each muffin in the glaze. Return the muffins to the wire rack to cool completely before serving.

From Ron Paul Restaurant and Charcuterie

 ## Cranberry Muffins with Nutmeg Sugar

To bite into one of these tart and tender gems is to awake from the fog of morning reverie. Consider the following recipe a rousing substitute for the more common blueberry contender.

Makes 14 muffins

1 cup cranberries

$\frac{1}{2}$ cup powdered sugar

2 cups unbleached all-
purpose flour, sifted

$\frac{1}{2}$ cup sugar

3 teaspoons baking powder

$\frac{1}{4}$ teaspoon salt

1 large egg

$\frac{3}{4}$ cup milk

$\frac{1}{4}$ cup vegetable shortening,
melted

$1\frac{1}{4}$ tablespoons granulated
sugar mixed with

$1\frac{1}{4}$ teaspoons freshly
grated nutmeg

1. Preheat an oven to 425 degrees F. Position a rack in the middle of the oven. Using two 12-cup muffin pans, butter or insert paper liners in 14 cups.

2. Pick over the cranberries, discarding any soft or crushed ones. Pat the cranberries dry with paper towels, then coarsely chop or halve them. Place in a bowl and sprinkle with the powdered sugar. Set aside.

3. Sift together the flour, sugar, baking powder, and salt into a large mixing bowl. Make a well in the center. In a small bowl, beat the egg until frothy. Beat in the milk and melted shortening. Pour the mixture into the well and stir quickly but lightly and just enough to blend. Do not over-beat; the batter will be lumpy. Gently fold in the sweetened cranberries.

4. Fill the prepared wells two-thirds full. Fill the unfilled wells with water so the pan won't warp. Wipe off any batter that spills on the sides of the cups. Place in the oven and bake until a tester inserted in the center of a muffin comes out clean, about 25 minutes. Remove the muffin pans to wire racks. Loosen the muffins with an icing spatula, tilting them so that the heat from the bottom is released. When cool, remove from the pan and sprinkle with the nutmeg sugar.

Huckleberry-Banana Muffins

The following muffins are fat and fluffy, with a Pacific Mountain undercurrent. With hot coffee, they are a terrific way to greet the morning. If huckleberries are not available, substitute blueberries.

Makes 14 to 16 muffins

2 large ripe bananas, peeled and sliced

$\frac{1}{4}$ pound ($\frac{1}{2}$ cup) unsalted butter

1 cup firmly packed light brown sugar

2 large eggs, lightly beaten

1 teaspoon pure vanilla extract

1 cup fresh huckleberries or blueberries

$2\frac{1}{4}$ cups unbleached all-purpose flour

2 teaspoons baking powder

1 teaspoon ground cinnamon

$\frac{1}{2}$ teaspoon salt

1. Preheat an oven to 350 degrees F. Position a rack in the middle of the oven. Using two 12-cup muffin pans, butter or insert paper liners in 14 to 16 cups.

2. Place the bananas in a food processor fitted with the steel blade or in a blender and purée. Measure out 1 cup purée and discard any remainder or save for another use.

3. Melt the butter in a saucepan. Remove from the heat and add the brown sugar, eggs, and banana purée. Mix well. Fold in the vanilla and berries.

4. Combine the flour, baking powder, cinnamon, and salt in a large mixing bowl. Make a well in the center of the dry ingredients. Pour the berry mixture into the well. Stir quickly but lightly and just enough to blend. Do not overmix.

5. Fill the prepared wells two-thirds full. Fill the unfilled wells with water so the pan won't warp. Wipe off any batter that spills on the sides of the cups. Remove any unfilled paper liners. Place in the oven and bake until a tester inserted in the center of a muffin comes out clean, 25 to 30 minutes. Transfer to wire racks to cool. Loosen the muffins with an icing spatula, tilting them so that the heat from the bottom is released.

 # Blueberry Streusel Muffins with Lemon Glaze

For most Oregonians, blueberry muffins are the real staff of life. In this version, they emerge from the oven with beautiful, buttery crowns. Finish with the lemon glaze and serve warm.

Makes 18 muffins

For the muffins:
1$\frac{3}{4}$ cups fresh blueberries
3 cups unbleached all-purpose flour
1 cup sugar
1 tablespoon baking powder
$\frac{1}{4}$ pound ($\frac{1}{2}$ cup) unsalted butter, at room temperature
2 large eggs, beaten

1 cup evaporated milk
1 teaspoon grated lemon zest
2 tablespoons unsalted butter

For the glaze:
$\frac{3}{4}$ cup powdered sugar
1$\frac{1}{2}$ tablespoons fresh lemon juice

1. Preheat an oven to 350 degrees F. Position a rack in the middle of the oven. Line two 12-cup muffins pans with 18 paper liners or butter 18 of the wells.

2. Pick over the blueberries, discarding any soft or crushed ones.

(continued)

3. In a large mixing bowl, combine the flour, sugar, and baking powder. Work in the butter with a pastry blender or your fingertips until the mixture resembles coarse meal. Remove 1 cup of the mixture and reserve it to make a streusel topping. To the bowl add the eggs and evaporated milk and stir to blend. Do not overmix. Gently fold in the blueberries and lemon zest.

4. Fill the prepared wells two-thirds full. Fill any unfilled wells with water so the pan won't warp. Wipe off any batter that spills on the sides of the cups. Melt the 2 tablespoons butter and drizzle it over the reserved streusel topping. Sprinkle a little of the topping over the top of each muffin. Place in the oven and bake until browned and firm, 20 to 25 minutes.

5. Meanwhile, make the glaze. In a small bowl stir together the powdered sugar and lemon juice. Remove the muffins from the oven and drizzle the glaze over the tops with a spoon. Serve warm.

 # Whole-Wheat Walnut Baguettes

Although not as significant to Northwest gastronomy as hazelnuts, walnuts figure prominently on local menus. Here they lend a bit of crunch and personality to a chocolate-brown baguette of exceptional flavor. If civility has not gotten the better of you, rip the warm loaf apart and slather it generously with creamy fresh butter. Or serve with a soft goat cheese—the tart white cheese is terrific against this dark, earthy bread.

Makes 3 baguettes

$2\frac{2}{3}$ cups lukewarm water (no hotter than 110 degrees F)

2 tablespoons active dry yeast

2 tablespoons light brown sugar

$\frac{1}{4}$ cup molasses

1 cup coarsely chopped
   walnuts
$\frac{1}{2}$ cup bran
2 tablespoons salt
4 cups unbleached all-
   purpose flour

$3\frac{1}{2}$ cups whole-wheat flour
1 large egg, lightly beaten
$\frac{1}{4}$ cup water

1. Place the lukewarm water in a small bowl. Sprinkle in the yeast and stir to dissolve. After a few minutes the yeast should be creamy. Set aside.

2. Combine the brown sugar, molasses, walnuts, bran, salt, and flours in a mixer fitted with a dough hook. Add the yeast mixture. Knead until the dough is smooth and elastic, about 5 minutes. To knead by hand, place the dough on a lightly floured board. Knead the dough with the heel of your hand, frequently turning it until the dough is smooth and elastic, about 15 minutes. Shape the dough into a smooth ball.

3. Heavily grease a clean mixing bowl and place the dough ball in it. Turn the ball once to coat lightly on all sides. Cover the bowl with plastic wrap and let the dough rise in a warm spot until doubled in bulk, 1 to 2 hours.

4. Punch the dough down and place it on a clean work surface. Separate the dough into 3 equal portions and form each portion into a smooth ball. Cover each ball loosely with plastic wrap. Place on a long board or in individual mixing bowls and set in a warm spot until doubled in size, 1 to 2 hours.

5. To shape each ball into a baguette, use your palms to roll the ball into a log about 16 inches long and 3 to 4 inches in diameter. Taper the ends. Set the shaped baguette on a baking sheet. Repeat the process with the remaining 2 balls. Cover the loaves loosely with plastic wrap and set in a warm spot to rise until almost tripled in volume, about 45 minutes.

(continued)

6. Preheat an oven to 450 degrees F.

7. When the loaves are light, swollen, and springy to the touch, use a sharp knife to slash a few diagonal cuts on the top of each. Make an egg wash by lightly beating together the egg and water in a small bowl. Brush the egg wash over the tops of the loaves.

8. Place in the oven and bake until tops are lightly browned and loaves have a hollow sound when tapped with a stainless steel knife, 20 to 25 minutes. Cool on wire racks before serving.

From Ron Paul Restaurant and Charcuterie

 # Hazelnut Rye Bread

Toasted hazelnuts, warm from the oven, are crunchy nuggets of flavor, and any recipe that includes them is usually enhanced. Such is the case with this rich rye bread, made with a hint of molasses and a heap of hazelnuts. It's wonderful hot from the oven with a platter of fresh cheese, ripe figs, and autumn pears.

Makes 2 baguettes

4 cups unbleached all-purpose flour mixed with 2 cups rye flour
2 tablespoons unsalted butter, melted
2 tablespoons active dry yeast
1 tablespoon molasses

1 tablespoon salt
$2\frac{1}{4}$ cups lukewarm water (no hotter than 110 degrees F)
2 cups coarsely chopped roasted hazelnuts (page 236)
2 large egg yolks, beaten

1. In a large bowl, stir together 3 cups of the flour mixture, the melted butter, yeast, molasses, salt, and lukewarm water until mixed. Gradually work in the remaining 3 cups flour mixture and the hazelnuts to form the dough.

2. Turn the dough out onto a lightly floured board. Knead until the dough is smooth and elastic, 10 to 15 minutes. Shape the dough into a smooth ball.

3. Lightly grease a clean mixing bowl and place the dough ball in it. Turn the ball once to coat lightly on all sides. Cover the bowl with a damp towel or plastic wrap and let the dough rise for 20 minutes.

4. Punch down the dough and divide it into 2 equal portions. On a lightly floured board, shape each portion into a long loaf. Line a baking sheet with parchment paper and place the loaves on it. Cover with a clean towel and let rise for 30 minutes. Meanwhile, preheat an oven to 400 degrees F.

5. Brush the loaves with the beaten egg yolks. Place in the oven and bake until tops are lightly browned and loaves have a hollow sound when tapped with a stainless steel knife, about 30 minutes. Cool on wire racks before serving.

From Briggs and Crampton's Catering and Table for Two

CHAPTER ELEVEN

COUNTRY PIES AND URBAN FRUIT TARTS

Sandy River Raspberry-Rhubarb Pie

Rhubarb and raspberries thrive in the foothills of the Sandy River basin, in the shadow of majestic Mount Hood. This down-home dessert captures a bit of the country with its filling.

Makes one 9-inch pie; serves 6 to 8

For the filling:
4 cups diced rhubarb
2 pints raspberries
1¾ cups sugar
¼ cup quick-cooking tapioca
Grated zest and juice of 1 small orange
1 tablespoon fresh lemon juice

For the crust:
2 cups unbleached all-purpose flour
¼ cup vegetable shortening

¼ pound (½ cup) unsalted butter, cut into 8 pieces
1 tablespoon sugar
Pinch of salt
⅓ cup water

To finish the pie:
¼ cup unsalted butter, cut into small bits
Sugar for sprinkling on the crust
1 cup heavy cream, whipped
3 to 4 tablespoons Grand Marnier, optional

1. To make the filling, combine all the filling ingredients in a large bowl. Stir together, then set aside for 1 hour to blend the flavors, stirring occasionally.

2. To make the pie crust, set a 9-inch pie plate in the refrigerator to chill. Place the flour, shortening, ½ cup butter, sugar, and salt in a food processor fitted with the steel blade. Process until grainy, about 15 seconds. Add the cold water and process only until a ball of dough forms. If the dough is too dry, add an additional tablespoon of water. Divide the dough into 2 unequal portions, one twice as large as the other. Wrap each portion in plastic wrap and refrigerate for at least 30 minutes.

3. Preheat an oven to 450 degrees F. Position a rack in the middle of the oven.

4. To finish the pie, lightly flour a work surface or pastry cloth. Using a lightly floured rolling pin, roll out the larger dough portion on the surface into a round about $\frac{1}{8}$-inch thick. Drape the pastry round over the rolling pin, then unroll it over the chilled pie plate. Gently press the pastry to fit the pan. Pour the raspberry-rhubarb mixture into the shell and dot with the butter. Roll out the remaining dough into an 11-inch round and fit it over the top of the pie. Pinch and seal the edges of the top and bottom crusts together. Using a sharp knife, slash a few steam holes into the top crust and finish with a sprinkling of sugar.

5. Place in the oven and bake until the crust is slightly browned, 20 to 25 minutes. Reduce the heat to 350 degrees F, cover the pie with a large piece of aluminum foil, and continue baking until done, about 40 minutes. Transfer the pie to a wire rack to cool. Serve warm or cold with whipped cream, plain or flavored with the Grand Marnier, folded in after the cream is whipped.

From Indigine

Hot Three-Berry Cobbler with Sour Cream Ice Cream

In this dessert, sweet pastry dough, cut into decorative stars and speckled with finely chopped hazelnuts, is artfully arranged over a violet sea of fresh berries. Any seasonal berry will work fine, but Lisa Shara Hall, a passionate Portland cook and the recipe's author, says a blend of marionberries, blueberries, and blackberries is smashing. This cobbler is delicious hot out of the oven served plain or with old-fashioned vanilla ice cream. But it is particularly heavenly with a scoop of Sour Cream Ice Cream (page 192).

Serves 10

For the dough:

½ pound (1 cup) unsalted butter, at room temperature

1 cup sugar

3 large egg yolks, lightly beaten

1 cup finely chopped roasted and skinned hazelnuts (page 236)

1¼ cups unbleached all-purpose flour

Pinch of salt

For the filling:

8 cups mixed seasonal berries

¾ to 1 cup sugar, depending upon the tartness of the berries

¼ cup Grand Marnier, kirsch, or framboise

½ cup unbleached all-purpose flour

¼ cup fresh lemon juice

2 tablespoons sugar for sprinkling on the top

Sour Cream Ice Cream (page 192) or good-quality vanilla ice cream, optional

1. To make the dough, combine the butter and sugar in a mixing bowl. Using an electric mixer, beat until light and fluffy. Beat in the egg yolks, one at a time, beating well after each addition. Fold in the hazelnuts, flour, and salt. Shape the dough into a ball. Cover with plastic wrap and chill for at least 2 hours.

2. Using a lightly floured rolling pin, on a lightly floured surface roll out the chilled dough about ¼ inch thick. Using cookie cutters and starting at the outside edge of the dough, cut out stars or other decorative shapes. Cut the shapes as close to one another as possible. Set aside.

3. Preheat the oven to 375 degrees F. Position a rack in the middle of the oven.

4. To make the filling, in a large bowl gently toss together all the filling ingredients, except the 2 tablespoons sugar.

5. Pour the mixture into a buttered 2½-quart baking dish or paella pan. Using a wide metal spatula, transfer the dough cutouts to the top of the cobbler, placing them about ½ inch apart. Sprinkle the 2 tablespoons sugar over the cutouts.

6. Place in the oven and bake until the crust is golden and the berries are bubbly, about 40 minutes. Serve warm or at room temperature, with a scoop of ice cream if desired.

From the kitchen of Lisa Shara Hall

 # Huckleberry and Crème Fraîche Tart

Although this handsome dessert takes its culinary lead from classical French cooking, no amount of gentrification will alter the down-home charm of mountain huckleberries. The pastry is infused with vanilla bean and the berries are folded together with sweet crème fraîche, which gives the filling a fierce creaminess. The recipe is an original by chef Karl Schaefer, a cooking wizard with passionate ideas about Oregon ingredients. Schaefer is now an organic farmer in Oregon City, but the tart was one of the many dishes that made his former restaurant, Le Cuisinier, Portland's premier restaurant during the '80s.

Makes one 10-inch tart, serves 8

For the vanilla bean short crust:
½ vanilla bean
2 cups pastry flour, or 1¾ cups unbleached all-purpose flour
10 tablespoons unsalted butter, at room temperature, cut into 1-inch pieces
2 large egg yolks, lightly beaten
3 ounces sugar

For the filling:
1 pint (2 cups) huckleberries
1 cup plus 2 tablespoons sugar
Juice of ½ lemon
2 cups crème fraîche (page 236)

1. To make the dough, cut the vanilla bean in half lengthwise and scrape out the seeds into a small bowl; set aside. Discard the pod or save for another use. Place the flour in a large mixing bowl. Using your fingertips, rub the butter into the flour until the mixture forms particles the size of small peas. Add the egg yolks and sugar to the vanilla seeds and beat until well mixed. Pour the vanilla mixture over the flour mixture, blending quickly with your fingertips. Gather the dough into a ball and flatten into a disk. Wrap in plastic wrap and chill for 15 minutes. Lightly butter and flour the inside of a 10-inch tart pan and refrigerate.

2. Lightly flour a work surface or pastry cloth. Using a lightly floured rolling pin, gently roll out the pastry on the surface into a round $\frac{1}{8}$ inch thick. Work from the center of the circle toward the outer rim, using short outward strokes. Fold the dough in half and then into quarters. Place it in the tart pan with the point in the center. Carefully unfold the pastry and ease it into the pan, pressing it in with your fingertips. Roll the pin over the top of the pan to cut away any excess dough. Refrigerate for 20 minutes.

3. Meanwhile, preheat an oven to 325 degrees F. Position a rack in the middle of the oven.

4. Line the chilled tart shell with a sheet of lightly greased aluminum foil that extends about 1 inch beyond the sides of the pan. Fill it with a layer of dried beans. Place in the oven and bake until the dough is set but slightly soft, 5 to 6 minutes. Remove the tart from the oven, remove the beans, and lift out the foil. Prick the bottom of the crust and return the tart to the oven until golden brown and firm, 12 to 14 minutes.

5. To make the filling, bring 1 cup of the berries and the 1 cup sugar to a simmer in a small pot. Skim the surface and simmer slowly for 15 minutes to thicken. Select a mixing bowl large enough to hold the small pot and partially fill it with ice. Remove the pot from the heat and nestle it in the ice to cool.

6. To assemble the tart, combine the cooled berries with the remaining cup of berries and the lemon juice. Place the crème fraîche in a clean bowl with the 2 tablespoons sugar. Whisk vigorously for a few minutes. Spoon three fourths of the crème fraîche over the bottom of the tart and smooth the top. Spoon the berry mixture over the crème fraîche. Refrigerate until serving time.

7. To serve, garnish each portion with a dollop of the remaining crème fraîche.

From Le Cuisinier

 ## Apple Tart in Ginger Pastry

Some of the Northwest's best-tasting apples can be found in Oregon's Hood River Valley, the land of fruit orchards, friendly folk, and fanatical windsurfers. With apples growing everywhere, cooks in the area have made a specialty of homemade pies and tarts. If you're the lucky recipient of homemade apricot preserves for the glaze, this dessert will be all the more exalted.

Makes one 9-inch tart, serves 6 to 8

For the crust:
$\frac{3}{4}$ **teaspoon finely chopped, peeled fresh ginger**
$1\frac{1}{4}$ **cups unbleached white flour**
$\frac{1}{4}$ **pound ($\frac{1}{2}$ cup) unsalted butter, chilled, cut into $\frac{1}{2}$-inch pieces**
3 tablespoons water

For the apple filling:
2 tablespoons unsalted butter
5 tart green apples such as Granny Smith or Newton Pippin, peeled, cored, and thinly sliced

3 tablespoons light brown sugar
Pinch of ground cinnamon
1 tablespoon slivered crystallized ginger

For the glaze:
$\frac{1}{3}$ **cup good-quality apricot preserves**
1 to 2 tablespoons apple brandy or Calvados

1. To make the crust, combine the ginger and flour in a food processor fitted with the steel blade and process to blend. Add the butter and blend briefly until the mixture resembles coarse meal. Add the water and process briefly until the pastry pulls away from the sides of the container. Shape the dough into a disk.

2. Lightly flour a pastry cloth. Using a floured rolling pin, roll out the dough on the surface into a round $\frac{1}{8}$ inch thick. Drape the pastry over the rolling pin, then unroll it over a 9-inch tart pan with a removable bottom. Gently press the pastry to fit the pan. Roll the pin over the top of the pan to cut away any excess dough. Refrigerate for 30 minutes.

3. Preheat an oven to 400 degrees F. Position a rack in the middle of the oven.

4. Prick the pastry and line it with a sheet of lightly greased aluminum foil that extends about 1 inch beyond the sides of the pan. Fill it with a layer of dried beans or pie weights. Place in the oven and bake until lightly browned, about 20 minutes. Remove from the oven, remove the weights, lift out the foil, and let cool.

5. To make the filling, melt the butter in a skillet over medium heat. Add the apples, brown sugar, and cinnamon and sauté until the apples are barely tender, about 4 minutes. Spoon the apples into the cooled shell. Top with the ginger.

6. Place in the oven and bake until apples are tender, about 30 minutes.

7. Meanwhile, make the glaze. Melt the apricot preserves in a saucepan over low heat. Strain the liquid into a bowl through a fine-mesh sieve. Stir in the brandy to taste.

8. Remove the tart from the oven and immediately brush the hot glaze over the surface. Let cool completely on a

wire rack. Remove the tart ring and slide the tart onto a serving plate.

From Briggs and Crampton's Catering and Table for Two

Nectarine and Plum Tart with Almond Filling

Ron Paul Restaurant and Charcuterie is one of Portland's best-known dessert spots. The architecture of chef Ron Paul's tart is classic: a baked pastry shell on the bottom, marzipan custard in the middle, and a fastidious arrangement of fresh fruit on top. Nectarines and plums work beautifully together, but you can experiment with other fruits, too. Pears are delicious with the almond filling; so are peaches, apricots, and pitted Bing cherries. For a smart finish, scatter a few fresh raspberries over the glaze.

Makes one 9-inch tart, serves 6 to 8

Pâte Sucrée tart shell, unbaked (page 189)

For the filling:
1 cup almond paste or marzipan
¼ pound (½ cup) unsalted butter at room temperature
2 large eggs

1 teaspoon grated lemon zest
2 teaspoons unbleached all-purpose flour
½ to ¾ pound ripe but firm nectarines and plums, pitted and sliced
½ to ¾ cup good-quality apricot preserves

1. Make the tart shell as directed, preferably using a tart pan with a removable bottom, and refrigerate until ready to use.

(continued)

2. Preheat an oven to 350 degrees F. Position a rack in the middle of the oven.

3. To make the filling, in the bowl of an electric mixer beat the almond paste to loosen it. Add the butter and beat to combine it thoroughly with the almond paste. Beat in the eggs, one at a time, beating well after each addition, and then mix in the lemon zest and flour.

4. Pour the filling into the chilled tart shell. Arrange the fruit in slightly overlapping concentric circles, starting on the outer edge and continuing until all of the filling has been covered. Bake until the tart shell is golden, the filling begins to puff, and the edges of the fruit begin to brown, 45 minutes to 1 hour.

5. Meanwhile, for the glaze, melt the apricot preserves in a small saucepan over low heat. Strain the liquid into a bowl through a fine-mesh sieve.

6. Remove the tart from the oven, transfer to a wire rack, and immediately brush the glaze over the top surface. Let cool completely. If using a pan with a removable bottom, remove the tart from the pan before serving.

From Ron Paul Restaurant and Charcuterie

 ## Blackberry and Lemon Cheese Tart

This recipe holds all the secrets to making a superior berry tart: an excellent pastry; a light, refreshing filling; and the biggest, sweetest berries around. The tart should be served the same day it's made since the pastry can get soggy if it sits too long. To increase its shelf life, bake the pastry shell and let it cool completely. Then lightly brush the interior with melted semisweet

chocolate. Chill until ready to fill. Any seasonal berry, from raspberry to loganberry, can be substituted for the blackberries.

Makes one 10-inch tart; serves 8

10-inch Pâte sucrée tart shell, fully baked (page 189)

For the filling:
$\frac{3}{4}$ cup fresh lemon juice
1 tablespoon gelatin
2 large egg yolks
4 large whole eggs
$1\frac{1}{4}$ cups sugar
1 pound cream cheese, at room temperature

$\frac{1}{4}$ pound ($\frac{1}{2}$ cup) unsalted butter, at room temperature
2 tablespoons grated lemon zest

For the topping:
$\frac{1}{2}$ to $\frac{3}{4}$ cup blackberries
$\frac{1}{2}$ to $\frac{3}{4}$ cup good-quality apricot preserves

1. Make the tart shell as directed, preferably using a tart pan with a removable bottom. Bake fully and let cool.

2. To make the filling, heat the lemon juice in a saucepan over low heat. Add the gelatin and stir to dissolve.

3. In a mixing bowl, whisk together the egg yolks and the whole eggs with a wire whisk until thick and lemon colored. Add the sugar and whisk until creamy. Turn the mixture into the saucepan with the gelatin mixture. Cook over low heat, stirring constantly with a wooden spoon, until the mixture has a custardlike consistency, 3 to 5 minutes. Remove from the heat.

4. In another bowl, combine the cream cheese and butter and beat with a wooden spoon until light and fluffy. Fold in the lemon zest and custard. Beat until smooth. Cover and chill thoroughly.

5. To assemble the tart, pour the chilled filling into the cooled tart shell. Pick over the berries, discarding any

(continued)

spoiled ones. If necessary, hull the berries. Remove the tart from the refrigerator. Arrange the berries over the top in concentric circles, starting at the outer edge and continuing until the filling has been covered.

6. Melt the apricot preserves in a small saucepan over low heat. Strain the liquid through a fine-mesh sieve into a bowl. Brush the warm glaze over the tart. This will preserve the moisture of the fruit and give the tart a nice sheen. Chill until ready to serve. If using a pan with a removable bottom, remove the tart from the pan before serving.

From Ron Paul Restaurant and Charcuterie

 # Rhubarb Tart with a Phyllo Cinnamon Crown

A top crust of crinkled phyllo dough and chopped fresh strawberries impart a bit of magic to this urban tart. Serve at room temperature, plain or with chilled crème fraîche (page 236) or slightly sweetened sour cream.

Makes one 12-inch tart; serves 8 to 10

12-inch Pâte Sucrée tart shell, unbaked (page 189)

For the filling:
$1\frac{1}{2}$ pounds rhubarb stalks, trimmed and cut into 1-inch pieces
$\frac{1}{4}$ cup chopped strawberries
$1\frac{1}{4}$ cups sugar
$4\frac{1}{2}$ tablespoons unbleached all-purpose flour

For the cinnamon crown:
12 sheets frozen phyllo dough, thawed in the refrigerator
$\frac{1}{2}$ **pound (1 cup) unsalted butter, melted**
2 teaspoons ground cinnamon
2 tablespoons sugar

1. Make the tart shell as directed, but build up a fluted edge. Chill for 30 minutes.

2. Preheat an oven to 350 degrees F. Position a rack in the middle of the oven.

3. To make the filling, in a mixing bowl, toss together the rhubarb, strawberries, sugar, and flour. Pour into the chilled pastry shell.

4. Next make the cinnamon crown. Working with 1 phyllo sheet at a time and keeping the others covered, brush the phyllo sheet with a little of the butter. Gather up the sheet so that it falls into pleats and place it over 1 edge of the filling. Continue the process with the remaining 11 phyllo sheets, using each to cover a portion of the filling. When finished, the filling should be totally covered with phyllo. Stir together the cinnamon and sugar in a small bowl and sprinkle the mixture over the top.

5. Place the tart in the oven and bake until the filling is set and bubbling and phyllo is golden brown, 45 minutes to 1 hour. Remove the tart from the oven and let cool on a wire rack before serving.

From Ron Paul Restaurant and Charcuterie.

 # Pâte Brisée (Short Pastry Dough)

This flaky, all-purpose pastry is well-suited for savories, dessert pies, and fruit tarts. The dough can be frozen for later use; it will keep up to three months. Thaw at room temperature at least 2 hours in advance of rolling.

Makes one 9-inch tart shell

$1\frac{1}{2}$ cups unbleached all-purpose flour

$\frac{1}{2}$ teaspoon salt

$\frac{1}{2}$ pound (1 cup) unsalted butter, chilled, cut into $\frac{1}{2}$-inch cubes

3 tablespoons vegetable shortening, chilled

5 to 6 tablespoons cold water

1. Stir together the flour and salt in a large mixing bowl. Add the butter and shortening and, using your fingertips, rub them into the flour until the mixture forms particles the size of small peas. Alternatively, using a pastry blender, cut the fats rapidly into the flour until the mixture resembles coarse meal. The key is not to overmix or let the butter soften any more than necessary.

2. Sprinkle in the cold water and blend quickly with a fork, pressing the dough against the sides of the bowl to form a rough mass. Gather the dough into a ball and flatten into a disk. Wrap in plastic wrap and chill for at least 2 hours or as long as overnight. Thorough chilling helps prevent the pastry from shrinking or losing its shape during the baking.

3. If you're going to prebake the shell, preheat an oven to 425 degrees F. Position a rack in the middle of the oven.

4. Lightly flour a work surface or a pastry cloth. With a lightly floured rolling pin, gently roll out the pastry on the surface, working from the center of the circle toward the outer rim and using short outward strokes. Roll the pastry $\frac{1}{8}$ inch thick; be careful not to stretch the pastry, or it will shrink when baked.

5. Lightly butter the inside of a quiche pan or a 9-inch tart pan. Fold the dough in half and then in quarters. Place in the pan with the point in the center. Carefully unfold the pastry and ease it into the pan, using your fingertips to gently press it in. Roll the pin over the top of the pan to cut away any excess dough. Alternatively, leave a small border and crimp the edges decoratively.

6. To partially or fully bake the shell, line the pastry shell with a sheet of lightly greased aluminum foil that extends about 1 inch beyond the sides of the pan. Fill it with a layer of dried beans or pie weights to prevent the crust from rising or shrinking. Place in the oven and bake until the dough is set but still slightly soft, 5 to 6 minutes. Remove from the oven, remove the beans (they may be saved and reused), and lift out the foil. Prick the bottom of the shell and return it to the oven. For a partially baked shell, bake until slightly browned, 3 to 4 minutes. For a fully baked shell, bake until golden brown, 12 to 14 minutes. Let cool on a wire rack before filling.

 # Pâte Sucrée (Sweet Short Pastry Dough)

This pastry brings to mind a superior shortbread cookie. As such, it's excellent for either pie crusts or dessert tarts. The dough freezes well for 3 months when tightly sealed in plastic wrap. Thaw at room temperature for at least 2 hours before rolling.

Makes three 9-inch tart shells or two 10-inch or 12-inch tart shells

$2\frac{1}{2}$ cups unbleached all-purpose flour
$\frac{1}{8}$ teaspoon salt
$\frac{1}{2}$ cup sugar
$\frac{1}{2}$ pound (1 cup) unsalted butter, chilled, cut in small cubes

1 large egg, lightly beaten
1 teaspoon pure vanilla extract

1. Place the flour, salt, sugar, and butter in a food processor fitted with the steel blade. Process briefly until the mixture resembles coarse meal. Add the egg and vanilla and

(continued)

process briefly, just enough to hold the ingredients to-gether. Alternatively, place the dry ingredients in a mixing bowl and use a pastry cutter or your fingertips to work the butter into the flour mixture; then quickly work in the egg and vanilla.

2. Gather the dough into a ball. Divide it into 3 equal portions for 9-inch tarts or in half for 10-inch or 12-inch tarts. Flatten the portions into disks and wrap each one in waxed paper. Chill for at least 2 hours or as long as overnight.

3. To roll out the dough, lightly grease the inside of the tart pans with butter. If you're making 2 or more tarts, roll out 1 dough portion at a time. Place the chilled dough disk between 2 pieces of floured waxed paper 20 inches wide. Roll out the dough about $\frac{1}{8}$ inch thick. Carefully peel off the top piece of waxed paper. Lift the dough, still attached to the bottom piece of waxed paper, and center it over the pan, paper side up. Carefully peel off the waxed paper and ease the dough gently into the pie pan, pressing lightly with your fingertips. Roll the rolling pin over the top of the pan to cut away any excess dough. Cover and chill until ready to bake.

4. To partially or fully bake the tart shell, follow the directions in step 6 for Pâte Brisée (page 189).

From Ron Paul Restaurant and Charcuterie

CHAPTER TWELVE

ICE CREAM WITH LOGANBERRY LIQUEUR AND OTHER TEMPTATIONS

Sour Cream Ice Cream

This ice cream, created in the Neahkahnie kitchen of pop culture writer and ice cream priestess Lena Lencek, gives new meaning to the concept of sweet and sour. Try it over your favorite berry pie or cobbler, or serve with freshly picked raspberries, blackberries, or huckleberries.

Makes 1 quart

1 cup light sour cream
1 cup heavy or whipping
  cream

$\frac{1}{4}$ cup sugar

1. In a mixing bowl, stir together the sour cream, heavy cream, and sugar until smooth. Pour into the container of an ice cream freezer and freeze according to the manufacturer's instructions.

From the kitchen of Lena Lencek

 # Oregon Berry Ice Cream

The Willamette Valley, a lush corridor sandwiched between the Cascade Mountains and the Coast Ranges, has been characterized as "God's gift to berries." This specialty from the Alsea, Oregon, kitchen of Pat Vidor can be enjoyed with any of the seemingly endless list of berries available in Oregon in summer, from blackberry to salmonberry.

Makes 1 quart

3 cups berries
2 cups heavy or whipping
  cream

4 large egg yolks
$\frac{3}{4}$ cup sugar

1. Place the berries in a blender or in a food processor fitted with the steel blade and purée. Strain the purée through a fine-mesh strainer into a bowl to remove the seeds. Measure out 2 cups purée and save any extra for another use.

2. Place the cream in a heavy saucepan over medium heat and heat until small bubbles appear along the pan edge; set aside. In a mixing bowl, beat the yolks and sugar until thick and lemon colored. Pour the yolk mixture into the top of a double boiler set over simmering water. Gradually add the hot cream, stirring constantly, until the mixture has a custardlike consistency and coats the back of a spoon, about 5 to 10 minutes. Do not let the mixture boil. Remove the saucepan from the heat and set aside to cool to room temperature.

3. Thoroughly combine the berry purée with the cooled custard. Pour the mixture into the container of an ice cream freezer. Freeze according to the manufacturer's instructions.

From the kitchen of Pat Vidor

Peach and Amaretto Ice Cream

Life is not all peaches and cream, but this recipe from Portland physician and entertainer extraordinaire Chris Maranze makes you wonder what else life could possibly offer. More than 30 varieties of peaches are grown in the Northwest, and the best appear June through September. The all-purpose Elberta is a reliable, full-flavored variety, but the somewhat tart Redhaven, with its firm flesh, or the luscious, bruise-resistant Redskin would both be lovely options.

Makes 2 quarts

For the vanilla custard base:

**2 cups heavy or whipping
cream**

2 cups milk

**1 vanilla bean, halved
lengthwise, or 1
tablespoon pure vanilla
extract**

3 large egg yolks

$\frac{1}{4}$ cup sugar

For the peach mixture:

**4 pounds peaches, peeled
and pitted**

$\frac{1}{2}$ cup sugar

$\frac{1}{4}$ cup amaretto liqueur

**$\frac{1}{4}$ teaspoon almond extract,
or to taste**

1. To make the vanilla custard base, combine the cream, milk, and vanilla bean (if you're using vanilla extract do not add it now) in a heavy saucepan over medium heat or in the top of a double boiler set over hot water and heat until hot. In a small bowl, whisk together the egg yolks and sugar until the mixture is pale and lemon colored. While whisking the yolk mixture constantly, slowly pour a little of the hot cream mixture into the yolk mixture to raise its temperature. When the yolk mixture is hot, whisk it into the cream mixture. Heat, whisking constantly, until the custard is thick enough to coat the back of a spoon, about 5 to 10 minutes. Do not let the mixture boil.

2. Pour the mixture into a cold mixing bowl. Remove the vanilla bean and, using a knife, scrape the pods so the seeds fall into the cream; discard the pods. If you're using vanilla extract, stir it in now.

3. To make the peach mixture, mince the peaches and measure out 8 cups. Place 2 cups of the peaches in a bowl with $\frac{1}{4}$ cup of the sugar. Chill. Combine the remaining 6 cups peaches with the remaining $\frac{1}{4}$ cup sugar in a heavy saucepan. Stir in the amaretto and bring to a simmer. Heat, stirring frequently, until the mixture is reduced by half of its volume, about 15 minutes. Remove from the heat and transfer the peaches to a mixing bowl. Cover and chill.

4. To make the ice cream, in a large bowl, combine the cooked peaches with the reserved 2 cups uncooked peaches. Stir in the vanilla custard and the almond extract. Pour the mixture into the container of an ice cream freezer. Freeze according to the manufacturer's instructions.

From the kitchen of Chris Maranze

 # Mocha Ice Cream with Roasted Hazelnuts

Homemade mocha ice cream, with its rich combination of bittersweet chocolate and strong coffee flavors, gets even better when roasted Oregon hazelnuts are figured into the formula. This recipe comes from Portland physician and art photographer Stu Levy, an ice cream fanatic who divides his time between the delivery room, the darkroom, and a deep freezer that holds an array of frozen fantasies.

Makes 2 quarts

For the vanilla custard base:
2 cups heavy or whipping cream
2 cups milk
1 vanilla bean, halved lengthwise, or 1 tablespoon pure vanilla extract
3 large egg yolks
$\frac{1}{4}$ cup sugar

For the mocha base:
1 cup roasted hazelnuts (page 236)
$\frac{1}{2}$ pound good-quality bittersweet chocolate such as Callebaut or Guittard
$\frac{1}{4}$ cup instant coffee powder or instant espresso powder

1. To make the vanilla custard base, combine the cream, milk, and vanilla bean (if you're using vanilla extract do not add it now) in a heavy saucepan over medium heat or

(continued)

in the top of a double boiler set over hot water and heat until hot. In a small bowl, whisk together the egg yolks and sugar until the mixture is pale and lemon colored. While whisking the yolk mixture constantly, slowly pour a little of the hot cream mixture into the yolk mixture to raise its temperature. When the yolk mixture is hot, whisk it into the cream mixture. Heat, whisking constantly, until the custard is thick enough to coat the back of a spoon, about 5 to 10 minutes. Do not let the mixture boil.

2. Pour the mixture into a cold mixing bowl. Remove the vanilla bean and, using a knife, scrape the pods so the seeds fall into the cream; discard the pods. If you're using vanilla extract, stir it in now.

3. To make the mocha base, coarsely grind the hazelnuts in a food processor fitted with the steel blade and set aside. Without cleaning the work bowl, grind the chocolate. Pour one third of the hot custard mixture into the container and process briefly to combine and melt the chocolate. Add the coffee or espresso powder and process briefly to blend. Scoop the remaining custard into a large bowl. Stir in the chocolate mixture, mixing well. Cover and chill.

4. Pour the chilled mixture into the container of an ice cream freezer. Freeze according to the manufacturer's directions. When the ice cream is partially frozen, fold in the hazelnuts.

From the kitchen of Stu Levy

 # Chocolate Truffle and Raspberry Ice Cream

At Portland's Panini restaurant, Linda Faes offers a dazzling combination of Oregon fruit, chocolate, and calories. This recipe is one of her specialties, and it is killer stuff—a potent

infusion of dark truffles and frozen berries with a deep coffee-flavored interior. If you really want to live it up, serve with your favorite raspberry sauce. Or garnish each bowl with a cocoa-dusted truffle.

Makes about 2 quarts

6 ounces semisweet chocolate, chopped
$\frac{1}{2}$ cup brewed espresso
$\frac{1}{4}$ cup crème de cacao
$\frac{1}{4}$ cup framboise, Chambord, or raspberry schnapps
$\frac{1}{4}$ cup water

$\frac{1}{2}$ cup sugar
6 large egg yolks
3 cups heavy cream
12 chocolate truffles, coarsely chopped
6 ounces frozen raspberries, coarsely chopped

1. Combine the semisweet chocolate and espresso in the top pan of a double boiler set over hot water and heat until the chocolate melts. Remove from the heat and let cool slightly. Stir in the liqueurs.

2. In a small saucepan, combine the water and sugar. Cover and bring to a boil. Remove the lid and continue to boil without stirring for 3 minutes.

3. Meanwhile, place the egg yolks in a bowl and beat with an electric mixer until light and lemon colored. Slowly add the sugar syrup and continue whipping until the mixture is fluffy and has increased in volume, 4 to 5 minutes. Reduce the speed to low and add the chocolate, mixing just until incorporated.

4. Using a chilled bowl and beaters, whip the cream until it barely begins to hold its shape. Fold it gently into the chocolate base.

5. Pour the mixture into the container of an ice cream freezer. Freeze according to the manufacturer's directions. Drop the chopped truffles and the raspberries into the ice cream just before the churning process is finished.

From Panini

Loganberry Ice Cream with Whidbey's Liqueur

There's an elixir at work in this transcendent dessert: Whidbey's Liqueur, a luscious loganberry drink brewed on Washington's Whidbey Island, a patch of paradise stretched over 50 miles. A number of liquor stores in the Northwest carry this liqueur, but if you can't find it, substitute a different brand of loganberry liqueur or even another fruit or berry liqueur.

Makes $1\frac{1}{2}$ quarts

$1\frac{1}{2}$ cups milk
$\frac{3}{4}$ cup sugar
3 large egg yolks, at room temperature
2 cups loganberries or other seasonal berries

2 teaspoons fresh lime juice
2 cups heavy or whipping cream
$\frac{1}{3}$ cup Whidbey's Liqueur or other berry liqueur

1. Place the milk in a heavy saucepan over medium heat until small bubbles appear along the pan edge. Reduce the heat to low and add the sugar; stir to dissolve. Remove from the heat.

2. Whisk the egg yolks in a bowl. Whisk $\frac{1}{4}$ cup of the heated milk into the beaten yolks, 1 tablespoon at a time. (This will heat the yolks slightly and prevent them from curdling.) Then add the yolks to the heated milk in a slow stream, stirring constantly. Return the yolk-milk mixture to low heat. Cook, stirring constantly, until the mixture thickens enough to coat the back of a spoon, about 5–10 minutes. Remove from the heat and let cool for 15 minutes.

3. Meanwhile, place the loganberries and lime juice in a blender or in a food processor fitted with the steel blade and purée. Strain the purée through a fine-mesh strainer.

OREGON'S CUISINE OF THE RAIN

In a large bowl, combine the berry purée, cream, and liqueur. Stir in the cooled milk mixture.

4. Pour the mixture into the container of an ice cream freezer. Freeze according to the manufacturer's instructions.

From Briggs and Crampton's Catering and Table for Two

 # Sorbet of Pear, Apple, or Peach

The key to a tempting sorbet—a pure and simple ice that provides a rush of fresh fruit flavor—lies in the fruit itself. Look for unblemished seasonal fruit, ripened to its peak flavor. If you're making pear sorbet, you can add 2 tablespoons pear brandy to the fruit purée or serve the purée with a splash of pear brandy. Apple sorbet can be spiked with apple brandy or Calvados.

Makes 1 quart

6 large ripe pears or apples, peeled, quartered, and cored, or 8 large ripe peaches, left whole

2 cups water
Juice of 1 lemon
Grated zest of 1 lemon
$\frac{1}{2}$ cup sugar

1. Cut a circle of waxed paper to fit the interior of a saucepan. Set aside.

2. Place the fruit in a saucepan. Add the water and lemon juice. If necessary, add more water if needed to cover the fruit. Add the lemon zest and sugar. Cover the fruit with the reserved waxed-paper round. Poach the fruit over low heat until it can be pierced easily with a sharp knife, about 8 minutes.

(continued)

3. Cool the fruit in its liquid. Strain and reserve the liquid. If you're using peaches, peel and pit them at this point.

4. Place the fruit in a food processor fitted with the steel blade or in a blender and purée. Add enough of the reserved liquid (which is now syrup) to make 1 quart.

5. Pour the mixture into the container of an ice cream freezer. Freeze according to the manufacturer's instructions.

From Ron Paul Restaurant and Charcuterie

CHAPTER THIRTEEN

CAKES, COOKIES, AND OTHER CREATIONS WITH SOURDOUGH, BITTERSWEET CHOCOLATE, AND MORE

Chunky Apple Walnut Cake

Every explorer of Oregon cuisine needs at least one fabulous apple cake recipe to celebrate the local harvest. Here, chunks of walnuts are buried in a thick batter threaded with orange zest and mingled with flavors at once fruity and rousingly spicy.

Serves 12

1 teaspoon fresh lemon
juice
1½ pounds tart cooking
apples such as Granny
Smith
3 cups unbleached all-
purpose flour, sifted
1 tablespoon baking soda
¼ teaspoon salt
½ teaspoon ground ginger
¼ teaspoon ground
cardamom
4 large eggs, at room
temperature

1 cup vegetable oil
½ cup fresh orange juice
Finely grated zest of 1 large
deep-colored orange
2 cups sugar
1 teaspoon pure vanilla
extract
1 cup roughly broken
walnuts
2 teaspoons ground
cinnamon mixed with
5 tablespoons sugar

1. Preheat an oven to 325 degrees F. Position a rack in the middle of the oven. Butter and flour a 10-inch tube pan.

2. Fill a large bowl with water and add the lemon juice. Peel, quarter, and core the apples and cut them lengthwise into thin slices. As soon as they are cut, drop the apples into the water to prevent them from browning while you assemble the remaining ingredients.

3. Sift together the sifted flour, baking soda, salt, ginger, and cardamom into a bowl. Set aside.

4. In a large mixing bowl, beat the eggs just to mix. Stir in the oil, orange juice, orange zest, sugar, and vanilla. Beat until light and creamy. Add the dry ingredients slowly and stir to combine thoroughly. Stir in the walnuts. Drain the apples well.

5. Turn half of the batter into the prepared pan. Add a layer of well-drained apples. Top with half of the cinnamon sugar. Cover with the remaining batter. Top with the remaining apple slices and cinnamon sugar.

6. Place in the oven and bake until a cake tester inserted in the center comes out clean, about 1 hour. Transfer the cake to a wire rack and let stand for 20 minutes. Invert the cake onto the rack and let cool completely. Invert the cake onto a serving plate. Serve at room temperature.

 # Bittersweet Chocolate Torte with Strawberries

When Nancy Briggs, Portland's top caterer, plans an early summer menu, Oregon's world-class strawberries figure somewhere in the game plan. In this recipe, the small, outrageously sweet berries are nestled between sheets of chocolate buttermilk cake that are amply spiked with brandy and espresso. Rosettes of whipped cream are then piped between the berries, and the whole affair is shrouded in sleek chocolate.

Makes one 8-inch cake; serves 8 to 10

For the cake:

$\frac{1}{4}$ pound bittersweet
  chocolate

$\frac{1}{4}$ cup brewed espresso or
  strong coffee

1 cup unbleached all-
  purpose flour

1 teaspoon baking soda

3 tablespoons vegetable oil

$\frac{1}{4}$ cup brandy

1 cup sugar

1 large egg

$\frac{1}{4}$ cup buttermilk

1 teaspoon pure vanilla
  extract

For the chocolate icing:

1 cup coarsely chopped
  semisweet chocolate

1 cup heavy cream

For the berry filling:

2 cups heavy cream

2 tablespoons powdered
  sugar

2 pints (4 cups)
  strawberries, hulled

1. Preheat an oven to 350 degrees F. Position a rack in the middle of the oven. Butter and flour an 8-inch round cake pan.

2. To make the cake, place the chocolate and coffee in the top pan of a double boiler set over hot water. Stir until the chocolate melts. Remove from the heat and set aside. Sift the flour and baking soda together into a bowl and set aside.

3. In a mixing bowl, combine the oil, brandy, sugar, egg, buttermilk, and vanilla extract. Add the chocolate and beat with an electric mixer to combine. Add the sifted flour and beat for 3 minutes at medium speed.

4. Pour the mixture into the prepared pan. Place in the oven and bake until a cake tester inserted in the center comes out clean, about 30 minutes. Let cool on a wire rack.

5. Meanwhile, clean the beaters of the electric mixer and chill along with a bowl.

6. To make the icing, combine the chocolate and cream in the top pan of a double boiler set over hot water. Stir until

the chocolate melts. Then whisk to combine the chocolate and cream thoroughly. Remove from the heat and set aside. The icing will thicken to spreading consistency as it cools.

7. To make the berry filling, pour the cream into the chilled bowl. Beat at medium-high speed, gradually adding the sugar, until soft peaks form.

8. To assemble the cake, remove the cooled cake from the pan. With a long, thin, sharp knife, carefully cut the cake horizontally into 2 layers. Carefully remove the top layer and set aside. Place the bottom layer on a flat cake plate. Arrange the whole berries over the bottom layer. Spoon the whipped cream into a pastry bag and pipe the cream over the berries to fill in the spaces, leaving a $\frac{1}{2}$-inch border uncovered around the edge. Place the top layer of the cake over the berries. Use a spatula to frost the tops and sides with the chocolate icing. Chill for at least 4 hours before serving.

From Briggs and Crampton's Catering and Table for Two

Black Beauty Cake with Raspberries and Custard Sauce

Much has been said about the perfect mating of chocolate and berries, and rightfully so. Here slices of flourless cake, supermoist and fudgy, are set off beautifully by naked berries spooned on both sides. The recipe comes from Lisa Shara Hall, one of Portland's best-known food mavens.

Makes one 8-inch cake; serves 8 to 10

$\frac{1}{2}$ cup water

$1\frac{1}{3}$ cups sugar

9 ounces unsweetened
chocolate, chopped

3 ounces semisweet
chocolate, chopped

$\frac{1}{2}$ pound (1 cup) unsalted
butter, at room tempera-
ture, cut into small pieces

6 large eggs, at room
temperature

Boiling water as needed

Raspberries or other
seasonal berries

1. Preheat an oven to 350 degrees F. Position a rack in the middle of the oven. Butter an 8-inch springform pan. Line the bottom of the pan with a round of parchment paper.

2. In a heavy 2-quart saucepan, combine the water and 1 cup of the sugar. Bring to a boil and cook for 4 minutes over high heat. Remove the pan from the heat and immediately add the unsweetened and semisweet chocolates. Stir constantly with a wooden spoon until the chocolates melt and are smooth. Don't worry if the mixture seizes. Next, stir in the butter, a few pieces at a time. Set aside.

3. Place the eggs and remaining sugar in a mixing bowl. Using an electric mixer, beat on high speed until the mixture thickens and triples in volume, about 20 minutes. Reduce the speed to low and add the chocolate mixture, beating only to incorporate.

4. Turn the mixture into the prepared pan. Set the pan inside a slightly larger pan and pour in enough boiling water to come halfway up the sides of the springform pan. Place in the oven and bake until a cake tester inserted in the center of the cake comes out clean, about 25 minutes. Do not bake longer than 35 minutes. Cool in the pan for 10 minutes, then run a sharp knife around the pan edge and remove the springform ring. When the cake has cooled, invert it onto a baking sheet and remove the pan bottom. Invert a serving plate over the cake and turn it upright.

5. Serve each slice of cake with a few tablespoons of fresh berries on either side.

From the kitchen of Lisa Shara Hall

 # Hazelnut Cheesecake with a Chocolate Crown

Whenever this cheesecake is served at a dinner party, everyone at the table wants the recipe. It is a creation of my dear friend Shirley Kishiyama, one of Portland's most gracious home entertainers. The filling, with its cool, custardy texture, is set in a buttery crust of hazelnuts and shortbread cookies, and a thin, chocolate–sour cream layer adds just the right amount of contrast to the delicate sweetness of the cake.

Makes one 8- or $8\frac{1}{2}$-inch cake; serves 10 to 12

For the hazelnut crust:
2 tablespoons sugar
$\frac{1}{4}$ cup unsalted butter, melted
3 ounces shortbread cookies or graham crackers broken into small pieces, or graham cracker crumbs
1 cup roasted and skinned hazelnuts (page 236)

For the cream cheese custard:
$\frac{3}{4}$ cup sugar, or to taste
1 pound cream cheese, at room temperature
2 large eggs, at room temperature, separated
$\frac{1}{2}$ cup Frangelico (hazelnut liqueur), or to taste

For the chocolate crown:
$\frac{1}{4}$ pound good-quality semisweet chocolate
$\frac{1}{2}$ cup sour cream

1. Preheat an oven to 350 degrees F. Position a rack in the middle of the oven.

(continued)

2. To make the hazelnut crust, combine the sugar, melted butter, and cookies or graham cracker crumbs in a food processor fitted with the steel blade. Process briefly to form a fine mixture. Add the hazelnuts and process just until the nuts are coarsely chopped. Press the mixture evenly over the bottom and 1 to $1\frac{1}{2}$ inches up the sides of an 8- or $8\frac{1}{2}$-inch springform pan. Bake until the crust is golden brown, about 12 minutes. Remove from the oven and let cool completely. Reduce the oven temperature to 325 degrees F.

3. To make the cream cheese custard, combine the sugar and cream cheese in a food processor fitted with the steel blade. Process until fluffy and completely smooth. Add the egg whites and process to combine. Then add the yolks and process to combine. Blend in the Frangelico. Taste and adjust the amount of sugar and Frangelico.

4. Pour the mixture into the cooled crust. Place in the oven and bake until the cheesecake starts to rise, about 25 minutes. Turn off the oven and open the door. Let the cheesecake stand for about 15 minutes before adding the chocolate crown.

5. To make the chocolate crown, place the chocolate in the top pan of a double boiler set over hot water. Stir until it melts. Remove from the heat and let cool to room temperature, 5 to 8 minutes.

6. Fold the sour cream into the cooled chocolate until thoroughly blended. Spread the mixture over the still-warm cheesecake. Cool to room temperature, cover, and refrigerate for at least 6 hours.

7. Let the cake stand at room temperature for 20 minutes before serving.

From the kitchen of Shirley Kishiyama

Poached Lemon Cheesecake

Portland's L'Auberge restaurant has a cult following for this lemony, dome-shaped cheesecake that is exquisitely light yet powerfully creamy.

Serves 8 to 10

3 tablespoons unsalted
  butter, melted
$\frac{3}{4}$ cup graham cracker
  crumbs
$1\frac{1}{2}$ pounds cream cheese, at
  room temperature
$\frac{3}{4}$ cup sugar
Juice and grated zest of
  2 small lemons

$1\frac{1}{2}$ teaspoons pure vanilla
  extract
4 large eggs
$\frac{3}{4}$ cup heavy cream
1 cup whipping cream
2 to 3 tablespoons powdered
  sugar

1. Using a pastry brush, paint the inside of a 6-cup metal bowl with the melted butter. Then coat the sides and bottom of the bowl with the graham cracker crumbs. Pour out any excess crumbs and reserve.

2. Preheat an oven to 350 degrees F. Position a rack in the middle of the oven.

3. In a large mixing bowl, combine the cream cheese, sugar, lemon zest and juice, and vanilla. Using an electric mixer, beat until light and fluffy. Add the eggs, one at a time, and beat in at medium speed, stopping the mixer and scraping down the bowl sides well between additions. Add the cream and beat in at low speed. Then use a whisk to reach the bottom and sides of the bowl to blend the ingredients well.

4. Pour the cheese mixture into the prepared bowl. Sprinkle the reserved graham cracker crumbs over the top. Place the bowl in a pan and pour in hot water to reach halfway

(continued)

up the sides of the bowl. Place in the oven and bake for $1\frac{1}{2}$ hours. Turn off the oven and let the cake cool with the door closed for 1 hour. Then cover and refrigerate the cheesecake for at least 3 hours.

5. Meanwhile, clean the beaters and chill along with a bowl.

6. Invert the chilled cake onto a flat cake plate. Run a warm, damp towel over the bowl to release the cheesecake and lift off the bowl.

7. Pour the whipping cream into the chilled bowl. Using the electric mixer set at medium-high speed, beat the cream, gradually adding the powdered sugar, until soft peaks form. Spoon the whipped cream into a pastry bag fitted with a large star tip and decorate the cheesecake in an attractive design.

From L'Auberge

Marionberry Cheesecake with Walnut Crust

In Oregon, cheesecake is distinguished from its eastern cousins by nutty crusts and fresh blackberries, which grow madly all over the state. The blackberry family is a large one that includes the sweet, bright black marionberry. Here marionberry conserve, available in many Northwest supermarkets and specialty food stores, is used in the filling. But any berry or fruit conserve may be substituted.

Makes one 9-inch cake; serves 10 to 12

For the walnut crust:
$1\frac{1}{2}$ **cups unbleached all-purpose flour**
$1\frac{1}{2}$ **cups ground walnuts**

6 tablespoons unsalted butter, chilled
1 teaspoon pure vanilla extract

For the filling:

2½ pounds cream cheese, at room temperature

1 cup sugar

4 large whole eggs

2 large egg yolks

¼ cup heavy cream

¼ cup unbleached all-purpose flour

¼ teaspoon salt

1 cup marionberry or other berry conserve

For the garnish:

Whipped cream

Marionberries or other seasonal berries

Walnut halves

1. To make the crust, combine the flour and ground walnuts in a food processor fitted with the steel blade. Cut the butter into chunks and scatter the pieces over the top of the flour. Sprinkle the vanilla extract over the butter. Process briefly, just until the dough is barely mixed. Pat the dough into the bottom of a 9-inch springform pan. Cover the pan and place in the freezer until the dough is firm, at least 2 hours.

2. Preheat an oven to 400 degrees F. Position a rack in the middle of the oven.

3. Remove the pan from the freezer and place it directly into the preheated oven. Bake until the dough is lightly browned, about 15 minutes. Remove from the oven and let cool on a wire rack. Reduce the oven temperature to 325 degrees F.

4. To make the filling, combine the cream cheese and sugar in a mixing bowl. Using an electric mixer with a paddle attachment or beaters, beat at medium speed until the cream cheese is smooth and the sugar is incorporated. Add the whole eggs and egg yolks, two at a time, beating well after each addition. Reduce the speed to low and slowly add the cream. Gently mix in the flour and salt. Fold in the marionberry conserve and stir until no trace of white remains.

(continued)

5. Pour the filling into the walnut crust. Cover the exterior bottom and sides of the springform pan with a piece of heavy-duty aluminum foil. Place the springform pan inside a large baking pan. Pour enough water into the baking pan to reach halfway up the sides of the springform pan. Place in the oven and bake until the cheesecake is firm around the edges but slightly soft and springy in the center, about $1\frac{1}{2}$ hours. Remove the cake from the hot water bath and let cool to room temperature.

6. Decorate the cake with rosettes of whipped cream, marionberries, and walnuts.

From Panini

 # Blueberry Sourdough Bread Pudding

Blueberries tend to burst when baked in the oven, but here, baked in a golden pudding with pockets of sweet custard throughout, they simply explode with goodness. For an interesting variation, replace the blues with huckleberries, tart little gems known to native Oregonians as wild blueberries. The recipe comes from I Dolci Bakery, a special-order operation located in the home kitchen of Jane Burkholder, who ranks high as one of Portland's most innovative chefs. I Dolci desserts are sought-after for dinner parties, weddings, and other celebrations.

Serves 8 to 10

1 loaf (24 ounces) good-
   quality sourdough French
   bread
$\frac{1}{4}$ pound ($\frac{1}{2}$ cup) unsalted
   butter
1 pint (2 cups) blueberries
4 large eggs

3 large egg yolks
2 cups half-and-half
2 cups milk
$\frac{3}{4}$ cup sugar
1 tablespoon pure vanilla
   extract

1 1/2 teaspoons ground
  cinnamon
1/2 teaspoon freshly grated
  nutmeg

1/4 cup sugar
Boiling water as needed
Heavy cream for serving

1. Cut about two thirds of the bread loaf into 1-inch-thick slices. Trim away the crusts and then cut the slices into 1-inch cubes. Place in a mixing bowl.

2. Melt the butter in a saucepan. Remove from the heat and let the butter cool. Add the blueberries to the bread cubes. Pour the cooled butter over the top and toss lightly.

3. Preheat an oven to 350 degrees F. Position a rack in the middle of the oven.

4. Butter a 2-quart baking dish or soufflé dish and fill with the bread and blueberries. In a mixing bowl, whisk together the whole eggs, egg yolks, half-and-half, milk, sugar, vanilla extract, 1/2 teaspoon of the cinnamon, and the nutmeg. Pour the mixture over the top of the bread and blueberries. Let stand for 15 minutes prior to baking. Combine the sugar with the remaining cinnamon, and sprinkle the top generously with the mixture.

5. Place the baking dish in a baking pan and pour in enough boiling water to reach halfway up the sides of the baking dish. Place in the oven and bake until the pudding is puffed and brown, about 1 hour. Remove the dish and pan from the oven and let the pudding cool in the water bath.

6. Serve at room temperature and pass a pitcher of cream at the table.

From I Dolci Bakery

Black Angus Brownies

These are simply the best brownies I've ever eaten, as dark as coal and rich enough for even the most devout chocolate cultist. Oregon's ubiquitous walnuts provide just the right amount of crunch. The secret here is a sparse allotment of flour, resulting in extremely moist, fudgy morsels with a thin, crackling surface.

Makes 16 squares

$\frac{1}{4}$ **pound ($\frac{1}{2}$ cup) unsalted butter**

2 ounces unsweetened chocolate

2 large eggs

1 cup sugar

1 tablespoon pure vanilla extract

$\frac{1}{3}$ **cup unbleached all-purpose flour, sifted**

1 cup coarsely chopped walnuts

Powdered sugar for dusting

1. Combine the butter and chocolate in a small pan over low heat. Stir until melted and smooth. Set aside to cool.

2. Preheat an oven to 350 degrees F. Position a rack in the middle of the oven. Butter and flour an 8-inch square baking pan.

3. Place the eggs, sugar, and vanilla extract in a mixing bowl. Using an electric mixer, beat until smooth. Beat in the cooled chocolate mixture. Add the sifted flour and beat for several minutes to blend thoroughly. Then fold in the walnuts by hand.

4. Pour the batter into the prepared pan and smooth the top. Place in the oven and bake until the brownies test done when a toothpick inserted in the center comes out clean, about 25 minutes. Let cool on a wire rack.

5. Dust liberally with powdered sugar; the top should be shrouded in the sugar. Cut into squares to serve.

 ## Hazelnut Ginger Shortbread

Crystallized ginger, once an imported luxury, today can be found in most specialty-food stores. Here it lends an intriguing note to nutty butter cookies. The recipe was created by cookie connoisseur Sara Perry, one of Portland's best-known food writers. The shortbread can be stored in a tin for up to 1 week or in the freezer for up to 3 months.

Makes 12 wedge-shaped pieces

$1\frac{1}{2}$ **cups unbleached all-purpose flour**

2 tablespoons coarsely chopped crystallized ginger

$\frac{1}{2}$ **cup plus 1 tablespoon sugar**

$\frac{1}{4}$ **cup plus 1 tablespoon ground, roasted, and skinned hazelnuts (page 236)**

$\frac{1}{4}$ **pound ($\frac{1}{2}$ cup) unsalted butter, at room temperature**

1. Preheat an oven to 325 degrees F. Position a rack in the middle of the oven.

2. In a large bowl, combine the flour, ginger, the $\frac{1}{2}$ cup sugar, and the $\frac{1}{4}$ cup hazelnuts. Cut in the butter with a pastry cutter until the mixture resembles coarse meal. Gather the dough into a ball.

3. Place the ball in an ungreased 8-inch tart pan with a removable bottom. Press the dough evenly into the pan. Pierce the entire surface with the tines of a fork. Then score the surface into 12 wedge-shaped pieces.

(continued)

4. Place in the oven and bake until golden brown, 35 to 40 minutes. Remove from the oven. While the shortbread is still warm, slice it along the scored lines and sprinkle the top with the remaining hazelnuts and sugar. Let cool completely on a wire rack before removing from the pan.

From the kitchen of Sara Perry

 # Hazelnut and Frangelico Cookies

Flavored with toasted ground hazelnuts and Frangelico (the seductive hazelnut liqueur produced by Franciscan monks), these rich, crispy, addictive cookies are from the kitchen of Pat Vidor, whose line of homemade cookies is a hot item at upscale Portland food stores.

Makes 4 dozen cookies

1 cup roasted and skinned
   whole hazelnuts (page 236)
2 cups unbleached all-
   purpose flour
1 cup butter, at room
   temperature

1 cup powdered sugar
1 tablespoon Frangelico
   (hazelnut liqueur) or pure
   vanilla extract
1 teaspoon pure almond
   extract

1. Preheat an oven to 350 degrees F. Position a rack in the middle of the oven. Butter a baking sheet.

2. Place the hazelnuts and flour in a food processor fitted with the steel blade and process until the nuts are ground as fine as the flour.

3. Place the butter in a mixing bowl. Using an electric mixer, cream the butter until light and fluffy. Add the sugar,

Frangelico or vanilla extract, and almond extract. Beat until blended thoroughly. Slowly mix in the hazelnut-flour mixture.

4. Scoop out $\frac{1}{2}$-inch balls of the dough with a melon scooper. Or use a barely rounded teaspoonful of dough for each cookie and roll the dough into small balls between your hands. Place the balls $1\frac{1}{2}$ inches apart on the prepared sheet. Bake until the cookie bottoms are lightly browned, about 10 minutes. Turn the cookie sheet once (reversing the front end of the pan to the back) during baking for even browning. Transfer the cookies to wire racks to cool. Store in a tightly covered container for up to 2 weeks.

From the kitchen of Pat Vidor

 # Apple Crisp with Amaretto Cookies and Apple Brandy Raisins

Oregon and Washington produce more than 200 varieties of apples, ripening from early summer through late fall. With such a selection, it's a shame to cling to the old supermarket standbys. Jonathons and Newton Pippins are ideal for autumn baking, particularly in combination with the local Spitzenburg, a flavorful apple that is also well suited for making cider. This apple crisp is terrific with either vanilla ice cream or whipped cream flavored with orange liqueur. For a variation, substitute chopped pitted dates or prunes for the raisins. Or use amaretto liqueur in place of the apple brandy. The following recipe comes from cookbook author Sara Perry. Look for imported amaretto cookies in the Italian section of well-stocked super-markets or in food-specialty shops.

Serves 6

1 cup raisins

$1\frac{1}{2}$ tablespoons apple brandy or Calvados

3 tablespoons Grand Marnier

5 cups sliced, peeled baking apples

$\frac{1}{2}$ teaspoon ground cinnamon

6 tablespoons granulated sugar

1 teaspoon grated lemon zest

1 teaspoon grated orange zest

$\frac{1}{2}$ cup sifted unbleached all-purpose flour

$\frac{1}{4}$ cup crushed amaretto cookies

$\frac{1}{2}$ cup firmly packed light brown sugar

$\frac{1}{4}$ teaspoon salt

$\frac{1}{2}$ cup unsalted butter, at room temperature

1. Place the raisins in a small bowl. Combine the brandy and Grand Marnier. Pour the mixture over the raisins and let stand for 10 to 15 minutes.

2. Preheat an oven to 350 degrees F. Position a rack in the middle of the oven. Butter an 8-inch square baking pan.

3. Combine the apples, cinnamon, and 2 tablespoons of the granulated sugar in a saucepan over medium heat. Bring the mixture to a boil. Reduce the heat to low and simmer, stirring frequently, until the apples are tender, about 5 minutes.

4. Remove from the heat and spoon into a bowl. Gently stir in the lemon zest, orange zest, and raisins with their soaking liquid. Turn the mixture into the prepared pan. In a bowl stir together the flour, cookies, brown sugar, salt, and the remaining 4 tablespoons granulated sugar. Add the butter and mix together with a fork until crumbly. Sprinkle over the top of the apple mixture.

5. Place in the oven and bake until the top is lightly browned, about 35 minutes. Cool slightly on a wire rack before serving.

From the kitchen of Sara Perry

 # Apricot Soufflé

Thin slices of coral-hued Northwest apricots give this high-minded soufflé its regional trademark and concentrated intensity. The sparkle of flavor comes from the essence of the peel, which is cooked down to a thick, sugary purée that is folded into the airy egg whites. The result is a lofty creation that is simply out of this world, especially with a dollop of liquored whipped cream.

Serves 6

Butter and sugar to prepare
  the pan
8 large, ripe apricots
Juice of $\frac{1}{2}$ lemon
$\frac{1}{4}$ cup water
$\frac{1}{2}$ cup granulated sugar,
  divided

6 large eggs at room
  temperature
1 cup whipped heavy cream
2 tablespoons Grand
  Marnier or apricot brandy

1. To prepare the pan, butter the sides and bottom of six 4-inch soufflé dishes. (If you wish to sugar the pans, sprinkle about 1½ teaspoons granulated sugar on the bottom of each dish. Turn and tilt to coat the sides; tap and shake out any excess.) If you don't have individual soufflé dishes, use a 1½- or 2-quart soufflé dish.

2. Peel the apricots, reserving the peels. Squeeze the lemon juice over the exposed fruit—this will not require the entire lemon half—and set aside. Place the peels in a 6-inch sauté pan with the water and ¼ cup of the sugar. Bring the mixture to a simmer and reduce it by half of its volume, about 3 to 5 minutes. Remove the pan from the heat and pass the mixture through a fine-meshed sieve into a clean bowl. Set aside to cool.

3. Preheat an oven to 400 degrees F. Position a rack in the middle of the oven.

(continued)

4. In the container of a food processor or blender, purée the reserved apricots with the remaining lemon juice and ⅛ cup of the sugar. Blend the purée with the cooled apricot peel mixture.

5. Separate the 6 eggs. Add 3 of the yolks to the apricot base. (Discard the other 3 yolks or save for another use.) In a clean, dry bowl (preferably copper), beat the 6 egg whites with a wire whisk or electric mixer until soft peaks form; add the remaining ⅛ cup sugar and continue beating until the whites stand up in stiff peaks but are not dry. Using a rubber spatula placed at the far end of the bowl, pour one third of the apricot mixture into the white peaks, carefully folding it in with a sweeping motion that goes across the bottom of the bowl and turning the mixture over the top. Continue this folding process, adding the remaining apricot mixture, one third at a time. Carefully spoon the mixture into the prepared soufflé dishes.

6. Place the soufflé dishes in the oven and immediately lower the heat to 375 degrees F. Bake without opening the door until the tops turn just brown—about 18 to 20 minutes for individual 4-inch soufflés and about 30 minutes with a 1½- to 2-quart soufflé dish. When finished, the soufflés should be golden and puffy, and when touched gently, there should be an indication of firmness. Serve immediately with whipped cream laced with the Grand Marnier or apricot brandy.

From Le Cuisinier

CHAPTER FOURTEEN

CONDIMENTS WITH WILD MINT, MOUNTAIN HUCKLEBERRIES, AND OTHER UNEXPECTED FLAVORS

Bing Cherry Chutney

Sweet and juicy, the scarlet black Bing is the Northwest's premier eating cherry. The following cherry chutney, a beautiful dark red condiment full of cinnamon, ginger, and pepper, can do amazing things for a grilled chicken, a roast turkey or loin of pork or a fillet of sturgeon.

Makes about 3 cups

$1\frac{1}{2}$ tablespoons chopped
   crystallized ginger
$1\frac{1}{2}$ pounds Bing cherries,
   stemmed and pitted
$\frac{1}{2}$ teaspoon freshly ground
   black pepper

$\frac{1}{8}$ teaspoon ground
   cinnamon
$\frac{1}{4}$ cup red wine vinegar

1. Place the ginger in a food processor fitted with the steel blade and finely chop. Transfer to a glass bowl. Coarsely chop the pitted cherries in the processor and combine with the ginger.

2. Stir in the pepper, cinnamon, and vinegar. Taste and adjust the seasonings. Cover and chill overnight. The chutney will keep for up to 1 week in the refrigerator. Serve at room temperature.

From Briggs and Crampton's Catering and Table for Two

 # Pear-Currant Chutney

Northwest cooks do marvelous things with chutney, the jam-like relish of sweet fruit and blazing spices that is the hallmark of East Indian cuisine. This fiery blend, which comes from Portland food writer Naomi Kaufman Price, can be used in many ways. Spoon a little over fish or chicken and bake for a

simple, delicious meal. Or serve with roast duck or quail, baked winter squash, or Crab Cakes with Aged Cheddar (page 18).

Makes about 2 quarts

4 pounds ripe but firm pears such as Comice, Bartlett, or Anjou	½ to ¾ cup chopped crystallized ginger
1 pound light brown sugar (3 cups packed)	2 tablespoons crushed black or yellow mustard seeds
2 cups white vinegar	2 cloves garlic, minced
1 onion, chopped	2 teaspoons salt
1 cup golden raisins	½ teaspoon cayenne pepper
½ cup dried dark currants	4 allspice berries, finely crushed

1. Peel, quarter, and core the pears. Slice the quarters crosswise about ¼ inch thick.

2. Combine the brown sugar and vinegar in a large pot over medium heat and bring to a boil. Add all the remaining ingredients and bring back to a boil. Reduce the heat to low and simmer, uncovered, stirring carefully on occasion without breaking the fruit, until the chutney thickens, about 50 minutes. (It will thicken further as it cools.)

3. Ladle the hot chutney into hot sterilized jars, leaving ¼-inch headspace. Wipe off the rims and seal the jars with sterilized rings. Process for 10 minutes in a hot water bath. Once the jars are opened, they can be stored in the refrigerator for up to 3 months.

From the kitchen of Naomi Kaufman Price

 ## Cranberry-Ginger Chutney

This spicy chutney makes a perfect sidekick for roast chicken, grilled lamb chops, or fresh salmon. Chef Millie Howe uses it to create an offbeat breakfast with a Northwest twist: She fills

omelets with a tablespoon of the chutney and a sprinkling of crumbled goat cheese.

Makes 2 quarts

$\frac{1}{2}$ **cup cubed, peeled fresh ginger**

8 cloves garlic

2 fresh jalapeño peppers, stemmed and halved

2 tablespoons cumin seeds

1 tablespoon peppercorns

1 tablespoon cardamom seeds

3 cups coarsely chopped onion

$4\frac{1}{2}$ **cups large, firm cranberries**

1 cup firmly packed dark brown sugar

1 cup red wine vinegar

1 cup water

2 tablespoons kosher salt

6 cinnamon sticks, each about 2 inches long

1. Combine the ginger, garlic, and jalapeño peppers in a food processor fitted with the steel blade. Process until finely chopped. Set aside. Combine the cumin seeds, peppercorns, and cardamom seeds in a blender or a spice mill and reduce the spices to an aromatic powder.

2. In a large pot, combine the reserved ginger mixture, the spice mixture, and all the remaining ingredients. Bring to a slow boil, stirring occasionally. Reduce the heat to low and simmer, uncovered, until thick and soft, about 30 minutes. Remove and discard the cinnamon sticks.

3. Ladle the hot chutney into clean, sterilized jars with tight-fitting sterilized lids. Process in hot water bath for 10 minutes. Once opened, the chutney will keep for months in the refrigerator or if unopened will keep for up to 1 year.

From Indigine

Oregon Peach Chutney

A dazzling variety of jams and condiments can be made with succulent Oregon peaches. This sweetish-sour conserve can be brushed over chicken or fish and baked as a glaze or served at room temperature and dabbed over all manner of curries and grilled foods. If you're experimentally inclined, consider substituting other fruits—from apples to pears—for the peaches. Apricots are also marvelous, although you will need at least a half dozen of them for this recipe. You can also vary the texture: The riper the fruit, the smoother the texture, so for a chunky texture use underripe fruit.

Makes 2 to 3 cups

1 cup dried black currants
5 underripe peaches, peeled, pitted, and diced
2 cinnamon sticks
10 cloves
6 quarter-sized slices fresh ginger, peeled and diced
Juice and grated zest of $\frac{1}{2}$ lime

$\frac{1}{3}$ cup good-quality white vinegar
$\frac{1}{3}$ cup firmly packed light brown sugar
10 grindings of pepper
$\frac{1}{2}$ teaspoon cayenne pepper

1. Place all the ingredients in a heavy 4-quart pot. Bring the mixture to a boil over high heat and reduce the heat to low. Simmer uncovered, stirring frequently, until the liquid turns glossy and thick enough to coat the back of a spoon, about 30 minutes. Remove from the heat and cool thoroughly.

2. Remove and discard the cinnamon sticks before serving. The chutney will keep for a week stored, tightly covered, in the refrigerator. Or pour the hot chutney into hot, sterilized jars. Seal and process for 10 minutes in a hot water bath. The chutney will keep for up to 1 year.

From the kitchen of Larry Kirkland

Fresh Herb Chutney

This nippy condiment is spectacular when fresh basil is the main player, but mint and cilantro also make a winning combination. Either adds rich color and luscious flavor to a variety of dishes: roast chicken, grilled fish, fresh tomatoes, and even omelets. It's also great with Cauliflower with Caramelized Onions (page 126).

Makes about 1 cup

2 cups fresh basil leaves or a combination of other fresh herb leaves such as mint, cilantro, tarragon, and Italian parsley
½ cup coarsely chopped onion

1 small fresh jalapeño pepper, seeded and finely chopped
¼ cup fresh lemon juice
2 teaspoons sugar
1 tablespoon kosher salt

1. Combine all the ingredients in a food processor fitted with the steel blade. Process until the mixture is just puréed. Taste and adjust the seasonings.

2. Serve immediately as a condiment; the dish will keep for only a few hours.

From Indigine

 # Wild Mountain Huckleberry Preserves

Oregonians have a serious passion for wild mountain huckleberries. These sweet, deep purple berries are usually hidden beneath a flaky pie crust, although they have a reputation for

garnering blue ribbons at county fairs when transformed into preserves. The following spread is a specialty of Pat Vidor, whose exceptional preserves are sold at Norm Thompson, Portland's answer to L.L. Bean.

Makes about $1\frac{1}{2}$ quarts

1 lime, coarsely chopped with peel
$3\frac{1}{2}$ cups sugar

$2\frac{1}{2}$ cups fresh huckleberries, stemmed

1. Place the lime in a small saucepan and add water to cover. Bring to a boil and cook over medium heat for 15 minutes. Strain the liquid through a fine-mesh strainer into a large, noncorrosive pot, pressing against the pulp with the back of a spoon. Discard the pulp.

2. Add the sugar and slowly bring the mixture to a boil, stirring frequently to keep the sugar from burning. Raise the heat to medium-high, place a candy thermometer in the syrup, and cook until the syrup registers 235 degrees F (soft-ball stage).

3. Add the huckleberries. Heat until the mass of berries and syrup is boiling rapidly (adjust the heat as necessary to prevent the mixture from boiling over). Continue cooking uncovered, stirring frequently, until droplets fall off a spoon in sheets (the soft-ball stage), about 30 minutes.

4. Remove from the heat and set aside to cool, stirring occasionally to distribute the fruit. Ladle the cooled fruit mixture into hot, sterilized jars, leaving $\frac{1}{2}$-inch headspace. Wipe off the rims and seal the jars with sterilized rings and lids. Process in a hot-water bath for 10 minutes. Store in a cool, dark place for up to 1 year. Once the jars are opened, they can be stored in the refrigerator for up to 3 months.

From the kitchen of Pat Vidor

Hot Chili Condiment

Seafood dishes often taste best when garnished with something sharp and unpredictable. Few things do the job better than this unusual blend of hot chilies and ripe tomatoes spiked with thyme and mint. It's the quintessential flavor booster for any soups, seafood stews, and grilled fish. It also does interesting things for lamb, chicken, and grilled vegetables. When stored tightly covered in the refrigerator, it will keep for several days.

Makes $1\frac{1}{4}$ cups

$\frac{1}{4}$ cup finely diced fresh
  serrano chili peppers
1 teaspoon minced fresh
  thyme, or $\frac{1}{3}$ teaspoon
  dried thyme
1 tablespoon minced fresh
  mint, or 1 teaspoon dried
  mint

$\frac{3}{4}$ cup diced, seeded Italian
  plum tomatoes
2 tablespoons red wine
  vinegar
1 tablespoon olive oil
Salt
$\frac{1}{4}$ cup diced, pitted green
  olives

1. Stir together all the ingredients in a small bowl. Taste and adjust the seasonings. Serve at room temperature.

From Briggs and Crampton's Catering and Table for Two

 # Cranberry, Port, and Onion Condiment

Cranberry bogs thrive on Oregon's southern coast, so it's no surprise to find the tart bog berry in all kinds of regional innovations. This colorful condiment is crisp, sweet, and biting. A few dabs will add spark to roast turkey, duck, or even grilled chicken breasts.

Makes about 3 cups

$\frac{1}{2}$ cup coarsely chopped red
  onion

1 cup port wine
1 cup cranberries

$\frac{1}{4}$ cup sugar

1 cup coarsely chopped,
   peeled apple

1. Combine the onion and port in a 2-quart saucepan. Simmer over low heat until the onion is soft, about 15 minutes. Add the cranberries, sugar, and apple, stir well, and simmer until the cranberries pop, about 10 minutes.

2. Remove from the heat and allow the mixture to cool completely. Cover tightly and refrigerate until serving. The condiment will keep for up to 1 week in the refrigerator.

From Briggs and Crampton's Catering and Table for Two

 # Sweet Pepper Relish

This chunky relish sizzles with the aroma of roasted red pepper and complements just about anything from the sea—fish soups, stews, or grills. When stored tightly covered in the refrigerator, it will keep for several days.

Makes 3 cups

3 red bell peppers, roasted,
   peeled, seeded, and
   deribbed (page 238)
$\frac{3}{4}$ cup chopped scallions
3 tablespoons chopped fresh
   tarragon

$\frac{1}{2}$ cup crème fraîche
   (page 236) or sour cream
2 tablespoons Dijon
   mustard

1. Cut the roasted peppers into strips.

2. Combine the pepper strips with all the remaining ingredients in a food processor fitted with the steel blade. Blend

(continued)

quickly to give the relish a chunky texture. Serve at room temperature.

From Briggs and Crampton's Catering and Table for Two

 # Hot Mint Relish

Northwest cooks do not hesitate to wed indigenous flavors with exotic seasonings from other lands. This homage to Oregon mint gets its edge from garam masala, *a highly aromatic blend of roasted spices popular in north India cooking. It can be purchased in specialty-food sections of supermarkets and in Indian markets. If you like explosive flavors, this mint relish will do the trick. Serve it with grilled fish, seafood stews, lamb, or roast pork. The recipe comes from the kitchen of Pat Vidor, whose Alsea, Oregon, farm kitchen is always full of seductive smells.*

Makes $1\frac{1}{2}$ cups

1 cup firmly packed fresh mint leaves
6 scallions
1 clove garlic
1 teaspoon salt
2 teaspoons sugar

$\frac{1}{2}$ to 1 fresh jalapeño pepper, seeded
1 teaspoon *garam masala*
$\frac{1}{3}$ cup fresh lemon juice
2 tablespoons water

1. Combine all the ingredients in a blender or a food processor fitted with the steel blade. Purée until smooth.

2. Cover and chill thoroughly before serving. Use within 3 days.

From the kitchen of Pat Vidor

 **Red Pepper Salsa**

Salsas, low in calories, fat, and cholesterol, have become popular enough to seriously challenge ketchup and onion dips as staples of American cuisine. These crunchy assemblages of raw ingredients make magnificent dips for chips or raw vegetables and are perfect for lathering on everything from roasted potatoes to fluffy omelets.

Makes about 4 cups

$1\frac{1}{2}$ **pounds ripe tomatoes, peeled, seeded, and diced**
$\frac{3}{4}$ **cup chopped scallions**
$\frac{3}{4}$ **cup chopped red bell pepper**
$\frac{1}{3}$ **cup fresh basil leaves, coarsely chopped**

$\frac{1}{2}$ **teaspoon salt**
Freshly ground black pepper
$\frac{1}{2}$ **teaspoon cayenne pepper**

1. Place the tomatoes in a colander to drain off any excess liquid, about 15 minutes.

2. Transfer the drained tomatoes to a mixing bowl and stir in all the remaining ingredients. Taste and adjust the seasonings. The salsa will keep tightly covered in the refrigerator for several days.

From Briggs and Crampton's Catering and Table for Two

 Apricot Mint Sauce

Clusters of wild mint thrive along the banks of virtually all waterways in the Northwest, from the creeks of the Coast Ranges to desert lakesides. These cool-scented weeds seem to

survive best on neglect, showing up year after year in ever-greater numbers. The following is a new twist on the traditional mint jelly served with lamb. It's also fabulous with grilled chicken or roast pork.

Makes about 1¼ cups

1 cup good-quality apricot preserves

¼ cup chopped fresh mint

2 tablespoons bourbon

1. Combine all the ingredients in a small saucepan over low heat. Simmer, stirring occasionally, until the preserves melt, about 3 to 4 minutes.

2. Strain the sauce through a fine-mesh strainer into a bowl. Spoon the hot sauce over lamb or pork as a finishing touch. Or pour the sauce into a serving bowl and pass it at the table.

From the kitchen of Pat Vidor

 # Mint Pesto

In this recipe, fresh Oregon mint takes the place of the traditional basil. Raspberry vinegar and roasted nuts add yet another new flavor dimension. The sauce is great on pasta but it is also marvelous with grilled foods, especially salmon, roast pork, or even a simple salad of fresh tomatoes.

Makes about ¾ cup

¼ cup pine nuts
4 large cloves garlic
1 cup fresh mint leaves
½ cup chopped fresh parsley
½ cup freshly grated Parmesan cheese

½ cup pure olive oil
2 to 2½ teaspoons raspberry vinegar

1. Preheat an oven to 350 degrees F.

2. Place the pine nuts in a small pan. Roast the nuts in the oven until golden, about 10 minutes.

3. Place the garlic in a blender or food processor fitted with the steel blade and process until minced. Add the mint, parsley, and roasted pine nuts. Process until the mixture is coarsely chopped, about 10 seconds. Add the Parmesan cheese and olive oil and use on-off pulses to blend. Do not overprocess. The mixture should be thick and smooth.

4. Transfer to a bowl and stir in the raspberry vinegar to taste. Serve at room temperature. The pesto will keep several weeks in a glass jar in the refrigerator when coated with a layer of olive oil and covered with a lid.

From Ron Paul Restaurant and Charcuterie

 # Wild Blackberry Compote

In this compote the blackberries retain their lovely shape and dusky flavor. The barely warmed fruit is added at the last minute to a gingery, citrus-scented syrup. Spoon it over pancakes, waffles, shortcake, or homemade vanilla ice cream.

Makes about 4 cups

1 cup fresh orange juice
1 cup sugar
1 tablespoon chopped, peeled fresh ginger
$\frac{1}{4}$ teaspoon ground cinnamon

1 lemon, cut in half
1 pint (2 cups) fresh blackberries, or $\frac{1}{2}$ pound (2 cups) frozen dry-packed blackberries thawed

1. Combine the orange juice, sugar, ginger, cinnamon, and lemon in a heavy noncorrosive saucepan over low heat. Bring the mixture to a slow boil, stirring constantly, and then turn off the heat. Remove and discard the lemon. Stir in the blackberries. Stir occasionally until the mixture is warmed through.

2. Serve warm or ladle into sterilized jars and close tightly. The compote will keep for 2 weeks in the refrigerator, or pack in plastic containers and freeze for up to 3 months. Reheat to warm before serving.

From The Heathman Hotel

CHAPTER FIFTEEN

NOTES ON BASIC
PREPARATIONS

 **Crème Fraîche**

Whether you call it French creme, crème double, *or sophisticated sour cream,* crème fraîche *seems to elevate the flavor of
anything with which it comes in contact. Creamy, silken, and
thick, with a most subtle sour undertone, it is the quintessential finishing touch. Fruit pies, hot soups, omelets, and pancakes are a few of the foods that benefit from its slightly nutty
flavor. It does not curdle, which means it can be stirred into
hot soups or sauces at the last minute. It's also easy to make at
home, although a commercial product is available at health-
food and upscale stores.*

Makes 1 cup

1 cup heavy cream
1½ tablespoons buttermilk

1. Heat the heavy cream in a saucepan over low heat until
lukewarm. Stir in the buttermilk. Pour the mixture into
a clean glass jar or ceramic container. Cover tightly and
place in a warm spot away from drafts until thick. This
will take 6 to 36 hours, depending upon the room temperature. Naturally, the warmer the room, the faster the
thickening will occur.

2. When thickened, stir the crème fraîche and cover with a
tight-fitting lid. Store in the refrigerator for up to 2 weeks.

 How to Roast and Skin Hazelnuts

*Hazelnuts (also known as filberts) figure prominently in the
new Oregon cuisine. They are rich and buttery, the sweetest of
all nuts, with a vague smoky undertaste. Local cooks frequently roast the nuts before using them, which brings out
their full complexity.*

1. Preheat an oven to 350 degrees F.

2. Place the nuts in a shallow pan. Place in the oven until the skins crack and begin to flake off, 10 to 15 minutes. Shake the pan occasionally to ensure even roasting.

3. Working with a few nuts at a time, place the nuts in a rough kitchen cloth. Rub vigorously to remove the skins. Most of the skins will come off, but don't worry if some cling to the nut. Cool the nuts completely before using.

 # Hazelnut Flour

This nutty flour is an interesting alternative to its all-purpose rival. It adds character to waffles, pancakes, pie crusts, breads, and other baked goods. Try it as a breading for fish in place of cornmeal; trout is especially good with a light dusting. And if you're breading chicken, consider this an innovative option.

Makes about $2\frac{1}{2}$ pounds ($8\frac{1}{2}$ cups)

1 pound roasted and skinned hazelnuts (page 236)

4 cups unbleached all-purpose flour

1. Preheat an oven to 150 degrees F.

2. Make sure the roasted nuts are completely cool. Place the nuts in a food processor fitted with a steel blade and reduce them to a powder as fine as flour. Be careful not to overgrind, or the nuts will turn into nut butter.

3. Spread the ground nuts on a baking sheet. Place in the oven and bake for about 3 hours, stirring every 30 minutes or so. Remove from the oven and let cool. Layer half

(continued)

of the all-purpose flour in a food processor fitted with the steel blade and top with half of the cooled nuts. Process briefly to combine thoroughly. Transfer to a clean, dry container with a tight-fitting lid. Repeat the process with the remaining ground nuts and all-purpose flour. The flour will probably have some small "clumps" in it. This is the result of the oil in the nuts and is fine.

4. Store in the refrigerator; the flour will keep up to 6 months.

From Harriet's Eat Now Cafe

 ## Roasted Bell Peppers

Sweet bell peppers—red, green, yellow, and more unusual colors like orange and a purplish black—take on a marvelous smoky flavor when roasted. The technique is not difficult to master and requires little more than an oven and a damp towel.

1. To oven roast, preheat a broiler. Place the peppers close together on an aluminum foil–covered baking sheet. Place the rack about 3 inches under the broiler so that the tops of the peppers are about 1 inch below the heat. Leave the oven door partially open so that you can watch closely and prevent the peppers from burning. Turn the peppers frequently with tongs until they are dark and blistered. Remove from the oven and wrap the peppers in a damp cotton towel for 5 minutes. Remove the towel and rub the peppers until the peels flake off. Trim the stems off the peppers. Cut in half and remove the seeds and ribs. The peppers are now ready to be sliced according to the recipe directions.

2. To roast using a gas stove, spear the pepper with a long two-pronged fork. Place the pepper over a gas flame and turn it continuously until the pepper is dark and blistered on all sides. Place the pepper in a damp towel for 5 minutes and proceed as for oven roasting.

 # Clarified Butter

When butter is clarified, the impurities are removed, resulting in superior flavor and color. Clarified butter doesn't burn either—a big advantage. It can be used in any recipe that calls for sautéing. The procedure must be done a day in advance, but the actual preparation time is quick.

Makes about 1 pound

1 pound unsalted butter

1. Melt the butter in a saucepan over medium heat. Refrigerate until the butter solidifies on top and the liquid settles to the bottom. Discard the liquid and remelt the butter as needed. Clarified butter will keep several weeks in the refrigerator.

 # Homemade Chicken Stock

A soup or sauce is only as good as its stock. The following is packed with essential flavor and produces enough stock to get you through numerous recipes. You can make a smaller amount if you wish, but, if you have a big freezer, it's better to make the whole batch, pack it in individual quart containers, then freeze for up to 6 months and use as needed.

Makes about 7 to 8 quarts

1 stewing chicken, 5 to 7 pounds, cut up

2 pounds beef flanken (kosher style) or boneless beef short ribs

1 veal bone, preferably with marrow

8 carrots, peeled, cut into 2-inch pieces

6 celery ribs, cut into large pieces

2 large onions, cut into large pieces

2 bunches fresh dill (16 to 18 stems per bunch)

Salt to taste

1. Remove any excess fat from the chicken pieces. Place all the ingredients in a 10-quart stockpot. Add water to barely cover. Bring the mixture to a boil and skim any surface scum. Reduce the heat to low and simmer, covered, until the meat is falling off the bones, 3 to 4 hours.

2. Strain the stock into a large container, pressing down on the solids to extract all the liquid. Pick out any chicken, beef, or vegetables from the sieve that haven't dissolved and save for another use. Season the stock with salt to taste. Cover with plastic wrap and chill overnight.

3. The following day, remove the congealed fat that has accumulated on the surface of the chilled stock. Save the fat for another use or discard. Reheat the stock or pack it into 1-quart containers, cover tightly, and freeze. Thaw as needed.

From the kitchen of Lisa Shara Hall

 # Fish Stock

The following is an all-purpose fish stock for Northwest soups. It can be prepared several days in advance and stored, tightly covered, in the refrigerator. Or freeze it for up to 1 month.

Makes about 2 quarts

2 pounds bones and
  trimmings from nonoily
  fish such as salmon, sole,
  halibut, and so on,
  including heads but with
  gills removed
1 small onion, chopped
1 celery rib, chopped
1 carrot, chopped
1 bay leaf
2 fresh thyme sprigs, or $\frac{1}{2}$
  teaspoon dried thyme
2 fresh parsley sprigs
4 quarts water

1. Combine all the ingredients in a stockpot and bring to a boil. Lower the heat and simmer for 1 hour, skimming off any surface foam.

2. Strain the stock through a fine-mesh sieve into a clean pot. Reduce the stock over medium heat to approximately 2 quarts liquid, about 30 to 40 minutes.

From Bread and Ink Cafe

Oregon's Trailblazing Chefs

Dennis Baker

owner/chef, Cafe des Amis

Right from the beginning, Dennis Baker knew he wanted to cook. While his college friends were flipping hamburgers, Baker was sweating over a pot of beef bourguignon. "I had the drive," he says. "I just studied the classics—everything you need to know is there."

Baker's dream was to run a restaurant that evoked the farmhouse foods of his Oregon youth. He got his chance in the late '70s when he opened Cafe des Amis, an Oregon-style bistro. Instead of duck à l'orange, Baker creates roast duck swathed in a sauce of backyard blackberries. His pâté is heady with apple brandy from a neighborhood distillery, and his rack of lamb is perfumed with hazelnuts from a local orchard. "I make up all the dishes in my head," says Baker, "but I am inspired by what is around me."

Chicken Liver Mousse with Figs and Apple Brandy (page 24); Gathered Greens and Field Flowers in Walnut Vinaigrette (page 55); Fettuccine with Clams, Mussels, and Spicy Sausage (page 144); Chicken, Mushroom, and Spicy Sausage Stew (page 89); Roast Rack of Lamb with Hazelnut Hollandaise

*(page 109); Duck with Wild Blackberry Sauce (page 97);
Chicken with Morels and Cream (page 91)*

James Beals and Kathleen Towers

chefs, L'Auberge

L'Auberge, like Oregon, is a study in rugged individualism. Owner Bill McLaughlin is a one-time college professor who holds a black belt in karate and a keen knowledge of Oregon wine; he keeps his service sharp by working the floor as a busboy. In his dining room, Oregon cuisine meets country French cooking. But in his upstairs bar you'll find fiery ribs, progressive music, and a faithful clientele of baseball fanatics.

McLaughlin has put together a wickedly intelligent kitchen crew. The lineup includes head chef James Beals, a demanding, self-taught purist, and pastry whiz Kathleen Towers, who helps L'Auberge keep its reputation as a den of caloric abandon.

Warm Goat Cheese Salad with Winter Greens (page 56); Roast Pork Loin with Raspberry-Prune Compote (page 111); Veal Scallops with Morels (page 115); Poached Lemon Cheesecake (page 209)

Nancy Briggs and Juanita Crampton

owners/chefs, Briggs and Crampton's Catering and Table for Two

There are two inviolable rules at Table for Two. You don't ask, "What's for dinner?" and you don't beg to bring "just one more person." A three-course lunch is the only meal there. It's served once a day—for *two* people only.

Welcome to the world's smallest restaurant, the dining room of a restored 1901 Victorian home in an old Portland neighborhood. Each day brings a new menu of Oregon's headiest dishes, intricately garnished with edibles from a backyard garden. The eating area is booked months in advance, and recipes are created in free-form cooking sessions, with an emphasis on bold color and unpredictable flavors. "We're not into the classics," says Nancy Briggs. "Since we don't know what we're supposed to do, we're free to do it our way."

Chanterelle Tart with Sugar-Roasted Walnuts (page 31); Sweet-and-Savory Grilled Chicken (page 94); Sauté of Spinach, Shiitake Mushrooms, and Comice Pears (page 134); Hot Chili Condiment (page 228); Sturgeon and Fennel Chowder (page 38); Dungeness Crab Salad with Warm Apple Dressing (page 62); Blackberries with Mint, Zinnia Petals, and Lime (page 52); Red Pear, Purple Cabbage, and Toasted Walnut Salad (page 52); Spring Greens, Asparagus, and Morels (page 53); Oregon Blue Cheese Dressing (page 65); Tarragon Vinaigrette (page 65); Hazelnut Rye Bread (page 172); Bing Cherry Chutney (page 222); Cranberry, Port, and Onion Condiment (page 228); Apple Tart in Ginger Pastry (page 181); Loganberry Ice Cream with Whidbey's Liqueur (page 198); Bittersweet Chocolate Torte with Strawberries (page 203).

Jane Burkholder

owner/chef, I Dolci Bakery

Dante's warning should be hung over the entrance of Jane Burkholder's bakery: "Abandon hope, all ye who enter here." Willpower melts fast in the face of a chocolate ganache cake lavished with marzipan-sculpted string beans and carrots. I Dolci is a well-kept secret among Portland's finest caterers and entertainers. Located in Burkholder's country home kitchen, it is *the* place for specialty ordered cakes and desserts. Burkholder uses Oregon produce as a springboard for new twists on classic American desserts. "I had a thing for bread pudding," she confesses, "and started adding blueberries, marionberries, raspberries, whatever was in season. Suddenly, it had these big wonderful veins of fruit running through it."

Blueberry Sourdough Bread Pudding (page 212); Autumn Pear and Goat Cheese Tart (page 30)

Linda Faes

owner/chef, Panini

Panini is Portland's nod to panini bars—Italian street corner shops specializing in "little sandwich rolls." With operatic arias filling the high ceilings and vigorous conversation at the espresso bar up front, this eatery does a worthy take on Italy's street-smart eateries. But it's desserts that make Linda Faes a shooting star on Oregon's restaurant scene. One patron goes as far as to have her latest pastry delivered to his house by cab.

Faes often finds inspiration in her own garden. Rose petals, pansies, and other elegant edibles are lightly brushed with beaten egg whites, dipped in sugar, then dried for later use as a finishing touch. "I like to keep decorations simple but detailed," she says. "And I like to go for flavor; if you're using lemon, really use it—on the inside as well as the outside."

Chocolate Truffle and Raspberry Ice Cream (page 196); Marionberry Cheesecake with Walnut Crust (page 210)

Amelia Hard, Joan Husman, and Catherine Whims

chefs, Genoa

At Genoa, Northwest ingredients meet northern Italy on a little corner of southeast Portland. It all comes together in a one-room dining chamber, dark and cozy, with little to distract diners from a procession of dishes designed with still-life precision and lyrical flavor. Menus change every fortnight, and ideas are drawn from the Old World as well as the new.

"My mother taught me that food is more than fuel," says Amelia Hard. "It's a vital part of life, a ritual that cements family and friends." Genoa's recipes join that spirit with an intense exploration of Oregon's bounty.

Chanterelle Cream Soup (page 41); Sweet-and-Sour Salmon with Fennel Greens (page 69); Pasta with Mussel Sauce (page 148)

Greg Higgins and George Tate

chefs, The Heathman Hotel

When talking about the Oregon food experience, Greg Higgins and George Tate are names that pop up early. During the late '80s, they were among the first chefs to blend sensory balance, visual harmony, and fiery ethnic Latin ingredients in a regional scheme. Seasonal menus at The Heathman are a triumph of color and presentation. Autumn, for example, is celebrated with colorful dishes such as roast duck surrounded by shock-red cabbage, bronzed hazelnuts, and forest greens with auburn edges.

Freshness, the chefs say, is crucial to the finished product. But so are sensible ideas about cooking: Master traditional techniques, suggests Higgins, and don't lean on trick dishes and fashionable ingredients.

Hazelnut Corn Cakes with Wild Blackberrry Compote (page 6); King Salmon Hash (page 11); Crab Cakes with Aged Cheddar and Pear Chutney (page 18); Game Pâté with Cranberry-Ginger Chutney (page 25); Oysters in Basil Nests with Quail Eggs (page 20); Steamed Clams with Garden Herbs (page 19); Chanterelle Sauté with Basil and Shredded Leeks (page 127); Grilled Venison with Cranberry-Pepper Sauce (page 113)

Pattie Hill

owner/chef, Bread and Ink Cafe

You never know what specials will be posted on Pattie Hill's blackboard, and that's part of the fun. It might be a sophisticated poached salmon or a homey dish of stuffed pears. One thing, however, is certain: The food meshes perfectly with Bread and Ink's warm and heady ambience.

Hill turned a teen-age passion for cookbook reading into a successful career. She read the 300 culinary tomes on her kitchen shelf like suspense novels, looking for clues to the world's great cuisines. She devoured the classics, tackled the esoterics, and researched Mediterranean styles. The best cooking, Hill concluded, "is not isolated as sensual pleasure, nourishment, or regional tradition, but all in balance." Her recipes maintain that harmony.

Pears Stuffed with Blue Cheese and Hazelnuts (page 28); Fruit Soup with Rhubarb, Berries, and Mint (page 48); Pacific Oyster and Spinach Bisque (page 36); Three-Onion Cream Soup (page 43); White Bean Soup with Fennel Pesto (page 44); Poached Silver Salmon with Rhubarb Compote (page 71); Lamb Braised with Quince, Cinnamon, and Apples (page 106); Summer Garden Ragout with Dark Greens and Fresh Herbs (page 135)

Millie Howe

owner/chef, Indigine

Millie Howe opened her first restaurant at age seven in a small Arizona town. Her City of Rocks Cafe had two paying regulars, her mother and grandmother, and the menu was drafted from '50s classics—Campbell's, Skippy's, and whatever else was found in the pantry. Twenty years later, in the early '70s, Howe opened what would become one of Portland's most original eateries, Indigine. Known for seafood pâtés and sourdough griddle cakes oozing apple cider syrup, Indigine was Oregon's first "regional and seasonal" restaurant.

Howe's concepts may not be new, but they are definitely unfamiliar. When she makes an enchilada, for example, it is a far cry from the usual shredded-cheese-and-hot-sauce number. She mingles Oregon influences with the Sonoran flavors of her youth to produce a sultry layering of tortillas, cheese, and local seafood. Asked to describe her creations, Howe says, correctly, "sensual."

Apple Cider Syrup (page 8); Bay Shrimp Pâté (page 23); Goat Cheese with Green Olives, Black Peppercorns, and Red Chilies (page 27); Oregon Shrimp and Scallop Enchiladas (page 76); Cauliflower with Caramelized Onions and Fresh Herb Chutney (page 126); White Lasagne with Scallops (page 159); Sandy River Raspberry-Rhubarb Pie (page 176); Cranberry-Ginger Chutney (page 223)

Ron Paul

owner/chef, Ron Paul Restaurant and Charcuterie

Homemade berry vinegars, pickled chanterelles, and crackling breads are displayed at Ron Paul's like Tiffany jewels on shelves as green as the Douglas firs that pepper the hills around Portland. Nearby, there's a handful of tables and a sit-down counter for patrons in search of a special brand of Oregon cooking.

Ron Paul is the kind of cook who shows up for a catering job with 300 chickens in clay pots, plus a ceramist as consultant. For a guest appearance at the James Beard Foundation in New York, he air-freighted Cascade Mountain mushrooms, Umpqua River mussels, and custom-smoked Oregon seafood.

Paul grew up in Tucson, Arizona, and traveled extensively throughout Europe with his family. "I was into frog legs and steak tartare when I was seven," he says with a laugh. "I ate things even my parents wouldn't touch." Trading a career as a mental health worker in the '70s to become a chef, Paul has never looked back. His innovations include a snappy regional pesto and bran muffins glazed with local pear brandy.

Ron Paul's Smoked Chicken Salad (page 61); Bran Muffins with Pear Brandy Glaze (page 165); Whole-Wheat Walnut

Baguettes (page 170); Braised Pheasant with Juniper Cream (page 100); Grilled Salmon with Mint Pesto (page 68); Nectarine and Plum Tart with Almond Filling (page 183); Rhubarb Tart with a Phyllo Cinnamon Crown (page 186); Blackberry and Lemon Cheese Tart (page 184); Pâte Sucrée (page 189); Sorbet of Pear, Apple, or Peach (page 199)

Nick Pierano

owner/chef, Nick's Italian Cafe

Oregon's wine country is defined by undulating hills, vintage farmhouses and hazelnut orchards that slice into blue-gray skies. Portlanders flock here each fall for annual wine-tastings. The vineyard-hopping ritual is often capped by a visit to Nick's Italian Cafe, a bastion of creativity on the main drag of McMinnville, 40 miles southwest of Portland.

This intimate eatery has been a serious player in Oregon's food and wine scene since it opened in the mid-'70s. Despite a growing national reputation, Nick's maintains a homey atmosphere enhanced by the owner's serious jazz collection and service provided by his two spirited daughters. Pierano uses a daily five-course menu to showcase his blend of northern Italian style and Oregon ingredients. Lasagne with hazelnuts and local mushrooms is the house signature, while Pierano's hand with locally raised beef borders on legend.

Hazelnut Lasagne with Oyster Mushrooms (page 154); Stuffed Sirloin Steaks (page 119)

Harriet Reed Greenwood

former owner/chef, Harriet's Eat Now Cafe

"This is no chic hangout," said an adamant Harriet Reed when she opened Harriet's Eat Now Cafe in 1983. The fast-rapping daughter of the Bronx didn't want her funky, low-tech eatery tagged as the latest "in" spot. She had her regulars to think about. But it was too late. Almost overnight word spread through Portland like a hot stock-market tip: For anyone looking for fabulous roadhouse eats upscaled with autumn fruits, hazelnuts, and all sorts of berries, this was the ticket. The culinary style was highly improvisational, thoroughly compulsive in detail, and often provocative in its juxtaposition of unlikely ingredients. Crowds flocked to the cafe, fighting it out for one of eight coveted counter stools.

Reed abandoned the business in the late '80s to pursue a career as a food writer, but she found love and marriage instead. Today, she lives with her husband, Jay Greenwood, and son, Wyatt, in Georgia.

Autumn Pear Waffles with Frangelico Maple Syrup (page 2); Gingerbread Pancakes with Apple Compote (page 3); Thin Cream Cheese Pancakes with Marionberry Syrup (page 5); Goat Cheese and Poached Pear Omelets (page 10); Aged Gouda and Sherried Apple Omelets (page 8); Hazelnut Flour (page 237)

Karl Schaefer

former owner/chef, Le Cuisinier

Karl Schaefer was the James Dean of chefs. With his dimpled baby face and slicked-back hair, the moody man in the kitchen looked like he would be more interested in a leather coat than a white chef's apron. Sure enough, when Schaefer came to Portland in the early '80s to open Le Cuisinier, he intended to be leader of the pack.

Until it closed in 1988, Le Cuisinier won four-star ratings for food that was the epitome of Oregon style. Schaefer combined local food, classical French techniques, and contemporary nutritional concerns. He picked fresh herbs from his garden, ordered chemical-free meats, and tracked down the best sources available, from morel hunters to mussel cultivators. Today, Schaefer runs a part-time catering business and lives on an organic farm in Oregon City, outside of Portland. But his dishes are still legendary on the local scene.

Petrale Sole with Champagne Sauce (page 80); Huckleberry and Crème Fraîche Tart (page 179); Apricot Soufflé (page 219)

Index

and sun-dried tomatoes,
145–46
and hazelnut stuffing in pears,
28–29
in orange salad with shredded
beets and raspberry vinai-
grette, 58–59
salad dressing, 65–66
Blue Heron French Cheese
Company, *xxxv*
Blueberry
Corn Bread, 162
discussed, xxx
Sourdough Bread Pudding,
212–13
Streusel Muffins with Lemon
Glaze, 169–70
Boletus mushrooms (boletes), *xlviii*
Bosc pears, *liii*
Bosker, Gideon, 154
Boysenberry, *xxx*
Braised foods
Fennel with Blue Cheese,
128–29
Lamb with Quince, Cinnamon,
and Apples, 106–7
Pheasant with Juniper Cream,
100–101
Bran Muffins with Pear Brandy
Glaze, 165–66
Brandied Currants with Pears,
131–32
Brandon's Food, *xxxv*
Brandy (*See also* Apple Brandy,
Pear Brandy and Clear
Creek Distillery)
discussed, xxxiii–xxxiv
Bread and Ink Cafe
discussed, 247–48
recipes from, 28–29, 36–37, 44,
46, 50, 72, 107, 136, 241
Bread Pudding
blueberry sourdough, 212–13

Bread(s)
Apple-Cheddar, 163–64
Blueberry Cornbread, 162
Hazelnut Rye, 172–73
Strawberry Applesauce, with
black currants and golden
raisins, 164–65
Briggs, Nancy, 38, 203, 244–45
Briggs and Crampton's Catering
and Table for Two
discussed, xxi, 244–45
recipes from, 33, 40, 52–54,
64–66, 94, 135, 138,
173, 183, 199, 205, 222,
228, 231
Broccoli with Toasted Walnut
Butter, 125–26
Brooks prunes, *liv*
Brownies, Black Angus,
214–15
Burkholder, Jane, 30, 31, 212,
245–46
Butter(s)
black morel, with asparagus,
124–25
clarified, 239
fennel pear, with McKenzie
Creek trout, 73
toasted walnut, with broccoli,
125–26

C

Cabbage, Purple
with red pear and toasted
walnut salad, 52–53
Cafe des Amis
discussed, 243–44
recipes from, 25, 37–38,
56, 64, 91–92, 98,
110, 145
Cake(s)
Bittersweet Chocolate Torte
with Strawberries, 203

Salad with Warm Apple Dressing,
62–64

E
Edible flowers
  discussed, xliv
  lavender, 10
  in salads, 55–56
  zinnia petals, 52
Eggs, quail
  with oysters in basil nests, 20–21
Enchiladas with Oregon shrimp
    and scallop, 76–78
English walnuts, *lxi–lxii*

F
Faes, Linda, 196, 246
Failing, Pat, 46–47, 149, 151
Fennel
  braised, with blue cheese,
    128–29
  discussed, xxxix
  greens with sweet-and-sour
    salmon, 69–70
  pear butter with McKenzie Creek
    trout, 73
  pesto, with white bean soup,
    44–46
  ramekins of fresh, with parsnips,
    129–31
  and sturgeon chowder, 38–40
  with wild rice, apricots, and
    hazelnuts, 141–42
Feta cheese sauce with linguine,
    151–52
Fettuccine
  with Blue Cheese, Walnuts,
    and Sun-Dried Tomatoes,
    145–46
  with Clams, Mussels, and Spicy
    Sausage, 144–45
Fig(s)
  and apple brandy with chicken
    liver mousse, 24–25

  discussed, xxxix–xl
  stuffed, with lemon chicken,
    86–87
Filberts. *See* Hazelnuts
Fillet fish, *xl–xlii*
Fish
  discussed, xl–xlii
  Stock, 240–41
Flank Steak
  in ginger-pinot noir marinade,
    116–18
  Willowdale, 118–19
Flour, Hazelnut, 237–38
Flowers. *See* Edible flowers
Forest Mushrooms
  with lemon rice pilaf, 140
  and scallops, 82–83
Frangelico
  and Hazelnut Cookies,
    216–17
  maple syrup, 2
Fresh Herb Chutney, 126–27, 226
Fruit (*See also individual fruits*)
  Soup with Rhubarb, Berries,
    and Mint, 48–50
Fruit preserves. *See* Preserves
Full Moon Mushroom Co., *xlix*
Fungi. *See* Mushrooms

G
Game
  discussed, xliii
  Braised Pheasant with Juniper
    Cream, 100–101
  Grilled Venison with
    Cranberry Pepper Sauce,
    113–15
  Pâté with Cranberry-Ginger
    Chutney, 25–27
Game Hens
  roasted, with corn bread,
    sausage, and apple brandy
    stuffing, 102–4
Garlic-mustard paste, 120

Gathered Greens and Field
Flowers in Walnut
Vinaigrette, 55–56
Genoa (restaurant)
discussed, 246–47
recipes from, 13, 41–42, 69–70,
148–49
Ginger
-Cranberry Chutney with Game
Pâté, 25–27
-Pinot Noir Marinade, 116–18
cranberry chutney, 223–24
hazelnut shortbread, 215–16
Mussels, 74–75
pastry, in apple tart, 181–83
Gingerbread Pancakes with Apple
Compote, 3–5
Goat cheese
and autumn pear tart, 30–31
with Green Olives, Black Pepper-
corns, and Red Chilies,
27–28
and Poached Pear Omelets,
10–11
Salad with Winter Greens, 56–57
Goat Cream Cheese
with potato gratin and thyme
leaves, 138–39
Golden Orchards, *xlii*
Gooseberry(ies)
compote, with roast duck, 95–96
discussed, xxxi
Gouda
Aged with sherried apple
omelets, 8–10
Granny Smith apples, *xxvii–xxviii*
Grappa(s), *xxxiii*
Gratin
Potato with thyme leaves and
goat cream cheese, 138–39
Gravenstein apples, *xxvi*
Greens (salad)
spring, with asparagus and
morels, 53–54

discussed, xliv
gathered, with field flowers in
walnut vinaigrette, 55–56
in summer garden ragout with
fresh herbs, 135–36
winter, in goat cheese salad,
56–57
Greenwood, Harriet Reed, 2,
250–51
Grilled foods
Leg of Lamb with Apricot-Mint
Sauce, 107–8
Salmon with Mint Pesto, 68
Sweet-and-Savory Chicken, 94
Venison with Cranberry Pepper
Sauce, 113–15

H

Halibut, Pacific, *xli*
Halibut with Hot Mint Relish,
81–82
Hall, Lisa Shara, 40–41, 48, 92–93,
177, 179, 205, 207, 240
Ham
in chanterelle lasagne, 157
smoky, with sweet onions and
potatoes, 14–15
Hard, Amelia, 246–47
Harriet's Eat Now Cafe
discussed, 250–51
recipes from, 3, 5–6, 10–11, 238
Harry and David (mail-order
company), *xxi, liv,* 59
Hash
King Salmon, 11–12
Hazelnut oil, *l*
Hazelnut(s)
and blue cheese stuffing in pears,
28–29
Cheesecake with a Chocolate
Crown, 207–8
Chicken in Hell's Fire, 92–93
Corn Cakes with Wild Blackberry
Compote, 6–7

K

Kesey, Ken, *xxiii*
King salmon
  discussed, lvi
  Hash, 11–12
Kippered salmon, *lviii*
Kirkland, Larry, 58–59, 70–71,
  118, 124–25, 131–32, 225
Kishiyama, Shirley, 207–8

L

Lamb
  Braised with Quince, Cinnamon,
    and Apples, 106–7
  discussed, xlvi–xlvii
  grilled leg of, with apricot-mint
    sauce, 107–8
  roast rack of, with hazelnut
    hollandaise, 109–10
Lasagne
  chanterelle, 157–58
  hazelnut, with oyster mush-
    rooms, 154–57
  white, with scallops, 159–60
L'Auberge (restaurant)
  discussed, 244
  recipes from, 13, 57, 100, 113,
    116, 209–10
Lavender
  with goat cheese and poached
    pear omelets, 10
Le Cuisinier
  discussed, 251
  recipes from, 81, 179, 181, 220
Leek(s)
  cream soup, 43–44
  shredded, with basil and
    chanterelle sauté, 127–28
Leg of Lamb with Apricot-Mint
  Sauce, 107–8
Lemon(s)
  Cheese and Blackberry Tart,
    184–86

cheesecake, poached, 209–10
Chicken with Stuffed Figs, 86–87
glaze with blueberry streusel
  muffins, 169–70
Rice Pilaf with Forest Musrooms,
  140
Lencek, Lena, 87, 89, 95–96,
  146–47, 192
Lett, David, *xxii*
Levy, Stu, 195–96
Lime(s)
  blackberries, mint, and zinnia
    petals, 52
  with chicken, blackberries, and
    fresh herbs, 87–89
  in Dungeness crab curry with
    roasted hazelnuts, and
    currants, 75–76
  mayonnaise with Hood River
    anjou salad, 59–61
Lingcod, *xli*
Linguine
  with Bay Shrimp and Roasted
    Walnut Pesto, 152–54
  with Feta Cheese Sauce,
    151–52
  with Scallops and Saffron Cream
    Sauce, 149–51
Liqueur(s)
  discussed, xxxiii–xxxiv
  Frangelico (hazelnut), 2–3
  loganberry, *xxxi–xxxii*
  Whidbey's with Loganberry
    Ice Cream, 198–99
Littleneck clams, *xxxvii*
Liver Mousse, Chicken
  with Figs and Apple Brandy,
    24–25
Loganberry(ies)
  discussed, xxxi–xxxii
  ice cream with whidbey's
    liqueur, 198–99
  liqueur, *xxxi–xxxii*

N

Native Game Company, *xliii*

Nectarine and Plum Tart with
    Almond Filling, 183–84

Nehalem Bay Crabs with Pasta and
    Blackberries, 146–47

Newton Pippin apples, *xxvii*

Nick's Italian Cafe
    discussed, 250
    recipes from, 121, 157

Norm Thompson Outfitters, Inc.,
    xxviii, liv, lix

Nova lox, *lviii*

Nut oils, *l*

Nutmeg
    Sugar with Cranberry Muffins,
        166–67

O

Oils
    discussed, 1

Olives
    green, with goat cheese, black
        peppercorns, and red chilies,
        27–28

Olympia oysters, 20

Omelet(s)
    Poached Pear and Goat Cheese,
        10–11
    Sherried Apple and Aged Gouda,
        8–10

Onion(s)
    caramelized, and cauliflower
        with fresh herb chutney,
        126–27
    in cranberry and port condiment,
        228–29
    sweet, *lx–lxi*
    sweet, with potatoes and smoky
        ham, 14–15
    cream soup, 43–44

Orange Salad with Shredded Beets,
    Blue Cheese, and Raspberry
    Vinaigrette, 58–59

Orchard Crest Farms, *xxxvii*

Oregon Apiaries, *xlvi*

Oregon Berry Ice Cream, 192–93

Oregon Blue Cheese Dressing,
    65–66

Oregon Harvest and Gifts, *xxxvii*

Oregon Mussel Chowder, 37–38

Oregon Peach Chutney, 225

Oregon Shrimp and Scallop
    Enchiladas, 76–78

Oregon Wine Advisory Board, *lxiii*

Oregon Winegrowers Association,
    lxiii

Oyster Mushrooms with Hazelnut
    Lasagne, 154–57

Oyster(s)
    in Basil Nests with Quail Eggs,
        20–21
    discussed, l–lii
    Pacific, and spinach bisque,
        36–37
    seviche of, with salmon and
        crab, 21–23

P

Pacific halibut, *xli*

Pacific Oyster and Spinach
    Bisque, 36–37

Pacific red snapper, *xli*

Pancake(s)
    Gingerbread with Apple
        Compote, 3–5
    Hazelnut Corn Cakes with
        Wild Blackberry Compote,
        6–7
    Thin Cream Cheese with
        Marionberry Syrup, 5–6

Panini (restaurant)
    discussed, 246
    recipes from, 196–97, 212

Paradigm Foodworks, Inc., *l*

Parchment–Baked Chinook
    Salmon with Peach
    Chutney, 70–71

Quail
  with Chestnut Stuffing and Warm
    Pears, 98–100
  Eggs with Oysters in Basil Nests,
    20–21
Quillisascut Cheese Company, *xxxvi*
Quince
  with cinnamon, Apples, and
    Braised Lamb, 106–7

R

Rack of Lamb with Hazelnut
    Hollandaise, 109–10
Ragout
  Summer Garden with Dark
    Greens and Fresh Herbs,
    135–36
Raisin(s)
  apple brandy, with amaretto
    cookies and apple crisp,
    217–18
  cider, with mashed pumpkin
    and cinnamon crème
    fraîche, 132–33
  golden, in applesauce strawberry
    bread with black currants,
    164–65
Ramekins of Fresh Fennel
    and Parsnips, 129–31
Raspberry(ies)
  -prune compote, with roast
    pork loin, 111–13
  -Rhubarb Pie, 176–77
  with Black Beauty cake and
    custard sauce, 205–7
  discussed, xxxii
  ice cream, and chocolate truffle,
    196–97
Razor clams, *xxxviii*
Red Bartlett pears
  discussed, liii
  purple cabbage and toasted
    walnut salad, 52–53

Red Pepper Salsa
  basic preparation, 231
  with roasted potatoes, 137–38
Red snapper
  Pacific, *xli*
Relish(es)
  Hot Mint, 230
  hot mint with halibut, 81–82
  Sweet Pepper, 229–30
Restaurants, Oregon, *xxi*, 243–51
Rhubarb
  -raspberry pie, 176–77
  berries, and mint with fruit
    soup, 48–50
  compote, with Poached Silver
    Salmon, 71–72
  discussed, lv
  Tart with a Phyllo Cinnamon
    Crown, 186–87
Rice
  pilaf, lemon, with Forest
    Mushrooms, 140
  wild, with apricots,
    fennel, and hazelnuts,
    141–42
Roasted foods
  Bell peppers, 238–39
  duck with gooseberry compote,
    95–96
  Game Hens with Corn Bread,
    Sausage, and Apple Brandy
    Stuffing, 102–4
  Pork Loin with Raspberry-Prune
    Compote, 111–13
  Potatoes with Red Pepper Salsa,
    137–38
  Rack of Lamb with Hazelnut
    Hollandaise, 109–10
Rogue River Valley Creamery,
    xxxvi
Rolling Stone Chevre (company),
    xxxvi
Rome Beauty apples, *xxviii*

Ron Paul Restaurant and
    Charcuterie
    discussed, 249–50
    recipes from, 62, 68, 101, 166,
        172, 183–84, 186–87, 190,
        200, 233
Ron Paul's Smoked Chicken
    Salad, 61–62
Royal Gala apples, *xxvii*
Ruhl Bee Supply, *xlvi*
Rye Hazelnut Bread, 172–73

S

Sablefish, *lix*
Saffron Cream Sauce with
    Linguine and Scallops,
    149–51
Saint Philibert, *xliv*
Salad Dressing(s)
    chipotle-mayonnaise, 61
    Honey-Bacon, warm, 54–55
    Oregon Blue Cheese, 65–66
    Raspberry Vinaigrette, 58–59
    Tarragon Vinaigrette, 65
    Walnut Oil, 55–56, 64
    warm apple, 62–64
Salad(s)
    Dungeness Crab with Warm
        Apple Dressing, 62–64
    Hood River Anjou with Lime
        Mayonnaise, 59–61
    Orange with Shredded Beets,
        Blue Cheese, and Raspberry
        Vinaigrette, 58–59
    Ron Paul's Smoked Chicken,
        61–62
    Spinach with Salmon, Straw-
        berries, and Warm Honey-
        Bacon Dressing, 54–55
    Spring Greens, Asparagus, and
        Morels, 53–54
    Toasted Walnut with Red
        Pear and Purple Cabbage,
        52–53

Warm Goat Cheese with Winter
    Greens, 56–57
Salmon
    Chinook Lox, 13–14
    discussed, *lv–lvii*
    grilled with mint pesto, 68
    king, hash, 11–12
    parchment-baked Chinook, with
        peach chutney, 70–71
    poached silver, with rhubarb
        compote, 71–72
    seviche of, with crab and oysters,
        21–23
    in spinach salad, with straw-
        berries, and warm honey-
        bacon dressing, 54–55
    sweet-and-sour with fennel
        greens, 69–70
Salmon jerky, *lviii*
Salsa, Red Pepper
    basic preparation, 231
    with Roasted Potatoes, 137–38
Salumeria di Carlo, *lvii*
Sandy River Raspberry-Rhubarb
    Pie, 176–77
Sardina, Roger (The Mussel Man),
    xlix, li
Sauce(s)
    béchamel, with lasagne and
        scallops, 159
    champagne, with petrale sole,
        80–81
    chanterelle sauce, with lasagne,
        157
    clam, mussel, and spicy sausage
        sauce, with fettuccine, 144
    cranberry pepper, with grilled
        venison, 113–15
    custard, with Black Beauty cake
        with raspberries, 205–7
    feta cheese, with linguine,
        151–52
    hazelnut hollandaise, with roast
        rack of lamb, 109–10

Squaw candy, *lviii*

Steak
 flank, in ginger-pinot noir
  marinade, 116–18
 sirloin, stuffed with garlic-
  mustard paste, 119–21

Steamed Clams with Garden
 Herbs, 19–20

Stew(s)
 Spicy Sausage with Chicken and
  Mushrooms, 89–90
 Summer Garden Ragout with
  Dark Greens and Fresh
  Herbs, 135–36

Stock(s)
 Fish, 240–41
 Homemade Chicken, 239–40

Strawberry(ies)
 Applesauce Bread with Black
  Currants and Golden
  Raisins, 164–65
 with Bittersweet Chocolate
  Torte, 203–5
 discussed, xxxii–xxxiii
 in spinach salad, with salmon,
  and warm honey-bacon
  dressing, 54–55

Strouse, Joan, 74–75

Stuffed Sirloin Steaks, 119–21

Stuffing(s)
 chestnut, with quail and warm
  pears, 98–100
 corn bread, sausage and apple
  brandy, with roast game
  hens, 102–4

Sturgeon
 discussed, lix–lx
 and Fennel Chowder, 38–40
 white, with hot chili condiment,
  78–79

Sturgeon caviar
 discussed, lix–lx

Summer Garden Ragout with Dark
 Greens and Fresh Herbs,
 135–36

Sun-Dried Tomatoes
 with Fettuccine, Walnuts,
 and Blue Cheese, 145–46

Sweet-and-Savory Grilled
 Chicken, 94

Sweet-and-Sour Salmon with
 Fennel Greens, 69–70

Sweet Pepper Relish, 229–30

Sweet Short Pastry Dough,
 189–90

Syrup(s)
 Apple Cider, 8
 discussed, xlii
 Frangelico maple, with autumn
  pear waffles, 2–3
 marionberry, with thin cream
  cheese pancakes, 5–6

T

Talarico's Meat and Seafood
 Market, *xlvii*

Tarragon Vinaigrette, 65

Tart(s)
 apple, in ginger pastry, 181–83
 Autumn Pear and Goat Cheese,
  30–31
 Blackberry and Lemon Cheese,
  184–86
 Chanterelle with Sugar-Roasted
  Walnuts, 31–33
 Huckleberry and Crème Fraîche,
  179–81
 Nectarine and Plum with Almond
  Filling, 183–84
 Rhubarb with Phyllo Cinnamon
  Crown, 186–87

Tate, George, 247

Thin Cream Cheese Pancakes with
 Marionberry Syrup, 5–6